BRAVO MAURICE!

BRAVO MAURICE!

A compilation from the autobiographical writings of Maurice Chevalier

Translated by Mary Fitton

London

George Allen & Unwin Ltd
Ruskin House   Museum Street

ISBN 0 04 920037 2

Translated from the French
BRAVO MAURICE!
© Julliard, Paris, 1968

Printed in Great Britain
in 12 point Fournier type
by Cox & Wyman Ltd,
London, Fakenham and Reading

Foreword

This book was first published, as a birthday tribute, when Maurice Chevalier was 80, with an introduction referring to him as 'one of our most illustrious contemporaries, world-symbol of all that France has contributed in the seemingly frivolous but in fact so essential domain of light entertainment, to song, music-hall and cinema'. It is made up of extracts from his own writings, 'which may serve to remind us of the unrelenting hard work, the conscientious professional approach and the awareness of humanity that have made the boy from Belleville into "our Maurice", and which take us at the same time through nearly eighty years of history, big things and trivial'.

English readers, unless they are devotees of theatrical history, may meet unfamiliar names, and the world of the *café-concert* is possibly unfamiliar too. It may, therefore, be useful to recall that when Chevalier began there were over 150 *cafés-concerts* in all parts of Paris, sometimes more than one to a district. They ranged from primitive and very racy little dives to bigger places where those patrons who did not stand in the promenade sat at their ease in the relative comfort of basket-chairs. The accepted drink was *eau-de-vie* with cherries in it, the stones being useful ammunition if anyone felt like criticizing the one-man turns, all of which fell into recognized categories. There were straight romantic singers – *chanteurs de charme*, as they were called – specialists in soldier-songs, in yokel-songs, tramp-songs and so forth. Performers, agents and composers congregated in and around the Faubourg Saint-Martin to be seen in the cafés, to buy new songs, look for talent or wait for jobs. The child from Belleville launched himself into this seedy, scintillating world and almost his only stroke of original luck was the fact that the professional mecca happened to be so near.

Many of the bars and tiny theatres where he worked have disappeared, pulled down or replaced by cinemas, and not a few of the larger establishments to which he graduated later have met the same fate. As for the great stars who were household names – Dranem of the bald head and diminutive, shallow hat; Mayol with his hair in a quiff and a calculated, graceful gesture for every phrase he sang; Harry Fragson, with his very English aura, accompanying himself at the piano; Paulus, of a slightly earlier vintage, with his rousing military numbers; plump Polin in a *poilu*'s uniform, with his infectious laugh; and Polaire with her wasp-waist and huge, magnetic eyes – well, you might find them on old music-covers or in postcard albums now. But their world went back to the Second Empire, almost to the Revolution, and its traditions are alive today; a world that was, until this year, Chevalier's.

Since this is a book of extracts there are, of course, gaps and fore-shortening, but it allows us to follow the juvenile low comedian as he turns into the dashing young song-and-dance man, and stands revealed at last as we remember him – a sort of madly attractive grandfather with a devastating accent and a passion for writing things down. Work and self-improvement are the key-notes. 'He is too modest a man', the French preface adds, 'to set himself up as an example, but there is nothing to stop his publisher, with the utmost delight, from doing so.' And for me, from all that people have told me, all that I have heard and read about Chevalier while making this translation, one remark stands out. Somebody on a television programme said: 'He never didn't smile in the work.'

M. F.

Summer 1972

Contents

Part Two: *A NOTEBOOK OF PEOPLE, EVENTS*
AND IDEAS SINCE 1945

Contents

Illustrations

Part One

*MY LIFE
TILL 1945*

STREET BOY'S EARLY LESSONS

I was born on 12 September 1888 at 29 Rue du Retrait, at the top of the hill in Ménilmontant, in the northern part of Paris. My earliest years were spent there and I recall nothing whatever about them. No sight or sound seems to have registered until the day when I became aware of myself as junior member of a group, consisting of my father, my mother, two brothers and me, all crowded together in two tiny rooms at 15 Rue Julien-Lacroix, a long narrow street that ran between the Rue de Ménilmontant and the Rue de Belleville.

It was in this cramped accommodation that I first began to notice just how much my remarkable mother managed to do in the course of a day: her housework, her braid-making, the cooking and ironing, and all the washing and mending for the other three, to say nothing of me, small though I was. She simply never stopped, and when the evening meal was over and my father and brothers, weary from their jobs, were half asleep before they reached their beds, I might wake for a moment and see her, the only one still moving about, washing-up quietly in the little, dim room. And then she would sit down carefully quiet as ever, the lamp beside her turned as low as possible, and stitch, stitch, stitch, to get some order finished that had to be ready by morning. Instinctively, even then, I knew her for what she was – the most noteworthy and beautiful of this lowly bunch with whom my lot was cast.

These early recollections are, inevitably, muddled. Some things I remember, then there are gaps, but I am quite definite about my first contribution to family life. As soon as I could walk and talk, I ran errands. I went to the horsemeat shop in the Rue de Ménilmontant for so-called beef-steak, or to the baker's, practically on our doorstep, for a loaf that hadn't turned out right. At the dairy opposite I got the butter – half a pound at a time, we were in no position to be extravagant – eggs and cheese. I liked the butcher and the baker best, for the former always gave me a scrap of horsemeat sausage as a titbit (a *pourmanger*, as it were, instead of a *pourboire*) and the breadshop provided a stale croissant from the previous night's baking. But the woman at the dairy never gave an ounce away and I never wheedled anything out of her, for all my melting looks and wounded astonishment at the failure of my juvenile charm; which probably explains why, to this day, I'd rather eat bread and meat than anything else.

My father's task was to collect the wine on his way home, and there we sat, waiting for supper, while he performed it by dint of enthusiastic potations in every bistro on the way. I scarcely knew my father, and it is only fair to testify that he was said to be an excellent worker and a very honest and good-natured man. But he was also a complete slave to booze, a fact which caused a great deal of misery and made my mother cry alone in a corner far too often. There was no self-pity in her tears, there were no explanations, and the small boy who watched her, grieving, was not old enough to understand.

We had a kind neighbour who not infrequently gave me the splendid sum of one sou to do her shopping for her, and when things weren't too bad Maman would find extra errands for me as an excuse for giving me something more. There was also the occasional stranger to signal me from my playmates, draw me out of ear-shot and ask me, in a shaky voice, to deliver a letter to some woman or other on such-and-such a floor at such-and-such an address near by, while he waited for the answer; there was always going to be an answer. A love-lorn admirer, maybe, or a husband pleading for her return after a row – the usual sort of drama in such circles. But my intrusion into the poor man's private life carried a kind of one-sou entrance-fee and if he seemed really anguished and altogether too miserable for words, then I went a bit faster and begged and prayed as well as I could to make the reply encouraging. The stings of love, do not forget, are as painful in low life as high; often more so, being nearer to nature and more sincere.

And what, you may inquire, did I do with all the cash? Well, I had two vices, even at that early age. One was sugared almonds and the other cigarettes, two of which were then sold for a sou. When there had been a lot of errands I stood myself so many sugared almonds that they more or less cemented me up and I next indulged in limitless debauch as, marooned in the lavatory, I puffed recklessly at my two cigarettes, one after the other. And soon enough I got what was coming to me, cold sweats, dizzy spells and what-have-you. I retired to bed, my eyes went funny and my mother's anxious face peered down at me, distorted and peculiar.

That is the most I can tell you of my earliest exploits before I went to the Charity School run by the priests in the Rue Boyer, to learn to read and write. In these new and different surroundings, among urchins of my own age, it quickly dawned on me that here, as anywhere else, the race is to the swift and the battle to the strong, whatever people say.

The others started picking on me from the word go. It began in the playground at the very first break.

'Ooh, look at him! Big-head!'

They were dead right, my head was indeed a size too big for the rest of me, though that was hardly my fault. But I was getting the backchat already.

'So, what's it got to do with you, prune-face?'

'Big-head, Big-head, Big-head!'

The group surrounding me grew larger and more menacing. By now I was being shoved about, had had my hair pulled by a boy on the side-lines and received a painful demonstration from behind that another was shod with sturdy hob-nailed boots. I shook all over. The situation was beyond me. I hadn't done anything, I didn't know any of them, so what was the object of it? They might – petrifying thought – knock me down and trample me underfoot. And I gave a sudden yell of revolt against the monstrous injustice of it all, such a yell that every voice was hushed and every eye in every horrible face was fixed on me. I had gone mad, completely mad. With no idea that I was in fact 'fighting', I lashed out in uncontrolled fury, like a human knuckleduster, at anything I could reach.

One child, entirely innocent, it seemed, of word or deed against me (but then, he shouldn't have been there in the first place) got my fist full on his nose, my head on his chin and my boot between his legs, and fell wailing to the earth. I glared around me, livid, and must have been a dreadful sight to see, for my attackers faded away in panic. Fear, not courage, had given me victory, and I was still shaking like a leaf; but all the same, as the bell recalled us to the classroom, I could feel that, if the roughs had put me in a spot, I had somehow done the right thing about getting out of it.

What else is there? The evening my mother first took me to a *café-concert*. It was at the Palais du Travail in the Rue de Belleville, and I watched acrobats and men and women singers in a daze of admiration. And then there was the day which found me at the foot of the steps outside our church, clinging to the rail in the square to observe a wedding procession move majestically forth. How imposing, rich and grand a sight! Mesmerized, with eyes like saucers, I failed to see that another eager spectator was leaning on the gate, which all at once jammed shut on my fingers. I shrieked so loudly that bride and groom took fright and nearly fell flat on their faces. Someone got my finger free, but the end of it hung down. The crowd pressed close.

'He'll have to go to the Ternon hospital with that, poor mite. What do they call you, dear?'

'Chevalier; Maurice.'

'And where do your people live?'

'Not far. 15 Rue Julien-Lacroix.'

As if in a nightmare, I saw them running off and felt myself fainting away. Then Maman was there. She stood still and never said a word, just looked. She looked at my finger, dangling and bloody, and her cheeks seemed to go hollow. Then she told them to call a cab, which meant she would have to work half a day to make up the fare of thirty sous. She clutched me to her and we drove away to the local hospital. I was in the most terrible pain, but I was also terribly proud. Proud because this accident was so very, very serious, and Maman was so upset; and oh, how very proud I was because we took that cab!

WOES OF THE WORKING CLASS

My finger had to be kept bandaged for a month in case the blood congealed, and held straight up in the air. Looking back, it might have been the starting-signal for a whole series of dismal events, some of them worse than others.

My father, to begin with. We had days of continual drunkenness and heart-rending domestic scenes, and then one evening – and I almost wrote one fine evening – he banged the door and lurched off, never to return. Wife and three children he left to their own devices.

That wasn't the end of it, either. The paternal role palled soon enough on my eldest brother, Charles, and there came the day when he announced that 'things' could not continue as they had been since father's walk-out. He was 20 years old, he informed our mother, 'with his own life to live'. Which meant, of course, that he had fallen in love and wanted to get married. He had officially proposed already and his workman's pay was not for us in future. Maman did not even protest that he should at least wait until our middle brother, Paul, was bringing home a grown man's wage; she accepted this desertion, too, and hid her disappointment beneath a smile of understanding.

Well, it was clear as daylight what would happen next. We were now a family of three, Maman, Paul and me, with Paul still an apprentice earning, I believe, three francs a day. That was our total income, three francs a day, so Maman, on top of her chores at home, looking after two boys and ruining her eyes with braid-work, had to go out cleaning for sympathetic neighbours to make ends meet. Her life became one long exhaustion. Toiling till all hours, doing without all kinds of things, she grew so weak that at last the doctor had to be sent for. Anaemia had so affected her eyes that she was slowly going blind. The lids had begun to bleed and in her feeble state she was having fainting-fits and collapsing several times a day. Trembling and haggard, she heard the doctor order her into hospital for a while. The *Hôtel-Dieu* ... a week or so, he thought ... but she had let things get serious, very serious; she must arrange to leave the children. Deathly weary, that stoical, marvellous woman faced an awful situation once again. To the sobbing Paul she explained about eating at the cook-shop downstairs, and being good and sensible; then, suddenly distraught and apprehensive, turned to me. Who was going to take charge of me, see to my meals, and general well-being?

The doctor reassured her. There was the *Enfants Assistés* in the

Rue Denfert-Rocherau, the big institution which cared for abandoned or unfortunate children whose mothers, either through illness or for any other reason, were unable to look after them. A certificate from him would procure my instant admission and one of the neighbours could take me there that very day. My poor mother made no answer, only threw her arms around me. I don't know how long we clung together, but all the strength she had left went into that embrace and they had to pull her from me. Slowly my young brain absorbed the fact that she was going away, all hunched and bent, with people holding her up on either side.

'She'll soon get better in the hospital, and you'll be really good, now, won't you? We'll go across to the *Enfants Assistés* now. That's what they *call* it, just for a name, you know, but it's more like a marvellous great school, and you'll have a lovely time, just while you can't be with Maman.' The woman from along the landing chattered away to an anxious child who had never before imagined there was anything on earth important enough to keep him from his mother. And yet, deep down, he didn't feel as awful about it as all that. An 8-year-old cannot imagine the worst. Youthful curiosity, aroused by the prospect of a marvellous great school where everything is going to be rather splendid, soon overcomes the novel, strangling sensation in the throat.

So there he was, that small boy, as near to smiling as he was to tears, in his suddenly strange circumstances. Leaving your mother, going on a more or less enforced journey to live with other people whom you had never seen before and never played with – he hadn't appreciated that such things could happen. Instinct told him to be brave. Certainly he must not cry – or would be wise to conceal the fact if he did.

Maman had whispered as she hugged him that he was 8 now, not a baby any more, and he must be a little man. So, holding the neighbour's hand and carrying his small bundle of possessions, the slum-child went off to the Poor Children's Home, which was nowhere near Ménilmontant but a long bus-ride away, the other side of Paris. Used as he was to his own monotonous street, the square, and his everyday walks, he found it an absorbing expedition. Maman made him keep to the home side of the local cross-roads, which was as far as he was allowed to go, so what he saw now might have been a scene full of animated toys who breathed and moved and ran about. But the bus stopped in front of a stern and dignified entrance, above which could be read the words, *Hospice des Enfants Assistés*. A glance at the tall grey buildings right and left warned him that toys are not the only things in life. The door opened.

The neighbour explained the position and showed his paper, smiled wanly, patted him on the back of his neck and left. He was taken into a room to wait with three other little boys. Intently he regarded them, realizing he was not the only one to whom these dreadful things could happen. When his turn came to go into the office he set his infant jaw. They gave him a blue lanyard with a numbered medallion on it and hung his uniform over his arm – navy-blue trousers, blue shirt and clean underclothes. He was then soaped under the showerbath and, clean from top to toe, left with the others.

They were of all ages, little ones, middle ones, big ones. (There were girls, too, but they lived in another building, opposite.) At 8, he was put with the middle ones and, wretched and ill-at-ease, resembled nothing so much as a small rabbit thrust into a cage with a lot of other small rabbits. One of these children, however, kinder and more sensitive than the rest, turned out to be a present help in time of trouble.

'She'll be better soon, your mother, just you see. And it's all right here, the beds are nice, all white and lavendery. Good meals, too. They even have pudding.' A desperate kind of friendship, welded in the playground at recreation times, grew up between the pair of waifs.

Orphans of the storm! Life for some of those children was so appalling that they didn't cry on arrival; they sobbed only when people came to fetch them away. But the little boy with whom we are concerned had been happy with his mother at home. He clenched his fists in his pockets and tried to look tough, and prayed in the dormitory when the others were asleep. Our Father, which art in heaven, make Maman better *soon*.

And it happened at last. One day at break-time he heard an

orderly calling his name. 'They've come for you. Run along and get changed. Your mother's better now.'

It was like a dream. He stumbled as he ran. The neighbour who, such ages ago it seemed, had brought him in, was there in the office by the main door with forms and papers in her hand. Wide-eyed, he stared at her, not yet daring to believe that it was true. But yes, it seemed all right. They went outside and got into the bus. He didn't bother about the ride across Paris this time, though. He was riveted by the thought of his mother's face; his heart pounded at the prospect of seeing and hugging her again. They were in the street, they were at Number 15. He took the stairs three at a time; into the room; and there she was, sitting, still weak and pale, her arms held out. He went straight into them, put his head down on her shoulder, in the hollow where he used to fall asleep at night, and began to be happy again. After this separation he knew, when he said 'Maman', exactly what he meant.

Not long ago I was visited by a miniature-painter who lives in Ménilmontant. He showed me delightful little pen-drawings of the *quartier*, all clear and neat as children's well-washed faces, each small picture in its delicate wooden frame. He is a craftsman-artist, doing beautifully finished work, clear-cut and honest, like himself. But for me his view of the church in Ménilmontant brought back one of the very worst days of my childhood. It was a great day, the day when all the boys and girls who were making their First Communion paraded past, elated and happy, with the district *en fête* for the occasion. Airy white dresses went rustling by, the boys had smart black suits all spanking new, with stiff shirts and white ties. Their eyes and their silken armbands shone. And at Number 15 I watched them from the window, crying softly, while Maman stroked and patted my hand, not knowing how to comfort me. We were going through a bad patch, and though I should have been there with the rest, couldn't possibly scrape together the few francs that the black suit would have cost, or the white shirt or the tie. And as for a fine silken armband, that was quite out of the question.

'CHEVALIER BROTHERS'

So Maman was back from the hospital and Paul was head of the family. We had lean weeks to get through still, but one Saturday night he came home with glorious news. He was apparently doing so well in his job of metal-engraving that his boss had decided to promote him three months earlier than usual to the status of fully-fledged workman at seven francs a day: There would be forty-two francs for housekeeping next week.

It was the beginning of a new life at 15 Rue Julien-Lacroix and we changed our lodging there by way of marking the improvement. We descended from the third floor to the first, with a window over-looking the street, if you please! We could have more outings too, and went off every Saturday, and frequently on Sunday as well, like a trio of boon companions. The pair of us and La Louque, as we called our mother, enjoyed the Palais du Travail or the Cirque d'Hiver, the Concert du Commerce or the Cirque Médrano.

I went completely overboard for some of the acts and the singers we saw and heartily envied the boys in the acrobatic numbers with their somersaults and balancing tricks. The way they jumped to the feet, shoulders or head of the supportman, to take off in what looked like a backwards dive, give a corkscrew twist and land again the right way up! When I got home I was possessed by dreams about it all – the lights, the applause, and then, the *money* they must be earning! Oh, to be an acrobat like the boys I clapped so zestfully and admired as lords of the universe; to be as they were, with a fortune to give La Loque! I thought of nothing else. I was 9 now, and together with some of the local urchins would do cartwheels and balancing-acts after school, in the Rue Sorbier. There in the sand-heaps I tried to explain to them the stunts I saw in the ring, as per-formed by all those born-and-bred acrobats who haunted my sleep every night of my life.

It was only much later that I discovered how circus families train their children in back and forward somersaults, with two men holding a cord round the pupil's waist, and how he does his first solo somersault only after much practice, when they are sure he is

safe to try it alone. Meanwhile, however, these professional proce-
dures were not for us. Devoted street-performers that we were, we
all plunged in together. The thing was a challenge.

'Bet you can't do a forward somersault!'

'Bet you I can!'

And the hardy one went at it, to collapse on his back or bottom,
or straight on to his head if he miscalculated badly. This, of course,
was why we favoured the sandheap. It cushioned the fall.

Nevertheless, spraining our arms and legs, bruising our backsides
and raising great bumps on our heads, we made definite progress
day by day. Some, more adept than others, managed to turn real
somersaults and actually land properly on their two feet, facing the
right way round. People gathered to watch us, and anyone who
brought off a successful jump got his round of applause.

For some reason – faith, perhaps, or it may be that the idea of
earning money at the business drove me to put more into it than the
others did – I was soon acknowledged as our leading light. Aware
of this local reputation and eager to keep it up, I rushed to the
improvised open-air gymnasium, whenever school was over, with
the speed of an Arab yearling. At night, seated at supper between
Maman and Paul, who was then 16 and growing rapidly, my
endless theme was acrobatics and *sauts périlleux*. The appreciative
onlookers we were attracting to our circus had finally turned my
head and, not very surprisingly, the inevitable happened. Big, strong
Paul heard me raving on the subject and caught the bug as well and
we began to lay plans for an acrobatic act of our own, to be per-
fected forthwith.

On our weekly expeditions we had always admired the litho-
graphed music-hall posters with English-style names. 'Brothers'
were the thing: Walton Brothers, Fernandis Brothers; Brothers here,
there and everywhere. We believed at first that 'Brothers' was a
Christian name like Louis or Jules, but when we learnt that it was
in fact the English for *frères* we really started thinking. High and
low we sought, until we found a printer with a stock of old litho-
graphs showing two jerseyed, acrobatic figures under the legend
'Martinon Brothers'. Paul's deft fingers quickly obliterated the word
Martinon with strips of paper and there we were – 'Chevalier

Brothers', and well-supplied with posters saying so. We were going to be the most marvellous Brothers ever heard of, have the most terrific success and earn so *much*! We hung one of our personal play-bills up in the room and, in raptures at the effect, endeavoured to raise La Louque's enthusiasm for an idea which we ourselves con-sidered little short of genius. And she smiled and said, indeed she didn't see why not – just so long as Paul kept on with his job and I stuck to my schooling.

So that was all right. We had the posters (the main thing, in our opinion), and could now turn to the trifling detail of the act itself. Paul was to be the base-man, while I sprang about on high, balanc-ing and doing somersaults. The Rue de Ménilmontant boasted a gymnasium, the Arras, where you paid five sous and stayed as long as you liked among the young men who practised Roman wrestling and swung their dumb-bells on its thick bed of sawdust. Acrobats used it for training, too; it was just the place we needed. Paul would join me in the evening after his work and we would set about re-hearsing the various routines we had mapped out. All Sunday and every holiday found us there.

My brother was at this time tall and thin, though perhaps a little stronger than he looked, while I was still small for my age, and fat. My family nickname, *Patapouf* or Fattypuff, was considered very suitable. I didn't in the least mind being fat. What I couldn't under-stand was why I sometimes felt full of vim and vigour and at other times too listless to answer when spoken to. I used to feel as though I had been stunned and drained of energy. Nor, alas, was the expla-nation forthcoming until considerably later, when it was found that I had had appendix trouble, intestinal and digestive trouble and lung trouble, all without anyone's guessing or worrying about it.

One night, then, Paul met me after work at the gymnasium to put the finishing touches to our act. Casually, as a muscle-building exercise, he began to imitate the weight-lifters, watching them care-fully, then picking up a 40-pound dumb-bell and trying to hoist it above his head. And as he did so I noticed for the first time how terribly bow-legged and thin he was beside all those sturdy men with their great arms and swelling chests. As I looked at his scrawny neck it came over me that my scheme for making an acrobatic

Brother of him might not be the happiest of inspirations, after all. I got a lump in my throat and a sudden urge to cry.

I felt absolutely miserable, for mingled with my tenderness for Paul was the involuntary realization that in my excitement I had pushed us into a path which neither of us was fitted to travel very far. You can imagine in what a turmoil I climbed on to his shoulders and tried my reverse somersault, or poised balancing on his head. (And I always think this was what strained his neck and gave him such a prominent Adam's apple later on.)

Nor was it long before I had to admit that my own arms and legs were not really strong enough either. I could go soaring aloft all right, but anything calling for true muscular effort was beyond me. It was the same with somersaults from a standing start, I lacked the lift and elevation. Instead of turning head-over-heels a couple of feet or so in the air, I couldn't produce enough spring and was tumbling more or less at ground-level. Sheer tenacity on my part kept us practising for ages, but it was clear to all at the Arras that our standard of acrobatics would never get the Chevalier Brothers on to the bill at the Palais du Travail.

In the middle of this crisis the date for my primary school examination came round and, in spite of being so depressed and under the weather and fully expecting another lamentable failure, I passed. This was a nice surprise, but what it meant was that, at $10\frac{1}{2}$, I had to leave and start learning a trade.

FIRST JOBS AND FIRST SUCCESSES

No, being an acrobat was definitely not for me. I put the glorious dream behind me and tried to find a job, scanning the 'sits vac.' posted up near the cable-tram stop at the bottom of the Rue du Faubourg-du-Temple, and duly presenting myself at the addresses I found on the list. After a few days of this, however, a ray of hope stole across my disillusion. If I couldn't be an acrobat, then why not be a singer? Why not, indeed? Except for the real vocalists, none of the comics and funny-men at the Commerce or the Palais du Travail had particularly good voices. There was a comic yokel act, for instance, and a comic soldier – I ought to be able to do as well as they did if I put my mind to it. That was the answer! Bitten with this new bug, I cast my former passion away like an ageing mistress and set to, making plans for my début as a comic singer. I had no intention of telling Maman what they were until later on, when I was sure of myself. Meantime, I decided to work at anything that turned up and to concentrate on learning songs to sing at my First Appearance.

We will not enter into details of all the jobs I had, and from which I was sacked regularly every fortnight. The tale would be much too long. I was a carpenter and an electrician: I painted dolls' faces, was employed as a printer and in a hardware shop and came to rest at last making tin tacks. It was while so employed that I had one of my dreamy interludes, with dramatic results. Thinking of anything but tin tacks, I rested one finger of my left hand on the mould and forgot to remove it as I pushed the pins out with my right. In a moment a piercing cry brought my fellow-workers to the spot, pale with alarm. My finger – the next one to the victim of the church railing – was crushed, flat, wrenched out, dangling. Maman was sent for at once, she took me to the hospital and we had the action as before.

But only a few weeks previously I had discovered a group of amateur singers who met in the back room of the Café des Trois Lions in the Boulevard de Ménilmontant. Now, during my enforced idleness after the accident, I summoned up courage to go to the *patron* and ask if I might sing a ditty or two on his stage the following Saturday; wearing a white glove, I said, to hide my bandaged finger. I was 12, and a small 12 at that, and he looked at me thunderstruck. Was I, he inquired, a local resident? When I said I was he told me to report at eight o'clock on Saturday with any paraphernalia I might need. And I could expect a cup of coffee for my trouble, nothing more.

Wild with joy, I announced the news at home. It made Maman and Paul laugh and they promised to attend my début as an amateur. I can see that evening still: our arrival together, and their buying tickets, and my going off behind the flowered curtain that screened the 'dressing-room'. I see myself setting out my bits and pieces under the amused regard of the stars of the Trois Lions, to all of whom, I suppose, I stood about knee-high. I put on my comic array, borrowed some of their make-up and daubed my nose and cheeks red. I then gave my two songs to the pianist and came up against a rather awkward question: he wanted to know what key to play them in. My determination was matched only by blithe unawareness. 'Oh, any key you like,' I told him.

Was I ready? someone asked. Was I ready! The pianist attacked a number called '*V'là les Croquants*'. I thought of the family and all the jobs I'd lost, and on a wave of elation, in my rural character get-up, stepped on to the stage.

The audience, at first surprised to see a toddler in this costume, soon began to smile at my air of confidence. Obviously a good beginning, and I fairly let them have it. Selecting a spot on the ceiling to help me concentrate, I opened my mouth and sang. The piano sounded splendid, though I did get an unaccountable feeling that we were somehow not as one; and even as I sang at the top of my voice, looking fixedly out and upwards, I could see from the corner of my eye that the pianist, still playing, was rising from his stool. They were calling me from the side, but nothing could stop me now. After one verse and a chorus the audience collapsed in gales of mirth, the men rolling about and the women in hysterics. I must be absolutely marvellous! What a triumph! Louder than ever I carolled, still gazing at the roof and, ending '*V'là les Croquants*' to clamour indescribable, left the platform to find the other performers – Georgel, Léon Delpierre and Brigham – in heaps, wiping their eyes in the wings.

I was all for going on again at once but, despite the mad acclaim, they held me firmly back. That was fine for tonight, they said, but next time I had better rehearse with the accompanist and arrive at some arrangement as to the key we were working in.

Why? I wanted to know.

'My dear child, you've been singing three tones higher than the piano, making an awful noise. That's what they were laughing at.'

I came to earth with a nasty bump. I wasn't mowing them down at all, I was making a fool of myself. It was a sad journey home with Maman and Paul, though they, too, could not help smiling at the recollection of my small figure and berouged face as I persisted, against wind and weather, through my three full verses and my three refrains. But they managed to console me, saying that things would be better next day if I did as advised and took counsel with the pianist. Poor old Fattypuff! Still, he had made his début, all by himself, up on a stage with an audience looking on.

And in the morning the whole Rue Julien-Lacroix, it seemed, was laughing too. It gave the impression, in its usual inelegant way, of hanging on to its sides and its bottom and falling about with laughter. Workmen in the bars had passed the word around: 'that lad of Madame Chevalier's was singing at the Trois Lions. You know the one I mean – little devil! The cheek of him! You should have seen him – they simply couldn't get him to stop. Went on and on in a little squeaky voice, forcing it like hell, so every note was cracked. Gazing up at the ceiling, too, as if he was blind or something. Didn't worry him a bit, though – just went on and on, faster, higher. Boy's potty.'

Sunday night at the Trois Lions was a repetition of Saturday, though I took it all more calmly. Evidently, stepping on to a stage wasn't going to kill you; I had learnt that much already.

Georgel and Léon D., as Delpierre was known, had taken pity on me and explained that pianist and singer could not possibly operate in different keys. I had made the audience laugh, agreed, but it had not been 'good' laughter, not the kind a professional artist wanted.

'Good laughter.' 'Professional artist.' The two phrases lodged in my eager brain and have stayed there ever since. So that was it! There was more to this whole process than merely making people laugh. The laughter had to be healthy and natural and free of mockery. You didn't just get up there and sing. You had to polish it, work at it. You had to be an Artist.

'Don't you worry, either of you,' I assured them, 'I see what you mean. You have to treat them properly, that's all. You have to be an Artist.'

And so it was dedicated to this great ideal that I set off to do the Monday morning errands. All the shopkeepers had heard the tale and wished to know the details, serving me, it seemed already, a shade more attentively than usual. The butcher produced some of the best horsemeat sausage, and I got a fresh croissant from the baker's wife.

'How did you get on?'

'Aren't you going to tell us about it?'

'Now, who put you *up* to it?'

'Wherever did you *learn* all that?'

How on earth should I know? I was in such a whirl at what I had done, anyway, that I might almost have been ill; it could all have happened in a fever. But it had happened, fever or no fever. The worst was over, and that was the main thing. All I had to do now was to sing better. Good laughter . . . being an Artist.

Every Saturday and Sunday I returned to the Trois Lions, and if there were, perhaps, less furore than on the night of my début, I was clearly making progress. I was in much less of a panic; I no longer confined my gaze to the ceiling; and I sang in the same key as the music. For those two evenings a week I was in heaven. It was that platform and that dingy back-stage that gave me courage to immure myself with the frightful tin tacks when the week-end was over. Then, all too soon, the café shut down for a while.

But I had heard of a tobacconist's in the Rue Ménilmontant with a big hall where a half-professional, half-amateur show called the '*Élysée-Ménilmontant*' was billed to open the following Saturday. I went to see about it and on the strength of my Trois Lions' reputation – can you imagine? – was booked to come and sing. For free, of course; a salary was still unthought of. And there, that Saturday night, fate took its decisive twist. Really, you never know what's round the corner.

ÉLYSÉE-MÉNILMONTANT

When it reached my turn the show was going well, the house warmed up and enjoying itself. *Le petit Chevalier* was announced. There was a murmur in front and I came on to laughter and applause. 'Isn't he small!' 'Only a child!' I gave them all I'd got and for the first time in my life I felt what actors call 'contact', the link when an audience is at one with you, that atmosphere in which you know you

dominate. They clapped when I finished and gave me a curtain-call.
I was too excited even to notice a jubilant hug from Paul. They were
still wanting me back but I had run out of songs.

'Just go and thank them, boy, and announce the next turn. Tell
them it's Gilbert, the Mayol of the Tourelles. Don't forget, now,
the Mayol of the Tourelles.' (Well, Mayol was a very top star and
the Tourelles a small *café-concert*.) I did as the stage-manager bade
me and stayed in the wings to watch the Great Professional.

And wonderful it was to see a real singer from such close quarters.
In a trance, with Paul at my heels, I regained my own little corner
of the dressing-room to change into ordinary clothes and gather up
my trappings. Gilbert, who had come from the Casino des Tourelles
already dressed and made up, was slowly getting into his overcoat,
winding a silk scarf round his neck, and he never took his eyes off
me all the time he did so. I was too frightened to speak and didn't
dare address him. But as I hurried to the door he called; 'I was
listening to you, boy. Been singing long?'

I glanced to left and right; he was talking to somebody else, of
course. But no, it was me he meant. I braced myself and answered:
'Only about six months, sir, so I'm not very good at it yet.'

He had a more refined sort of face than the other singers I had
come across and his expression was friendly and gentle. Kindness
radiated from him. He continued,

'What are they paying you a week here?'

'Paying? Oh, nothing. My goodness, it's marvellous of them to
let me come at all!'

This apparently gave him a moment's reflection. Then he said,

'You be at the Casino des Tourelles at eight o'clock tomorrow
night, Sunday, and bring your songs and your costume. I'll ask the
manager if you can do a public audition. If you go over well, and
I don't see why you shouldn't, he'll offer you a job for a week or a
fortnight at what he thinks you're worth. And you'll have something
for your bus-fare if he doesn't, so you can't lose.'

I opened my mouth to accept with fervour and failed to produce
a sound. All I could manage was a sort of gurgling noise as I swallowed once or twice. Then I pulled myself together. I should be
there . . . how could I ever thank him . . . and so on and so forth.

When we got home, Paul helped me to persuade La Louque that the audition would show definitely whether I were any good, and that Saturday night I lay awake to all hours, wondering whether the whole thing could possibly be true. I listened to the others breathing and finally fell asleep, my heart bursting with love for them and I resolved to prove it by making their Patapouf someone who counted in the world.

As for the vital Sunday evening in December 1901, it will stand out in my memory if I live to be 100. Paul and I arrived an hour too soon. The Casino des Tourelles, not too far away, up near the Porte des Lilas, was silent. The matinée had ended over an hour before and the company was in the middle of its dinner at a little eating-place near by. The doorman knew nothing about me and refused to let us in, so we had plenty of time to steady our nerves by walking up and down the Avenue Gambetta for forty-five minutes, me with my bundle in my hand. The public were admitted at eight and we were back at the stage-door at a quarter to. Gilbert himself welcomed us and took me to the manager, an ex-actor named Rithier, who listened to his proposal, and at length, with a shrug of the shoulders, agreed. I could appear at number 3 on the programme, after a lady singer and a comic called Caron. Caron had a rollicking reception and when he made his exit a board was exhibited with the word AUDITION in large letters. It was my turn.

The audience was still rollicking and scarcely noticed me above the noise as I came on. It took them several minutes to settle down, and as I was neither old enough nor big enough to command their attention properly, I entered, did my act and finished without a vestige of that famous contact. A few of the women clapped and some of the men did glance in my direction as they continued to savour Caron's witticisms. They were getting over their transports by the second song and displayed a little more interest, and though they didn't laugh much, at least they seemed to have some idea of what they were laughing at, but I went off dismally convinced of failure. Forlornly I was waiting for the agreed pittance when Rithier and Gilbert came bursting in.

'*Petit gars*, they like you! That was very good. You'll have to

1. Maurice Chevalier's mother

Maurice Chevalier, aged 13,
posing for a postcard photo

2. Aged 14: two photos from his song turns

work at it, but you amused them all right. They thought you had guts.'

Guts. Courage. Again the word struck me. It did indeed seem that courage was needed to keep on being funny for an audience that wasn't responding to you. But I couldn't muster a syllable in reply, feeling absolutely wretched and sure they were only saying it out of pity, trying to cheer me up.

'Now, listen, child. You can start here next Thursday. We open four nights a week. Thursday, Saturday, Sunday, Monday, two houses a night. How much do you want?'

'Wh ... what?' I said.

The offer knocked me sideways, and I hadn't the faintest idea. I could only stammer at them.

'Wh ... whatever you think. I don't know.'

'Right, then, listen. You're here for a fortnight, twelve francs a week. Three francs a day, that is, for every day you work. If you change your songs, and if you do well, you can have a bit more. Suit you?'

There were nods and winks from my brother, as if to say, Oh, that's fine, you'd better accept, and I did a quick sum in my head. Twelve francs was two francs more than I achieved in the most profitable week at the tin-tack factory. And no more factory, either. Free all day, and a professional entertainer, what was more! Rapturously I said yes. Arms linked, Paul and I rushed off home, down past the Ménilmontant reservoir, in such a state of delirium that we landed in our own house as though shot from catapults.

'Maman! Maman! Guess what's happened!' we yelled in chorus. At last I shouted my brother down and told how I was going to be an Artist with two francs more a week than tin tacks yielded at their very best. And how wonderful to think the daytime would be free, for I should be fully occupied 'going down to town', finding and learning new songs for the programme. I couldn't possibly attend a factory.

She watched our exalted faces with that calm look of hers that had so much love in it, and when we had finished her expression seemed to say: 'Well, if that's the way it is, we'll see how things work out.'

'But,' she added, 'if there are no more engagements after this one, promise me you'll go back to the factory. Promise.'

ARTIST AT LAST

Only soldiers and labouring men can appreciate how glorious it really is to lie late in bed in winter-time. When your life revolves around having to be at work at seven o'clock in the morning you know all about the ghastly leap up, still half asleep, and the rush to put your head under a tap of ice-cold water with the barbarous object of shocking yourself awake. When I was circulating hopelessly from job to job, Paul and I would rise valiantly and douse ourselves together before we sat down to the good hot coffee La Louque had waiting for us on the table. Then, depending on where I happened to be employed, we often went some of the way together before parting for the day. Now, staying in bed was the immediate advantage of my new career, but that first Monday I was not happy about it. I watched Paul get up unaccompanied and go through to the kitchen to drench himself in the inhuman tap-water; come back alone to the table, and then set forth into the chilly fog of early morning. If my lot had improved, his hadn't, and the thought rather spoiled my warm comfort under the bedclothes. What made it worse was the fact that he gave no sign that he minded my lying there like a lord while he had to get on with the same old hard routine. He hadn't minded before, when I was out of work or having to nurse my finger, but this time it marked the beginning of a whole new life. Indeed, our two lives were different already, and I had unexpected pangs of remorse. He was so good and sweet-natured, Paul; no resentment or bad temper. Yet affection and remorse did not, I fear, prevent me from rolling over and drifting off for another two hours while Maman did the housework. It was utter bliss. Then came *café au lait au lit* – terrific. It had been a marvellous idea of mine, this being an Artist. I was literally drunk with freedom, and the *café au lait* went to my head like fiery armagnac.

My new position as an Artist called also, I considered, for some sartorial gesture on my part. I had to cut a bit of a dash. Once fixed up at Les Tourelles, therefore, the next thing was to visit Les Économes, a big ready-made-clothes shop in the Rue de Ménilmontant. My mother came too, and we chose a magnificent overcoat with a velvet collar. It cost nine and a half francs and the material was shocking. And to go with it, what better than a fine, three-franc French-Revolution-type tall hat of the sort known as a Girondin? As I have mentioned already, I was little and dumpy with a very large head, so the Girondin for me had to be wide and, of course, correspondingly tall. I hope I make the picture clear – something like a gnome in giant's headgear. I decided to cherish this outfit against the day I opened at Les Tourelles. That day I would don overcoat and stove-pipe hat and knock the whole Rue Julien-Lacroix cold as I passed elegantly through on my way to rehearsal.

The longed-for Thursday came. Our concièrge, I noticed, failed to respond when I nodded and bade her good-morning. Stunned, poor woman. The first few yards of my progress in the street produced a similar uncanny silence. People saw me coming and the words died away on their lips. But by the time I got to the Passage Ronce, which was then one of the black spots of the district, I could hear things like: 'Oh, *ben alors*, have you *seen* the child?' What was wrong? Had I by any chance done something silly? Or were they just jealous because I looked so smart? It was the Girondin that upset them, I could feel it was: my exiguous self, huge hat, huge head.

Oh, well. Too bad. No going back now. I straightened up and continued along the crowded Rue de Belleville, where further unpleasing comment greeted my Girondin, and arrived safely at the theatre.

There I rehearsed my songs. Caron, the comedian, inquired when he could expect to see me in a tail-coat and topper, the others said I was a dandy and teased me good-humouredly. Then, not without misgiving, I started for home. All down the Rue de Belleville I walked so fast that sweat ran from the Girondin on to my velvet collar.

'Good God, child! Hang on to your hat!'

'Here comes the mayor!'

'Afternoon, Doctor!'

They barracked me the length of the street. Misgiving became fear, then panic. I broke into a run until I reached Rue Julien-Lacroix, within sight of the house. Two hundred yards or so, and I was safe. Were those shadows, lurking at the corner of the Passage Ronce? No, I was tired. I must be seeing things. But I was not seeing things. First one lanky figure stepped out of that murky alley-way, then another, and another. It was an ambush, ready and waiting. My cry for help was curtailed by a clout on the crown of the French-Revolution hat which crammed the wretched thing down to my chin, while through it could be heard hoots of guttersnipe laughter.

I never even tried to get it off, but rushed, terrified, blind and headless in the general direction of Number 15. I stumbled, fell and was picked up. With much ado, somebody fished me clear of the Girondin. Trembling, I related my misfortunes and fled to my mother, weeping bitterly at the humiliation of it all. I, who had thought myself so beautifully dressed! I may as well confess that I was 18 before I dared put a hat on my head again, and it is probably why I have preferred caps ever since. But still, it made no difference to my being an Artist. That great, that central fact, remained.

TRIAL TRIPS

Our family expeditions on Sunday afternoons were often to the Concert du Commerce in the Rue Faubourg-du-Temple, and here I had become acquainted with Boucot. He was less impressed than I could have wished when I told him that I, too, was now an Artist but said we should see more of one another as I had the days to myself. We went 'down to town' together, and soon I was going down alone, complete with velvet-collared coat and nice new cap, acquired since the Girondin fiasco.

I called constantly on the music publishers in my search for new material, and they all got to know me. Some of them were quite interested in the tale of my career so far and in their offices I was meeting men and women performers all the time. The famous ones were the more friendly to an aspirant so young and small, but the less famous and the definitely unheard-of (and that meant most of them) took pointed exception to me, on the ground that I was doing somebody out of his place in the profession and ought to have been at school.

I was a few months past my thirteenth birthday and alone in their world. Despite the marvellous kindness of Gilbert in giving me a start, he could not help me three weeks later when the manager of Les Tourelles said he was making changes. He liked my work and they'd certainly have me back – another time. Thanks to Boucot I got a booking at the Concert du Commerce, but alas, it was only five francs for a weekly five performances and I took it with a heavy heart for this was a drop of seven francs and, I thought, signalled the end of my days in the business if I were to play fair with my mother. But she could not bear to see my disappointment when I broke the sad news and, astonishingly enough, said I should not give in so easily. I must try for a week or two longer and then, if nothing turned up, it would be time to put a good face on things and go back to the workbench. Meanwhile, she said, get going; chase every job you can, and make an all-out effort.

I had an audition at the Ville Japonaise, a *café-concert* in the Boulevard Strasbourg, where they took me on at twenty-one francs a week. This was my best ever, and lasted several weeks. Still, I had to be thinking of the next step, and applied to the Casino de Montmartre – another public audition and engagement on the same terms, three lovely francs a day for matinée and evening show. This kept up my weekly rate, which was all I worried about.

The Casino de Montmartre was on the Boulevard de Clichy, opposite the Quat'z Arts and under the same management. It was a low-class, crowded place with a matinée audience of droppers-in and all the ponces, pimps and bullies for whom Montmartre was the capital of Paris. Some of these gentry, rather than sit about playing cards all afternoon while their women were on the beat, preferred to sit about listening to songs, and passed the waiting hours at the *apéritifs-concerts*. Not a particularly savoury public, I think you will agree, and you soon knew where you were with them. It was here I first saw people really slaughtered on the stage, heard an audience shouting abuse and found poor wretches in tears in the dressing-rooms as they wearily wiped off their make-up.

Our patrons were basically tolerant of the ordinary professional artists, considering them properly qualified, but pitiless to the candidates for public audition, and since they knew that the supply of quaking victims would never fail, audition matinées were hugely popular. The management knew it too, and welcomed every trembling aspirant who came. The more abysmal his effort, the more the house enjoyed itself.

Whether they thought I was too young to be roasted alive, or whether they detected some latent possibility of improvement, they paid very little attention to begin with and let me get on with it; and as time went on actually became mildly enthusiastic. Those afternoons at the Casino in Montmartre were my first real struggle with savages, and the fact of survival increased my confidence for the future.

There were on that bill two ladies, alas unresponsive, who played havoc with my heart. One was a ravishing brunette called Fernande Déprat and the other was Spinelli. At my tender age, that adorable little Parisienne upset me terribly. She was only 16 herself, with a dream of a figure, tip-tilted nose and silky black hair that framed her face, and her arrival caused a sensation on both sides of the curtain. The hard-bitten matinée customers gazed at her in silence, like so many stock-breeders at the sight of a promising filly, and behind the scenes she had the effect of a small charge of dynamite, appearing in our midst to sing, in the most artless way and with vigorous contortions of her already curvaceous person, about the *p'tit coup de piston* that helps so much when you want a good position.

> It's no great shakes,
> But the difference it makes.

Well, a *coup de piston can* mean a little bit of influence, but you may imagine how the song developed in this case. It was, to be explicit, most explicit.

La Spi, as we used to call her, was incredibly beautiful in those days and still not fully conscious of her own sex-appeal. I would hang about until she came on to the stage and peer at her through a crack in the scenery. They clapped and recalled her and not a soul was paying the slightest attention to a word she sang in that throaty voice of hers. Then back she came into the wings, all impact and youth and beauty, and everybody's eyes popped out, mine farther than any. I must have looked like a fish. She soon noticed me, of course, but it didn't mean a thing. Everyone was after her and no one ever got anywhere; Spi was already in love and, I presume, living with an artist who, stupid fellow, didn't even bother to collect her from the theatre. As for me, I nearly yearned myself silly.

After several weeks there, my next engagement was for three days at the Fourmi, on the Boulevard Barbès. I had programmes now, to prove my professional standing, and took them with me when I went to see the manager. He was busy getting his next bill together.

'There's one spot, number 2 on the programme. Three days, thirty-five francs. Take it?'

Take it! He must have been joking. All records broken and the asking price was going up. Maman was delighted.

At this point my friends introduced me to a variety agent named Dalos who booked me for seven days at the Concert de l'Univers in the Avenue de Wagram, a renewable contract at five francs a night, twice nightly and the Sunday matinée. His commission was 5 per cent. Thirty-five was now my settled salary and I seemed to have a future to look forward to.

The director of the Concert de l'Univers was old Hamel, a bull-dog sort of a man and an occasional hard drinker, though said to have a kind heart beneath it all. During the show he was often to be seen pacing up and down the gangway at the back of the stalls, addressing the singers on the stage. 'Very good, that number of yours,' he might proclaim. 'Well done! Good lad!' Or: 'Any more of that muck and you're out! I'm warning you!' His total expenses were forty francs a day for eight of us, all playing twice nightly for five, and it was an easy-to-please audience, mostly *petits bourgeois* and domestic servants. They soon began to make more fuss of me than I had ever known before. From watching people like Boucot, Sergius and Dorville I had by now concocted a comic style, with bits

of one and bits of another, and a little dash of the great Dranem
added to them all. I sang his hits and also recited monologues by
Claudius, including a gem called '*Volonté d'Fer*' or 'Display Determination'.

> Display determination,
>   It's the main thing that I know –
> The male part of the nation
>   Had better let it show.

A revelatory hitch of my hands in my trouser pockets emphasized
the words, a gesture of lamentable vulgarity that made our lamen-
tably vulgar patrons fall off their seats. The more innuendoes and
obscene by-play I treated them to, the funnier, considering my small
stature and childish aspect, they found the whole foul performance.

I was kept on for nearly three months at the Univers, travelling
by Métro between Ménilmontant and the Place des Ternes, and to
vary my repertoire and make sure the regulars were constantly
amused, I had to learn half a dozen new songs a week. As I have
said, what they relished was the combination of my immaturity and
the excessively dirty jokes I had the nerve to prattle at them. And
the dirtier the better, I thought, being unable to see straight and
having nobody to give me sensible advice. The more they laughed
the deeper I plunged into the murky depths, convinced that I had
got the hang of pleasing them week after week. Very short-sighted
of me.

A REAL LITTLE MAN

The long sojourn at the Concert de l'Univers was followed by a stint
among the *cafés-concerts* and low halls of Paris. Sometimes Dalos
fixed the bookings for me, at other times I asked for the auditions
myself. One way and another, I worked at the Café Persan in
the Boulevard Sébastapol, at the Bateaux Parisiens in Auteuil, in the
Rue du Faubourg Saint-Martin at the Galeries Saint-Martin, at the
Café de la Presse in the Rue Montmartre, La Poste in the Rue
Saint-Dominique, and many more. Then Dalos came up with my

first provincial contracts – thirty-five francs for three days at the
Folies-Bergère at Le Havre, fares paid and my first sight of the sea;
a week in a little place at Amiens at ten francs a day; the Alcazar at
Tours, twelve francs, ten days. And here it was that I had a horrible
adventure.

One night, after my turn, a commercial traveller invited me to
lunch with him next day at a restaurant somewhere near Tours. He
was alone in town, he said. He thought I looked a pleasant type – why
not go out and enjoy ourselves? He seemed quite a pleasant type himself and his enjoyment was such that after our first drink he insisted
on two more. I was happy enough with the second, and the third
went straight to my head, so that I walked into the restaurant laughing uproariously and swaying about: a new sensation and, I must
say, an agreeable one. We washed down an excellent lunch with
excellent wines, my friend appeared without guile and life – my life
– well, I thought, where could you find anything to beat it?

After coffee we adjourned to a *brasserie* for a little glass of something. I had never tasted hard liquor before. 'Oh, but now's the time
to begin!' My host ordered two rums, I found mine far too strong at
first; it burned, and made me splutter. But then there came a seduc-
tive warmth, an unusual glow of well-being, and I was floating gaily
above all human contingency. How far below me everything was, to
be sure; how easy all the answers were!

'What about the other half?'

'Why not, why not?'

'Waiter, two more rums.'

There was somehow much less difficulty about this other half. It
slid down to join the first with no trouble at all and didn't scald my
throat. Voices from the surrounding tables began to echo strangely.

'Have another?'

'Certainly. Yes! Delicious.'

Another rum went down with a rush. We were still safely seated
and I had no inkling that I was doing anything stupid. The commercial traveller, of course, was having great fun. It gave him a
wonderful laugh, seeing a boy get stoned who'd never been stoned
before.

'Waiter!' he cried. 'Two more rums.'

By now my own voice was sounding new and different. I listened astonished. How very peculiar! It was me talking all right, but how could I be producing that strange noise? Absolutely nothing to do with me. Funny, very funny. It made me laugh ... and laugh ... and laugh. Like an avalanche the rums kept coming and we drank them all. Eight, nine, ten rums, all down the hatch. Still I was safe on my chair and, apart from the impression that I had somehow passed into another world, I felt no ill effects. We lifted our elbows in unbroken rhythm the entire afternoon and when I saw it was time to be getting to the theatre I rose to my feet for the first time since lunch.

The place spun round. Extraordinary, the way it spun. I couldn't stand upright and had to sit down again. A fine state to be in with a show to think about. My companion merely laughed at me.

'First taste of the stuff – good heavens, boy, serves you right!'

But I wasn't laughing any more. I had my work to do and how in God's name was I going to do it? My charming friend was himself incapable of movement, but I had to get up, and get to my dressing-room; and get myself ready; and get on the stage and sing. I muttered *au revoir* and thank-you to the drunken fool, made a desperate effort, staggered to the café door through a dizzying whirl of objects and onlookers and covered the short distance to the Alcazar clinging to the walls.

The passers-by, seen through a fog, seemed to be expressing amazement, exchanging remarks and cackling at the sight of me. I could see their eyes, and I could see their lips moving, but not a word penetrated. I felt ghastly and everything had grown unreal, save the knowledge that I had to overcome the ghastliness and sing. Soaked in sweat, I dragged myself to the dressing-room and saw in a mirror a livid face I didn't recognize. I began to take my clothes off. One of the company, dressed and ready, inquired if I were ill, but when I tried to answer not a sound emerged, though the whirling sensation got worse. Bells were clanging and my head was hitting the roof. What the *hell* was happening?

I was, I am told, picked up dead drunk in a pool of vomit and carried to my digs. They put me to bed and one of the girl singers kindly came to the rescue with cold compresses. Need I add that the show that night went on without me?

'The Chevalier boy's making a good start, I must say. Dreadful for a child of his age. A hard case, that one!' So ran the comments at the theatre.

Such, then, was my earliest encounter with the demon drink and it reminds me, since we are on the subject of failings, of how I started gambling. Though I can claim to be cured, for the moment at any rate, I must have been like a sitting duck to begin with. There was a game called *la passe anglaise*, which we lesser lights would play backstage at the Casino de Montmartre, usually with next week's pay-packet, rolling a pair of dice on the floor or a table-top. Your hopes soared when a seven or eleven came up, and sank to despair at deuce, three or twelve. By 1905 or 1906 I had the fever so badly that one evening – it was at Tourcoing, I remember, when the Exhibition was on – I was on the point of losing all I had at *petits chevaux*. My entire earnings for the whole engagement were melting away, five francs at a time. The man in charge of the *petits-chevaux* gadget had regarded me thoughtfully for a while. Then, though you could hardly tell that he was speaking, muttered.

'What are you doing here, boy?'

I confessed, rather shamefacedly, that I got an odd thrill out of risking my money.

'How much are you down?' he asked.

I told him. He went on with his job and paid no more attention to me. Then at the end of a round, I heard the ventriloquist voice say, 'Twenty francs on number 3.' I put down twenty francs, number 3 came up and I collected what was for me a fortune. He never moved a muscle, he seemed not to see me and I could not think of anything to say to him. Then he spoke, through closed lips, again: 'Now, get out and don't let me see you in here any more!' I whispered my thanks and never re-entered that gaming-room. I have played since, spasmodically, but came to the conclusion that the pleasure of winning doesn't make up for the awful feeling when you lose. Some-one once told me that the punter's chances of being ahead when he leaves the tables are a possible nine to one, and that someone knew what he was talking about. If you gamble you are a loser before you start and only the most incredible good luck can alter the fact. And many a loose-liver assures me that gambling is, of all the vices, the quickest road to ruin.

COMING OF AGE OF A WAIF AND STRAY

A fury of work now seized me, as though I needed to get the disgraceful incident at Tours thoroughly out of my system. The management there had written to Dalos complaining of my behaviour and I didn't dare go back to him for bookings, but luckily the Casino de Montmartre re-engaged me at five francs a day, and after that I earned seven at the Univers, so things looked up once more. We took this opportunity to leave the Rue Julien-Lacroix and rent a small two-roomed courtyard apartment at 15, Rue de Faubourg-du-Temple, at the end near the Place de la République.

So all was going well when Paul met a girl from Belleville, fell head over heels in love and announced to Maman that he wished to be married. It was the well-worn theme. Wishing to be married was apparently a family failing. We asked him to put it off until I was a little older and trotted out every argument we could think of, but it was no use: had to live his own life; Love with a capital L. Still, he was a kind soul and promised to help us out with part of his weekly wage. There were tears all round. Maman wept, Paul wept, I wept to keep them company. Then it was just La Louque and me, alone against the temptations and cruelty of the world. Suddenly I had to be my own father and my mother's sole support. The household consisted of her and me and I was head of it, captain of our fate. At $14\frac{1}{2}$.

The gap left behind by Paul was for some days deep and grievous. Then all at once I realized that Maman had only me to look after and began to take full advantage of the situation. We grew even closer than before. Over our meals I chatted to her about my friends and my job and sang her my new songs to hear what she thought of them. She devoted herself to me entirely and we lived in increased and happy accord. I didn't have to share her with anyone, and obviously nothing could be nicer. I simply adored her, knew that she depended on me for a livelihood and was acutely aware of my responsibility.

I had a long run at the Concert de l'Univers, then broke new ground on the boulevards, at the Petit Casino on the Boulevard Montmartre. This place was regarded in the profession as the springboard for a successful career. Its situation and its highly critical patrons made it a kind of test-run for lesser performers, a trial before an audience who knew what was what. All the singing stars had started there and so it was a great moment for me when, at 15 or so, I waited to step on to its stage.

And my first song evoked only icy astonishment. In the whole long auditorium there was no response to my would-be amusing antics and no reward but a few scattered handclaps. Scenting defeat, I tried to avert it by emphasizing the coarser bits of business in my monologue. Looking small and being priapic had never yet failed to do the trick in the Avenue de Wagram and I thought the best thing to do was to look more priapic still. To my horror and surprise it didn't raise a smile. There was even what sounded like a buzz of criticism as I went off, instead of clapping. In my third number, a veritable triumph at the Concert de l'Univers, I was a messenger-boy delivering a box containing a petticoat, some corsets and a pair of pants for a lady customer. I opened the box at the first chorus and donned the petticoat over my own attire, wrapped myself in the corsets during the second verse and the end, when I got to the wide-legged pants with bits of petticoat hanging out in front and behind, was guaranteed to produce a belly-laugh. It never missed; you could rely on it anywhere.

But not this time. Not at the Petit Casino. When it reached the point at which my stony audience should have thawed at last, I heard not laughter but a loud, demanding protest. 'That's enough of that. Disgusting! Pack him off to school!' No one contradicted, so presumably everyone agreed and there followed a general outcry, with shouts of: 'Children shouldn't do that vulgar stuff'; 'It ought to be stopped'; and 'Shameful, absolutely shameful, no other word for it.'

I remained rooted to the spot, stupefied and unable to believe it was happening. But it was happening all right, with boos and cat-calling. Finally I came to and made a speechless exit, head hung low. The stage-manager, an old actor now on the shelf, sniggered at me: 'Well, they did it to Paulus, they can do it to you.' (He adored Paulus of the rousing songs and extravagant gesticulation, and had been a follower of his.) That finished me. I went down to the dressing-room and cried for an hour or more. I couldn't stop, assuming, in utter despair, that every performance was going to be the same. I hadn't much self-confidence in the first place, and now I was afraid.

I met Paul after work when the matinée was over and between sobs told him all about it. I could not face that stage again. I was frightened, so frightened that I shook, but he comforted me as best he could and we resolved to wait and see what the evening show was like before deciding what to do.

That night I was so abashed and terrified that I could have sung in a Church orphanage without offence. Nobody clapped, but at least I didn't get the bird. I had the same icy reception all the week and spent a miserable time. I lost every scrap of confidence and faith in myself and knew, deep down, that decent people were justifiably shocked to see a brat of my age blandly churning out smut. All the same, why had none of my friends warned me sooner? Was I the only one who had to learn life's every lesson in this painful way? I was enormously depressed and ashamed and imagined that the entire Faubourg Saint-Martin knew of my mishap.

The summer season was upon us and work was harder to find. I was often unemployed for weeks in a row. La Louque and I had no savings – it is rather difficult to see how we could have amassed any – and we lived in real want, on baked potatoes and herb tea. My shoes were full of gaping holes and all summer I couldn't have them mended; I padded them with thicknesses of newspaper, I remember, to save treading through. Paul helped a bit, but he had his own home to keep going and very little money. I did all I knew to get a job, but nothing went right. I had hit a bad streak.

There was an occasional Sunday when I earned ten francs at some *guinguette* by the river, and that fed us for a week. I was dreadfully down and resentful, not on my own account, for I loved my work and didn't mind being poor, but because I was not providing for my mother more successfully. Moreover, I had said good-bye to the factory, and with it the chance of learning a trade. If my songs, already, failed to keep the wolf from the door, the outlook was bleak indeed.

Sadly, I began to see that I might have to quit a profession that wasn't even feeding me, go cap in hand back to that bench and get down to a proper job. Fair enough. But that meant beginning again at an apprentice wage of a franc a day, and how were we going to live on that, the pair of us? Then I found an advertisement in a newspaper. Someone with good, clear handwriting was wanted to address envelopes for three francs a day; application to be made by letter as a specimen of penmanship. My application was our last hope. I roughed it out laboriously several times and sent it off.

Anxiously we looked for the post every morning and prayed for a favourable response. Two days went by, then three, then five. Ten days, and still no word. We were more than poverty-stricken now, we were desperate. I would have taken any job anywhere, from anybody. The worst was going to happen, all right.

The letter that finally came for me was headed from the Parisiana *café-concert*. In a turmoil, I opened it. Would I call the following day at two o'clock? If a good fairy had dropped suddenly into our humble abode she could not have been more welcome. Laughing, crying, La Louque and I hugged each other. Was it the turning-point? Was the sun going to shine for us again?

Next day I duly presented myself, all spruced up in my shabby suit and broken shoes, at the big music-hall on the Grands Boulevards. Its new proprietor had come across my name in some old programmes while arranging his autumn revue, and before I left his office had engaged me for the whole run of a show called '*Satyre Bouchonne*'. I was to sing in the opening number, do bit-parts and chorus work. Eager to make the most of my luck, I had demanded ten francs a day and would have been only too happy with five. We compromised at nine and signed the contract.

A big revue of this sort, in a first-class theatre, usually ran for six months at least. For so long, therefore, I could reasonably count on my nine francs. What a night that was! How delicious our baked potatoes were, and how the brew of cherry-stalk tea went straight to our heads! We resolved to put half my earnings aside from the very beginning, for sickness and rainy days, and never get into such a mess again. Life had taught us the meaning of thrift, a word we had not understood before. So now we should live on twenty-one francs a week, which Maman said was quite enough; I should have a franc and a half to spend, and every day four and a half francs were earmarked for the *Caisse d'épargne*, where I went and got a fine new bank-book without delay.

We felt we had been saved from drowning. Our struggles were over, though not forgotten, and all my hopes returned. A sure six months at nine francs a day was a fortune. And I may as well confess that had any manager offered me a life-contract to follow that revue, and slipped in a clause that gave him anything I ever earned over ten, I should have signed my whole career away and kissed his hand into the bargain.

PARISIANA

My friends and I passed the time until the season opened by going to see all the great stars, and some chastening expeditions we had. As we, who were nobodies, listened to the giants of our profession, a certain melancholy would overtake us and there would be no more joking or larking about on the way home. How unattainable they seemed, how endless the road that lay between us and them, paragons that they were, with their personalities, their captivating voices, talent and public following. Looking at ourselves in the cold light of reason, we were, we clearly saw, bereft of every attribute they had. And none of us, if the truth were known, really aspired so high. We should all be quite satisfied to be good, average singers, and very happy too.

Posters were all over Paris by September and the papers were full of announcements that Parisiana, under new management, would re-open with a *café-concert* programme. The star was Vilbert, whose soldier-songs, it was claimed, were newer and better than those of Polin. Vilbert was going to wipe the floor with Polin.

3. Aged 19, with his mother

LA REVUE DE L'ALCAZAR
Chevalier *dans l'Hygiénique*
Moi j'suis hygiénique avant tout

4. Two photos taken of his performance in Marseilles in 1908, aged 20

CHEVALIER

PHOTO BONFORT - MARSEILLE

Certainly this lively and engaging southerner, with his shrill tenor voice, contributed something new to the art of the *café-concert*, but all the same his style, set against Polin's unruffled and unarguable talent, caused no revolutions and he found his true line with low comedy later on. Interestingly enough, every great music-hall figure has had to contend at some point with a newcomer rocketing to fame and seeming to challenge his position. Often the challengers have had very successful careers of their own, but the originals always kept the lead without too much trouble: they had got where they were by virtue of what they were, without fighting anyone, and because their way of amusing or moving an audience was their own, and individual. No enduring reputation was ever founded on any sort of deception of the public. A real professional career lasts too long, for one thing. There is ample time to see through the merely clever, the merely adept, if the genuine gift is lacking. You can fool some of the people some of the time, you cannot fool all of the people all of the time. (Not my phrase, but the sentiment appeals to me.)

I can see the coxcomb Vilbert as though it were yesterday, perfumed and elegant, bidding me admire his yellow shoes, made to measure, he assures me, at Marseilles and sent on to him in Paris. 'Seventeen francs, my dear young Chevalier,' he flutes in his slightly off-key tenor. 'Seventeen francs they cost me. Now what do you think of that?'

I could only register admiration and experience envy, for my first fortnight's salary had not yet been paid and it was thanks to folded newspapers and nothing else that I had any shoes at all.

MARSEILLES

Nothing special happened during the Parisiana run. What I remember most is being a head shorter than anyone in the company when it began and a head taller when I left. I shot up at an incredible rate; I had a friend who always said it gave him a crick in the neck to watch. Height, unfortunately, didn't make them renew my contract when the show finished, but I ended up with a tidy 500 francs

in the savings-bank and re-equipped with a new, or almost new,
wardrobe of suits and shirts and shoes. Maman and I had held firm
to our plan of keeping half my earnings in reserve and had done the
re-equipping in the huge covered flea-market of the clothing trade
in the Rue du Temple. All the old clothes dealers in Paris operated
there, behind serried rows of stalls, their wares spread out before
them. It was open until midday and there was nothing you couldn't
buy – academic robes or the tattered remnants of a general's uniform, a brassière, a rupture-belt or lacy underwear discarded by
some high-class tart. Here one morning, in my quest for an outfit, I
came across what seemed to me an absolutely staggering costume: a
suit, very wide in the shoulders, very much in the American style of
the day, generously draped. Its previous owner had evidently been
a portly man. The dealer's price was fifteen francs, but after heated
argument I beat him down to twelve and carried away the prize.
Maman altered it for me as well as she could and, the picture of the
modern sporting type, I strolled off to the Boulevard Strasbourg to
take a turn round the block and display my finery.

I was an enormous growing boy and very thin, and must have
resembled a bean-pole in all those folds and drapes. It was painfully
clear from the reaction of my friends that, when it came to tailoring,
I had a lot to learn. What was more, I no sooner set foot in the
theatre that evening than the great Fragson inquired, in his rasping
voice: 'Wearing our grandfather's suit tonight, Chevalier?' Duti-
fully his entourage, male and female, tittered at the sally and I
blushed scarlet.

Shame was an emotion I could never master. I have always been
prone to feel stupidly and constantly ashamed. The failing got
worse instead of better as time went on, and here was another case
of it. I told Fragson that if he didn't like my suit he could well
afford to pay his tailor to make another for me, shrugged my shoulders at him and turned away before I said anything really rude. But
I was bitterly humiliated because all the girls were laughing, and I
am so constituted that that trivial remark stood between Fragson
and me as long as I knew him. Never once did I meet him, see him,
congratulate him, but the words, 'Wearing our grandfather's suit
tonight, Chevalier?' seemed to hang blazing in the air as we parted.

I never could make a friend of him in the years that followed, for all my professional admiration. Yet far nastier things said and done by other people have faded from my memory without a trace. Perhaps I am at the same time too humble and too proud. Or it's probably just a touch of personal idiocy.

With the glorious title of Chevalier, M. of Parisiana, I now began the round of the agents, job-hunting once more. I called myself Chevalier, M. in imitation of several near-stars of the period such as Roger, M. and Darius, M. and to avoid confusion with a successful eccentric comedian of a generation back, Louis Chevalier, to say nothing of Émile Chevalier, the provincial actor. But nothing very thrilling turned up, so I took an offer to play a Thursday, Saturday and Sunday at the Eden-Concert at Asnières. Only thirty-five francs, though. Could this portend a slipping back to the hand-to-mouth existence I had known before? Despondency returned.

I went to Asnières on the Thursday to do my three days: an attractive, well-proportioned theatre in the main street, an audience of kindly-disposed suburbanites, local bookmakers and ordinary folk. And I was a hit from the word go.

I was using some of Dranem's songs, but by now my own particular blend of Dranem and Boucot, Sergius and Dorville, had developed a special savour of Ménilmontant that was all my own. I improvised backchat from the stage with this charming audience, and they loved it and put new heart into me. They laughed, and went on laughing. Without my knowing it, my act had evolved and changed. I had ceased to be a child and was a young man whose occasional innuendoes were no longer out of place.

They called me back, they stamped their feet, and I made my exit dazed with success, for I had forgotten I could ever earn genuine applause like that. I wanted to laugh and cry, and almost before I had my make-up off the manager and his wife came round with congratulations and asked me to do an extra week. That blessed extra week stretched into two, three, ten. I stayed the whole season. The place had adopted me. I was known as the Holy Child, *le petit Jésus* of the Eden of Asnières, part and parcel of the establishment, and I look back gratefully to the weeks I passed in happy relation with its delightful customers. With them I built up my self-confidence and there, popular and accepted, I first became aware of, then started to express, my true personality. Before I was properly on the stage they were calling out, '*Bonjour, p'tit Jésus,* how are you today?' I didn't have to imitate anyone any more.

The close professional world of the *café-concert* took note of my success and Asnières led to a week at the Scala in Brussels at twenty francs a night. When I went home with this tremendous news, La Louque and I stood ourselves a dinner for two at Druant's to celebrate.

That was a magnificent summer, not a bit like the one before. Brussels was Asnières all over again and I was there a month, happy with the audiences, happy in my work and loving that beautiful, smiling city. To follow I found nothing better than the palais d'Été at Lille at fifteen francs for two shows a day but I accepted it. I had learnt by now that the worst thing you can do in this business is to do nothing. If you don't work you not only don't earn, you also spend more, which puts you in the soup twice over.

Lille, like Brussels, was another Asnières and I played there for two months. It was past belief, the way it was all suddenly so easy. The applause started before I even opened my mouth, tycoons invited me to lunch and supper. I went back to Paris with 2,000 francs saved up and the reputation, acknowledged on the Boulevard de Strasbourg, of being a young man worth watching.

The old troupers discussed me with thoughtful expressions on their faces (I was 16, remember), but their juniors seemed more than pleased to see me.

'Maurice, my boy! I hear you knocked 'em in Brussels and Lille!'

'I say, I've written to the management – you wouldn't like to put in a good word, would you?'

The director of the Alcazar in Marseilles, in town to arrange his winter bookings, had apparently heard my name and sent for me. I emerged with contracts for a three-month tour that would include Marseilles, Nice, Lyons, Bordeaux, Avignon, Clermont-Ferrand, Algiers and other places at a salary varying from twenty to thirty francs a night, according to the town. I was treading on air, impatient to begin. It seemed like years before my opening Friday in Marseilles.

But it dawned at last and there I was, stepping out of the train in Marseilles railway station at about ten in the morning. With a suit-case in each hand I set out for the Alcazar in the Cours Belzunce in the lower part of the town, passing as I went the huge posters for that night's performance. Dalbret was on the top line as star attrac-tion and my name was in big print, half-way down. The sight of it was like a blow in the midriff. I stopped in my tracks, sick with anxiety.

'You do know this is Marseilles, don't you?' I said to myself, 'the place you hear so much about? Where everybody's out to get everybody else. Gangs in the gallery at the Alcazar, and gun-fights, too, if they happen to meet. Not very funny, I should think.'

I called to mind the tales they told in the Faubourg Saint-Martin; the howling audiences, the organized apache gangs. Marseilles, the Chicago of tomorrow. Wonderful or terrifying city, depending on one's point of view.

I was greeted at rehearsal by the manager, Franck.

'Good morning, there you are. Get your stuff ready, it's your turn.'

A troupe of acrobats were fixing their apparatus, while stage-hands set scenery for the different numbers and the orchestra was in attendance to run through with the singers. My turn. Diffidently I explained my requirements to the conductor. The music struck up, and so did I.

The feeble croak I produced drew glances of surprise from the orchestra pit. What the hell was this? Franck was obviously per-turbed and Marius, his lighting-man – gas lighting, for the theatre had no electricity then – gave a fatalistic shrug. The one-eyed stage carpenter, François, scratched the back of his head. There was gloom and presentiment on every side.

'Down a tone, perhaps?' suggested the conductor, out of the kindness of his heart.

'No, no, Monsieur. It'll be all right tonight, I'm sure. It's the journey, you know. It'll be all right with an audience.'

'Tonight!' said the glances. 'They'll murder him tonight.'

The Alcazar was packed, stalls, circles, promenade. Shall I ever forget that promenade or the row upon row of heads, most of them with caps on, and everyone yelling and shouting? The short first half of the programme was just girls and steady uproar and nothing startling happened in the second until the appearance of a song-and-dance man called Bertho, who had a very high-pitched voice. He didn't exactly sing, he baa-ed. Tonight his normal goat-like tones were exaggerated by panic and he was baa-ing worse than ever. The gallery baa-ed threateningly back at him once or twice during his first two songs but it was a cartwheel during a chorus that led to real catastrophe. It triggered off a general explosion, heralded by a man in the stalls who rose to his feet with a stentorian *Bravo!* turned to the fascinated public and cried *Bravo!* again. Bertho stood looking at him, hypnotized, and everybody started laughing. Once more the man shouted, 'Bravo, what a *dancer!*' in accents of feigned enthusiasm, and sat down with the air of a satisfied connoisseur. At that the storm really surged over orchestra and stage. Beside himself with fury, Bertho rushed off into the wings in a terrible taking and cannonaded straight into the wall.

Next, a rather pretty woman did some Montmartre songs, including a satirical effort on the Russo-Japanese war. The last line of the chorus, *Down with General Oku!* was based on a popular tune and referred to some Oriental commander. But the Marseilles theatregoers did not, at that date, much relish the acid wit of Montmartre and this song, like all its kind, had a great many verses. The house grew restless again. For the fifth time round the singer expressed her scorn of General Oku and as she began the sixth verse you could feel impending crisis. She went into the famous last line of the chorus with no variety whatsoever of tone or beat, and was promptly drowned by a voice from the gallery, where a big, strapping man, in a seat near the proscenium-arch, bellowed,

'You can stick your General Oku!'

This created quite an effect, for Oku, in the accent of Marseilles, became *au cul*, reinforced by an unmistakable V-sign. The singer beat a retreat, the intervener received an ovation; the orchestra began my introductory music and I made my entrance, more dead than alive.

Laughter at the Oku joke had not yet subsided. All over the house people were literally rolling about in their seats, convulsed with merriment. I stood and waited, at a loss for what to say or do. Eventually, at long, long last, they settled down and I started my first number. My voice came out muffled and weak, worse than useless with that audience, who were more intractable than ever after their recent diversion. My three verses were met with a deathly hush. This was frightful, but I tried to carry on as though I hadn't noticed and began a comic monologue on atavism, of all subjects. Try if you can to put yourself in my place for five minutes – looking like a clown and having to make an unsmiling audience laugh. But there it was, appalling.

There was a sort of rippling noise as I made for the wings. Stricken, I sought the stricken regard of Franck, Marius and François. The rippling sounded more distinct. Desperately, before they finished me off, I launched into my third song, '*Le Rondeau Populaire*', a list of favourite song-titles strung together into a lyric. And then – could I have heard aright? They were laughing. Nicely, in a friendly fashion. They couldn't be! But they were, again and again and again, and applauding loudly at the end.

The atmosphere changed completely. I sang each chorus marching round with a child's uniform kepi on my head, blowing a toy rifle like a trumpet, and they loved it. The laughter was continuous. I had won.

Circling the stage after the first verse, I could see Franck's beaming face as he craned out of the wings, crying: 'That's fine, my boy. Go on, you've got them!' The rest of my turn went like clockwork and when I had done they shouted and wanted me back, but I had some experience now and after an escape like that I was going to make them wait. As the stamping feet grew deafening Franck took me by the shoulders and said: 'Right, my boy, off you go for now.' A quick, very brief encore to avoid the risk of overdoing it, and I was crumpled up in the dressing-room with legs that felt like cotton wool. The manager's voice came out of a dream.

'You know what this means, boy? You've conquered the whole Midi, that's what. We're more or less the Paris Opera House where this game's concerned.'

But I had had a mauling too, that left me quaking at the thought of the narrow margin between triumph and disaster. Ours is a profession where extremes meet.

The night we closed I signed a contract for the following season: thirty-five francs this time. I was sad to be leaving and arranged to meet Bertho at the station next day. He was bound for Paris, I for Clermont-Ferrand, and I anticipated a last exchange of jokes on the platform as we said good-bye, a burst of laughter to carry us out of sight. But over the farewell handshakes our glances were suddenly serious and I couldn't laugh at all. We had had a fortnight of sheer cameraderie and perfect understanding which had assuredly found a place in my ever-vulnerable heart. I was speechless and my eyes filled with unexpected tears. For the first time I was doing what we, who take the road to peddle our bright and cheerful wares, have to do all too often, and at cruel cost. I was tearing myself away from a friend.

BOXING, ENGLISH STYLE

By now, 1907, I was having some success. People like Mayol, for instance, then at the height of his career, might have been irritated by this, but it could not possibly affect them; Mayol was like the Rock of Gibraltar. But there were others.

Every day, from noon onwards, the second and third rank of the music-hall used to congregate at a café in the Rue du Faubourg Saint-Martin run by a couple named Pagès. None of its customers was in the top flight, for the big names wouldn't have risked being seen there, but all the rest came to eat and drink and talk shop and mix with kindred spirits, while Madame Pagès – Félicie to the regulars – presided like a benevolent grenadier. Here, one night after my tour, I found myself under attack from an ageing, embittered comedian. He had given me old-fashioned looks on many previous occasions – which I had thought it best to ignore – but this particular evening, perhaps with a drink too much inside him, he wasn't shilly-shallying.

'Now then, star of the century! Condescended to mix with the untalented horde, have you?'

Unprepared for this assault, I said that was a stupid remark and must be the drink talking. The crowded café fell suddenly silent as the unusual spectacle of an older man taunting a young one unfolded before a professionally appreciative audience. I was petrified and stood there abashed with my mouth wide open. Pop-eyed with rage, the other lost all control and yelled at me.

'Star my arse', he said, 'and if that's not enough for you, you can come outside! Come on out into the Passage de l'Industrie and I'll fix you so you'll never know what's hit you, you dirty little show-off.'

So now what? Did I accept his challenge? If I didn't, my reputation would sink to zero with them all. I must accept it. Yet I could not bring myself to do so. Seeing me hesitate he bore menacingly down upon me, his distorted face making me feel worse than ever.

I haven't the faintest idea what I babbled back at him. That street-fighting wasn't my line; that I hadn't been raised as an urchin, didn't know what was biting him. . . . The top and bottom of it was, I was plain scared.

It was an undramatic conclusion. The onlookers turned back to their cards and chatter, casting looks of scorn in my direction, although la mère Pagès, as we called her, said: 'That's right, Maurice. You fight him and you'll have to take the whole place on. They're every one of them jealous.' Her support effectively closed the incident and I departed, white as a sheet, to slink off home and there collapse in a paroxysm of shame. I was a coward, no doubt about it. I had been afraid, quite simply afraid. I never slept a wink.

This was the time when the vogue for English boxing had just reached Paris, and French boys were gradually learning to stand up to fighters from Britain and America who looked all set to murder them at first. A dancing-teacher friend of mine, Stilson, happened to be managing a young French boxer named Mongevin, and with that dreadful evening fresh upon me I told him the whole story of fear and cowardice, chagrin and shame, and begged him to get his protégé to teach me how to box; it would help him on a bit, for I was willing to pay for lessons. I simply couldn't be risking these insults and never know how to say boo to a goose. Something had to be done.

Daily, buoyed up by the thirst for revenge, I took my boxing-lesson and followed it with a few minutes in the ring with Mongevin. In a month he said my speed and dash were well above average. I was taking far more than I was handing out, of course, but I was also getting used to giving and receiving blows. Stilson came to watch the lesson one night and casually suggested that we might spar a little. I agreed, expecting him to make hay of me, for he was tall and strong and quick on his feet. But thank heaven, he danced better than he boxed. From the first few exchanges I knew I was on top and attacked him boldly. Stilson, with a bloody nose, gave in. It was a joyous feeling. His fighter Mongevin had done the umpiring and was literally crowing, not only as my instructor, but because I, his pupil, had knocked his own manager about before his very eyes.

As for me, with a bruise or two on my face, I was treading on air. Only one thing remained before perfect harmony ensued between me and the universe at large, and that was to go back to the café and bid defiance to my former challenger. I knew now that blows were rarely very serious, and Mongevin had certainly given me more than that hysterical funny-man could deliver, even if he hit me.

I had the whole fight planned in my head. I should hold him off for a while with my left, then, if that worked, go into the attack, always relying on my left, and try for his nose until he saw stars. And the minute he appeared to be slowing down I should get him just where I wanted him for a one-two, right-left to the jaw.

I waited in a frenzy until every last *habitué* was assembled in the café Pagès and made a rapid inspection through the window. My man was there all right, having his game of cards. I drew a deep breath and went in, straight past the bar, on a beeline for his table. I tapped him on the shoulder and he turned. I suppose I must have gone a pale but decided green, and suddenly everything around was dead quiet.

'You said some very insulting things to me a month ago, if you remember.'

'Oh, yes? And you recall what happened?'

'You wanted to knock the living daylights out of me.' My throat was dry and I could hardly frame the words.

'So I did. And then?'

'Nothing, then. But I've been thinking it over and, you know, I don't see how an oaf like you can really do much damage. So now's your time. Let's go out and get it settled.'

'Bravo, Maurice!' The voice of Madame Pagès.

All eyes rested on the surly comedian and there was the pregnant pause that heralds some sensational event. But the event when it came was a sad let-down, a mere attempt to shrug the matter off. Whether he had heard about my lessons in the noble art, or thought I was all worked up and capable of thrashing him; whether he took alarm at the rigid set of my mouth or just got panic-stricken in his turn, I do not know. At any rate, he spluttered excuses for having forced a quarrel on me when he wasn't sober. The drink had made him touchy. Nothing in the world against me – why not have a drink now and forget the whole thing?

Sure of myself, conscious of having retrieved my position, I assumed an air of loftiest calm.

'I don't drink with little girls,' I said. Then, high and disposedly, I proceeded to the bar and invited Madame Félicie to share a glass. But ah! the might-have-been!

THE ELDORADO MUSIC-HALL

I was, physically, rather at a loss after this abortive battle. I had been all keyed up for a storm of blows and the peaceable outcome left me in the air and nervy. About now I happened to be working in Lille and went one afternoon to a gymnasium owned by François Descamps, who was not then the famous manager he later became, to ask whether I might have a round or two with any of his pupils. All the pupils, I was told, had other jobs in the daytime. All, that is, save one youngster he was bringing on, a 14-year-old, by name Georges Carpentier; but he thought, on reflection, that I should be too much for him. I was not exactly a killer, I protested, but

Descamps got terribly agitated. 'That's all very well,' he said, 'it begins all right, everything nice and gentle, then you warm up and you start hitting harder. Can't risk your doing any damage to my little Georges!' His little Georges! He really was worried lest I injure the cherished starlet, which seemed reasonable enough at the time and too silly for words a few years later. However, I mention it to Georges occasionally, to remind him that once my strong arm made him tremble.

Since boxing had helped me to put a braver face on life I was grateful to it, and commissioned a short sketch, entitled *English Boxer*, in which I appeared in striped jersey and ten-ounce gloves and ended up shadow-boxing with myself. This was hailed as a splendid innovation, and, again, was something new in my act.

Meanwhile I was working full tilt, *d'arrache-pied* as we say, and my feet were certainly doing their share, for I practised tap-dancing every morning, and modern Anglo-American-style dance routines. I always wound up two or three of my songs with a dance and liked to vary my steps and my acrobatic evolutions and the comic business for my exit. The song-writer Henri Christiné was taking an interest in me and the songs he wrote for me were tailor-made. In one especially, '*Le Beau Gosse*', I could dance to my heart's content, and it was a huge hit with the young.

La Louque and I were leading an ideal life these days. We had already moved to 118, Rue du Faubourg Saint-Martin, and now took a bigger apartment at the same address, where for the first time we had a view out on to the street. My contracts were getting better and better and even with our rule of spending only half my fees we ate and drank like kings. I often brought friends home to dinner, and Maman had a welcoming smile for them all and saw that they enjoyed themselves. Sometimes Milton came, or Georgel, who had turned professional with great success, or the witty Bohemian Georges Roger. No, things couldn't have been more pleasant in that new flat of ours.

When we ate alone I had to tell her all I had been doing (or nearly all, anyway), and demonstrate any new songs which had been written for me. English and American numbers were becoming more and more popular in Paris and she used to learn them from me like a child. We would hum them together over dessert, she taking the melody while I harmonized in thirds. Rather silly, I suppose and yet, when I look back, it means so much.

Then it would be time to leave for the theatre. Then there was the show, and supper at a restaurant, and occasionally sundry other amusements, too, before I got home. But that beloved voice called good-night from her room however late it was. Until I was safely back she could not sleep.

'Heard the news?'

'No. What news?'

'Young Chevalier. Dranem's gone on tour and he's booked to replace him at the Eldorado.'

'Good God, you're joking! *Chevalier* filling in for *Dranem*? At the *Eldo*?'

'That's what I said.'

'Well, you could knock me down with a feather.'

'Didn't have to do a thing about it, either; they came and asked him. Begged and prayed him almost. He told them he wasn't ready for it, not enough experience and so forth, but it was him they wanted and he wound up saying yes. Never lifted a finger!'

'What's he getting?'

'Thousand a month, two full months. Top of the bill, too, never mind about Montel, and Bach, and Georgel.'

'Heavens above!'

'I think it's a bit too much too soon, myself. Can you imagine – billed ahead of turns like that at his age! Never heard of such a thing.'

'Oh, I don't know, probably do him good. But my God! Only 19 and filling in for Dranem! You certainly needed a bit more behind you before you got your stripes in my time.'

From the Boulevard Saint-Martin to the Boulevard Strasbourg, all was in ferment. There was only one talking-point, a single topic of conversation. Some hoped for success, others saw disaster looming.

I told my mother about it all. '*Petite Louque*, I simply couldn't believe them. Madame Marchand had told them to get me, and she's the boss's wife, and so they had to. They'd have paid me twelve or

fifteen hundred a month if I'd dared to ask, I know they would.'
The scene left nothing to be desired. Mother gazed at me speechless
and her chin quivered for sixty seconds at least before she burst
into tears. And on the opening night I, too, stared transfixed at the
posters outside the theatre. CHEVALIER was there in large
letters, with Montel, Bach and Georgel trailing behind; and they
were the best in the business, if you didn't count Mayol, Dranem,
Polin and Fragson, the four very top names.

I sang at the Eldorado for two months, and though Montel was
far from pleased the audiences were kind, which helped to compensate for his provoking ways. I was 19 and I had made it.

One night a report came round that P. L. Flers was in front. It
was as though we had all received an electric shock. Flers was the
Napoleon of the music-hall, director of the big revues at the Folies-
Bergère, and everyone gave of his or her best in the hope of attracting his attention. When not actually on the stage we peered eagerly
through holes in the scenery, trying to read the great man's thoughts.
Personally, I was not over-concerned. I was on top of the world,
anyway, and happy with things as they were.

And so it never occurred to me, when a Folies-Bergère letter was
handed to me next night, that the summons came for me alone. I
inquired round the green-room who else had heard, and silence fell.
Nobody else had heard. Montel said nothing, but his face went
suddenly tight, and I shut up. But the evening after that I took home
a contract for three consecutive winter seasons at the Folies, starting
at 1,800 francs a month, with a 500-franc rise every year.

Maman was used to the onward and upward trend by now and
these things no longer surprised her. We were going on beautifully
at home, with nothing to upset her save, occasionally, the dawning
irregularity of my love-life. But news of my fabulous contract was
all over the neighbourhood in twenty-four hours, and most embarrassing it was. That footloose band of players with their perpetual
packing and unpacking, their journeyings to and fro, could sense
that one of their number was on the way up. I was about to leave
the fold, and we were not at ease together any more.

THE FOLIES-BERGÈRE AND THE AMBASSADEURS

The first song I ever sang at the Folies-Bergère was a parody on a famous play by Henri Bataille, '*L'Enfant de l'Amour*', it was called, and it had a chorus that went,

> From the moment I was born,
> Child of love, that's me.

These recurring lines I accompanied with one of my suggestive hitches, jerking forward in a way that usually raised a cosy laugh we could all share together. But this evening it did nothing of the kind. Throughout that introductory number, through all my patter and posturing and eccentric dance-steps, there came no gleam of encouragement, never a smile. Just rows of frozen faces, rapidly turning bored. My second and third songs underlined the failure. Too well-bred to go in for noisy disapproval, this audience made its feelings horribly clear by contemptuous non-demonstration. I was shaken and utterly bewildered. This was my début before people who mattered and I had obviously gone badly wrong. It was like the Petit Casino again after my triumphs in the Avenue de Wagram, and in very similar circumstances – the changeover from one kind of public to another. This was scarcely on the same level, though. The leap this time was from the Eldorado up to the Folies-Bergère, and it felt like receiving a slap in the face.

The next night they put me on earlier and cut my third song out, to shorten my turn, and I had been so terrified of getting the sack that I was almost grateful to them. But the day after that the *Figaro* critic, enthusing over the rest of the show, literally felled me in his review. 'And where', he inquired, 'can they have found this clumsy booby, and who let him loose in our leading music-hall? Vulgar beyond belief. His song based on Bataille's masterpiece is nothing but filth.'

A slating like that, when I thought I was on my way to the stars, brought me crashing down with a bump. Were the best audiences, then, so very hard to please? Certainly, at this moment, I decided that they must be. I just didn't know enough, hadn't enough brains, to satisfy them. I should have stayed in the *cafés-concerts*, where folk were perfectly happy so long as you made them laugh, and didn't argue the toss about how you did it. Convinced this time the sack was coming, I sought an interview with Flers. A low comedian was manifestly no good in these exalted circles, and would he please release me from my contract and let me go back to where I belonged? I had neither talent enough, nor anything else, to justify their expectations here.

Flers heard me out with a faint smile, fixing me as he did so with his keen, melancholy glance. By the time I had finished I was practically sobbing at him. Then he patted me lightly on the cheek and said,

'You haven't found yourself yet, my boy. Salad days. But you listen to me carefully and pay attention to what I say and you'll be a star-turn of the winter show by the time we get to the dress-rehearsal next month. Till then just tone it down a bit. Less effort, and not so much business. And when it comes to the revue, you do as I tell you. That's all.'

And in that big winter revue, partnering Jane Marnac as the only dance-man comic in the show, I was the obvious choice to play opposite the women stars. I was young, fit and energetic, with a mixture of comedy, song and dance that distinguished me from the rest. My up-to-the-minute topical numbers went over better than the cleverest stuff that other people sang, for rhythm is a mysterious thing, with more power over an audience than any verbal wit. The lyrics Flers wrote, if not unduly subtle, were nevertheless streets ahead of the material I had been using, and that awkward public admitted me freely, now, to its good graces. I turned my back upon vulgarity. I would watch Claudius and Morton from the wings and profit by what I saw, their unforced style and lightness of touch. There was nothing heavy, I noticed, no lingering over comic effect. I was learning to value that rarest of stage virtues – quality.

With the onward and upward trend continuing like this, we could afford more improvements on the domestic front and, after many longing glances at a 'Flat to Let' notice in the Boulevard de Strasbourg, Maman and I decided to treat ourselves to much more comfortable quarters. We took two rooms overlooking the Passage de l'Industrie, with a bedroom for me and a kitchen on the court-yard side, on the second floor at Number 18. Progress!

When I was engaged by the manager of the Ambassadeurs and of the Alcazar d'Été, the open-air *café-concerts* in the Champs-Élysées, for three summer seasons to alternate with my three winters at the Folies-Bergère, I seemed to be settled for life. I didn't enjoy revue as much as working alone, but the life was a great deal more pleasant. Now I went into the provinces for no more than a couple of months, and was in Paris for the rest of the year. Moreover, I was reaching the sophisticated public, as I could never have done with the kind of songs that started me off so badly at the Folies. Night after night I polished my style, and reaped the benefit every time I stepped on to the stage. Discarding vulgarity, I grew better at my job. And then, one night in June, I was opening at the Ambassadeurs, when a few short years before I had been lost in the crowd of hopefuls who patrolled miserably round the place, on the outside looking in. Now I was up there, with everybody clapping; you can imagine how I felt. What with one thing and another, this summer engagement of mine was proving just about perfect.

After the show I often went to the popular nightclub, Chez Fisher, where Fisher put himself at the top of the bill and did the last turn of the evening. But the presiding goddess, here as in any other night-spot where she chose to appear, was of course Fréhel. Fréhel was an entirely contradictory creature, hard to describe; one minute all crystal purity, and the lowest imaginable guttersnipe the next. She was about 20, I suppose, and it would have been an under-statement to say that she was beautiful. Very slim, with a bewitching oval face and an inborn poise and elegance which gave her an English look. She had thoroughly French eyes, though, and a warm hoarse voice that seemed to well straight from her stomach. She kept the most shocking hours and was for ever either losing her voice and deciding to die of consumption, or singing with incredible resonance and giving fantastic performances. It was always one extreme or the other and I presume the late hours had something to do with it. Without the slightest effort she could make an audience laugh or cry. Fréhel had the lot – looks, that odd, compelling voice and natural, direct ability that rang absolutely true. She was individual, a great

E

artist and more sought-after than most in the pleasure-loving Paris of those days. But as a result of the wild life she led she tangled herself up in one disconcerting love-affair after another, when she would have done better to keep her head and get on with her career.

But Fréhel had, alas, no head at all and her whole history was a regrettable demonstration of the fact. She burnt herself out, physically, in what seemed to her admirers an impossibly short time, and was a sad loss to the French music-hall. With that wonderful, abounding temperament she could have been the greatest *chanteuse* of her generation, had she managed to keep even a little of her youthful beauty. But our profession is a hard taskmaster. You may think it calls for nothing but grace and gaiety; what it demands is discipline, constant sacrifice and slavery. Fail to embrace any of these with a smile on your face, and you may do quite nicely for a while but there'll be a big bill to pay in the end.

However, to return to Fisher. He was a man with no voice, few physical endowments and much insidious charm. He seemed to feel, rather than sing, his songs and I remember how, an untaught street-Arab newly arrived in his world, I found him very puzzling. How did he do it? He wasn't young, he wasn't slender; he couldn't really sing and he didn't make beautiful gestures as did all the other romantic soloists, from Mayol down. At one fell swoop he made nonsense of everything I thought I had learnt about a job in which I was proceeding, in any case, by sheer instinct. The rowdiest set of revellers, after buckets of champagne, went suddenly quiet, as though Fisher, with a couple of lines and a chorus, had touched the most sensitive spot they had. How did he do it?

It has taken me years and years to find out how. Many years, during which life has had to teach me what I could doubtless have gathered long before from books had I been less benighted, had I realized that books could have supported and enriched me, and generally clarified my thinking. Fisher could make almost immediate heart-to-heart contact with his hearers. He had 'charm'. And it wasn't the shoddy, milk-and-water charm of an ageing Don Juan trying to be young. Fisher's was the charm of a temperate, sensible man who had been in love with love and who, instead of lamenting, turned his disillusion into tender songs on the folly of loving too much. He first made me see that in our profession, where the important things are contact and fluidity, it isn't a man's age and appearance that matter, so much as what he can bring out of the depths of his own nature and lay before an audience. The elegant ladies and gentlemen in Fisher's club sat there and listened to what was in his heart and almost, as they did so, he renewed their souls. I cannot think that many of them ever understood the process, but it is a lesson which I have to thank him for: sincerity first, technique second.

MISTINGUETT

Returning when summer was over to the Folies-Bergère, I was in for a glorious surprise: they had engaged my admired Mistinguett. My more than admired Mistinguett, if the truth were known. I had rather a crush on her and now, I hoped and prayed, I might be dancing with her.

The whole company gathered on the stage for the allocation of parts at the first rehearsal, and my heart was going like a sledge-hammer when they came to her scene. Then Flers called my name and I stepped forward.

'Do you know Mademoiselle Mistinguett, Chevalier?'

We had, in fact, met and I was able to say yes.

'Good. Right, then, you have the main comic number, *La Valse Renversante*. I'll give you an outline.'

He motioned me to sit beside her while he described the sketch. Some amusing dialogue to begin with, of which she took the lion's share and I made do with what was left; this developed into an argument, in which she hit me as hard as she could for several minutes and I remained dumbly on the receiving end; and finally, entwined and dancing dizzily round, we sent the furniture flying. Cannonading into the sofa, we got involved in the carpet and rolled ourselves up in it completely. We finally unrolled, waltzing all the time, waltzed abruptly through the window, and off. The stage was to be ours from eleven to twelve every morning, from the next day onwards, to rehearse alone.

Next morning, in my practice-clothes and dancing-pumps, I was ready and waiting before the star, in a restrained and stylish suit, arrived. She changed into something fetching and practical, and together we set about the most entrancing rehearsals I have ever known.

What a woman she was! What temperament she had, and what fun she got out of her work! Her joking persistence until some step or figure came exactly right filled me with admiration. There was an immediate bond between us, too, for we sprang from the same humble background. She, the great Mistinguett, treated me as an equal from the first. With her I never felt awkward for being no grander than I was and I soon saw that my urchin witticisms, coming from one who was so recently a street-urchin himself, were making her laugh aloud. The people she mixed with now, she said, never laughed like that; far too clever, they were, and not cheerful enough.

The sketch was progressing nicely, and if its reception at rehearsal were anything to go by it was sure to please an audience. I was happy being near her, just being with her, and for her part she seemed relaxed and confident when we were together. I had vowed to keep my emotions to myself – it would only spoil everything if she said no – but the hours I spent away from her were very long and empty. We knew that we made a good team; the complicated dance, coming so easily, proved that beyond a doubt. And we spoke the same language, too, common or garden working-class. The cracks with which I enlivened our labours must have made a refreshing change from the high-toned conversation of the nobility and gentry she mixed with nowadays; and I suppose she could sense my feelings when I held her in my arms. Keep all these things in mind, and you will perhaps understand what eventually happened at one of those rehearsals. Rolling ourselves in our carpet, with Mistinguett clinging to me, away from the rest of the world, we realized naturally, unmistakably, without a word spoken, that this, for both of us, was it. We unrolled much more slowly than usual, and no one, for that day at least, suspected that the Mistinguett-Chevalier partnership, with all its private joys and all the public praises, had just embarked upon its long and pleasurable career.

I was 22, still painfully shy and ill at ease anywhere save backstage at the Folies or in the Boulevard Strasbourg, where, to some extent, I was buoyed up by professional success. To be sure, I was doing a whole lot better than all the middling and minor artists living in our district, but there were great gaps in my non-education and elementary schooling, and I was dreadfully awkward. I got the shakes going into a smart restaurant or a modish haunt like Fisher's and felt uncomfortably inferior to everybody present. Shame engulfed me and I thought all the fashionables were gloating over my embarrassment. As soon as possible I would retreat to less exalted company, and the first dinner-jacket I had made was about as relaxing as a suit of armour, so tense and starchy did I feel whenever I 'dressed' to go out. All this Mistinguett knew, considered feeble and was determined to cure.

She still had a few nights to do at the Variétés in '*La Vie Parisienne*' before coming to the Folies and gave me two tickets for the show. I was to go round in the second interval and visit her in her dressing-room. So behold me in the third row of the stalls, duly wearing my dinner-jacket, and my mate Milton, who had not yet attained the heights of tailor-made evening clothes, perched there beside me. A prey to varying emotions, I watched that revue: the lavish scenery, the polished acting, the beautiful women, and Mist herself like an explosion of down-to-earth gaiety among them all. When she was not on the stage the rest of its distinguished company, with Max Dearly at their head, were enough to make me more aware than ever of how little I knew and how vulgar I was. I felt like a peasant invited up to the château for the evening, out of kindness.

But when she appeared the others vanished and I gazed as though I could eat her up, trying to believe my new happiness was real. Singing and dancing, outshining everyone, she knocked me endways. I was proud and grateful, and terrified already of proving unworthy of all she had given me since our wordless declaration in the carpet at the Folies-Bergère. Now and then, when she had the chance, she let her magnificent eyes dwell on me for a second, glowing and soft, before she went rollicking back into her role once more. I was madly in love with her. Professionally I admired her tremendously and as a woman she was so much more wonderful than any other I had ever met that I didn't know whether I was on my head or my heels.

All the same, I couldn't see her again until next day's rehearsal. She wasn't free after the show. 'Someone' was calling for her. 'Someone' was taking her to supper at Viel's or Maxim's and then, no doubt, back to the flat on the Boulevard des Capucines. And how well I knew its windows and balconies, having stared across at them often, as to the promised land, from the pavement opposite.

Well, what else did I want? I ought by rights to be deliriously happy, sharing the biggest, best-deserved success of a superb revue with the greatest leading-lady of the music-hall, becoming over-night the darling of its choosy public. And yet . . . and yet. . . . Good God! I thought, don't be a bloody fool. You had to say good night as though you were just friends. Well, that's how it is, what more can you expect? She isn't free, remember, and she hasn't made you any promises. She likes you, yes, but that doesn't mean she has to burn all her boats on your behalf. You'll see her alone in her dressing-room tomorrow and it will all be different. Tomorrow. And now get off home to bed, you with the splendid career. Pull yourself together. Pull yourself together and tell La Louque what a marvellous time you had. Go and kiss her, she's lying awake waiting for you to come in. Say how tired you are. Then you can shut your own door and lie down and have a good old sob about the whole thing. Shouldn't even get undressed, if I were you.

Jealous, are you? Hurts, does it? Well, it's something to cry about all right, but you be sensible and keep it under your pillow. Probably proves you have a delicate nature, anyway. You really can't have everything in this life, and when you think of the Rue Julien-Lacroix you're not doing too badly, by and large.

FIGHT THE GOOD FIGHT

It was somewhere about this time that the Home for Retired Music-Hall Artists at Ris-Orangis asked me to help at its charity gala matinée. English-style boxing was still a novelty in France and somebody had the bright idea that it might be an attraction to have a bout between well-known fighters, one white and one coloured. Then somebody else thought, why not ask me to appear on behalf of the white races?

I cannot say I was over-keen. I could box all right, but knowing how to box is not quite the same thing as standing up to a professional. They then said, not to worry, the fight would be fixed. They had persuaded young José Gans to get knocked down in the third round without having given me too much punishment in rounds one and two. This being so, I accepted.

Came the great day, and I entered the ring with Carpentier, Hogan and Bernard in my corner, all in the secret and laughing their heads off as they did their stuff. Our announcer, a celebrated M.C., proclaimed in stentorian tones 'a fight of ten rounds between Young José Gans' – he pointed to him and the Negro rose to his feet; applause – 'and Maurice Chevalier'. I stood up in my turn to cries of enthusiasm. The umpire then called us into the centre for his short address on fighting fair and no hitting below the belt. I was beaming like the sun. (Mistinguett, I should add, was in a side box with a gang of companions, all eager to see how her wonder-boy would fare.) I even tried to beam at my opponent, but he failed to meet my eye. The man was a damn good actor! Back to the corner, off with the robe, and the bell went for hostilities to begin.

Out I bravely came, as ready for him as if I had been prancing into boxing-rings my whole life long. I extended my hand, or rather, my right glove. He grunted vaguely but hardly touched it with his own and what happened one second later was a shattering surprise.

They had assured me, as I told you, that there was no shadow of risk. The tiger's claws were clipped, he would only pretend to bite and nothing could possibly go wrong. I took my time assuming a pretty guard in approved Carpentier fashion, up on my toes and weaving nicely, chin tucked snugly into my left shoulder, feinting harmoniously the while. With all this I was far too occupied to see what the other was doing, and, while I was still busy with my stylish stance, he pounced. The breeze of his left-hand glove went past my jaw, which I automatically drew back, his fist landed like a cannon-ball between my stomach and my liver and the breath went out of my body. Like someone who had dropped some money and was searching for it on the floor I lurched round the ring bent double, uttering groans of Oh! and Ah! What the hell was going on? He wasn't supposed to be doing this. I straightened with an effort and he knocked me over again with all the strength he had. Reflex action from the pain helped me to dodge the worst of it, but even the draught was terrifying. I went to pieces entirely until Georges, voice brought me to my senses.

'Use your left and parry, Maurice! Left and guard!'

Gans fell on me without a pause and pushed me round the ropes as if I were a child. Obeying Georges mechanically, in sheer self-preservation, I stopped him with an extended left and didn't linger. In this way I managed to land five desperate lefts on his nose and break away before he could attack. They must have hurt him, for the whirlwind abated a little. I was feeling better, if still far from aggressive, and as I circled him I muttered behind my gloves,

'Have you gone mad or something? You know the arrangement.'

Never shall I forget his diabolical look, the grin on that dark face, nor the glint in his eye.

'Me no fraud,' he cackled, 'me no fraud.'

As if the words had set his wrathful war-dance off afresh, he leaped upon me like a beast unchained. From then on it was less a boxing-match than a foot-race round the ring. I never would have believed that terror could have changed me into a grasshopper. I got in a punch with my ever-reliable left, then sprang a yard to one side of him, or even behind. I wouldn't swear that I didn't actually jump over his head. But I was never just where he thought I was and always got him from some unexpected angle – a quick punch on his dirty great nose and off out of range. Even so, he was more infuriated than tired by these last-ditch tactics when the bell sent us back to our corners.

Carpentier, Hogan, Bernard and the umpire were fuming. What had been intended as a friendly take-off of a sporting event had turned into something serious. Young José, in spite of having taken his money in advance, was obviously going to press for a knock-out. Hogan went over to tell him that if he persisted there would be another fight as soon as this one finished, the two of them with bare fists in a locked dressing-room – and Hogan was at the time the middle-weight champion of France. The Negro gave him a crafty, mulish look and answered as before: 'Me no fraud.'

We had a less spectacular second round, for I kept out of trouble by using my left and some of the steam seemed to have gone out of him; or perhaps he was tiring and saw his chance of hurting me grow less. Not that I was very scientific. All I could hope for was to bang away with that left and avoid as many blows as possible.

Then, in the interval, he announced that he would bite the dust at the beginning of round three, and this he did. Shaking in my shoes, I weakly tapped him with my right. He appeared to reel at the impact and fell flat on the floor. The audience were tepid but un-protesting; they must have suspected something fishy. The Negro had done his undivided best to fell me in the first round when I, with all my airs and graces, was expecting a very different tale. But than what happened? Had he taken fright, perhaps, at the thought of what Hogan and Carpentier would do to him? Or had I, tittupping round like a ballet-master, actually managed to tire him? Had all that business of left hooks to the nose had some real effect? Well, we shall never know, and I don't suppose anyone's very interested.

My bruises gave me a few days' agony and faded away. But a persistent rumour ran in the Boulevard de Strasbourg that Young Gans had in fact collected twice, once from our side to get himself beaten and again, to some considerable tune, from a former 'friend' of mine to lay me low. I never discovered which friend, nor really bothered much. Charming fellow, whoever he was.

BOUCOT

Winter of 1909–10. Things seemed to be going splendidly without much effort on my part, but I couldn't help touching wood, all the same. *Pourvu que ça dure*, we say in French; let's hope it lasts. And I felt I was marking time in a profession where you should always be going something new if you want to hold your public. Mean-while, my old acquaintance, Boucot, was making a name for himself by doing just that. 'They' said he was absolutely new, a revelation.

And what had Boucot got these days that so appealed to 'them'? One had better go and see.

He was a serious man with a lugubrious voice, and unimpressive at first glance. His opening number drew no more than polite applause, as though his hearers were waiting for the real thing. After the next they began to exchange remarks and questioning looks in the stalls, but then he announced his third song and the miracle took place.

Its title, 'Compensations', did not sound particularly promising. He had been losing their attention and it is hard to analyse the sudden change. So far he had been a surprise in the bad sense of the word; people had heard exaggerated reports of him and were tense with anticipation. And now – but wait till I tell you.

The introductory music was followed by a few bars ad lib., played over and over again as the orchestra waited for the singer to begin. Mock-serious, unhurried, Boucot removed an imaginary pair of gloves, rolled them up and put them in his pocket. Then, still to the same few bars, he started to hum, in harmony, a totally different tune and to match his improvisation with words that sounded vaguely English, though they were in fact a nonsense language of his own.

> Ouan dignenigne dignenigne Nousnaille
> Ouan dignenigne Mousmaille
> Trafalgar Square e Troufignon street.

It just might have been 'When dining, you'n I'.

So he continued, on and on until the audience yielded to the novelty and originality of the thing – copied since by many others – and broke into laughter. This, then, was the departure 'they' enjoyed so much. After the verse he hummed again to the ad lib., full tilt and always solemn as a judge: the 'Mountaineers' Chorus' and bits of 'Lakmé' and whatever else occurred to him. It was revolutionary. Nobody was doing anything like it on the Paris stage and it was irresistible. The whole theatre dissolved.

A second lunatic verse, then he went back to his 'Ouan dign-enigne...', approaching the side of the stage as he sang. Still singing, he bowed to a pretty woman in one of the boxes, sat him-self down on its velvet rim, kissed her hand and mimed a passionate

declaration. The audience was going wild by now and after the
initial shock the lady's escort, or husband, or whoever he was, joined
in and laughed with them over his large cigar. Boucot sniffed the
smoke and wagged his head appreciatively. The man, still laughing,
took out his case and proffered it. More applause. Boucot, unruffled,
selected a cigar, graciously allowing the donor to light it for him,
savoured it slowly, and blissfully relaxed. Then, in the most natural
way in the world, he picked up the woman's handbag, opened it
and looked inside, found the mirror and peered at it. Bold as the
innovation was, it was so completely fresh and unexpected that the
whole house went into stamping hysterics. This chap Boucot –
they'd never seen anything like him! Still humming madly, he made
his exit and the audience, sick with laughter, cheered him to the
echo and went on laughing for most of the next turn.

It was indeed a revelation. I left the theatre quite bemused and
for hours all I could say as I thought of him was, 'Well, you old
devil! Well, you old devil!' while for days the disjointed ideas
banged round my head like empty barrels in a drifting cargo-boat.
Boucot went on his way, triumphant.

Then, at the end of the season, I had something to worry about
at last. They cancelled my engagement at the Ambassadeurs and
the Alcazar d'Été by registered letter. I had been getting stale, the
public were fed up with me and the management, instead of keeping me for the three seasons agreed upon, felt they had had enough
of me after two. It was a bitter blow but I think it did me good, a
brutal lesson on how quickly the barometer of success can rise and
drop. I had believed that my up-to-date style was proof against
competition of the – highly unexpected – Boucot variety, and I sat
down to cool consideration of the facts. They were plain to see. I
had to acknowledge that Boucot was making progress while I, just
as unarguably, was falling back. The question was, why?

I knew perfectly well why. It was a year now since I had gone on
tour, or left Paris, or done anything about finding any new material,
or worked out any new business. And obviously a tour was the solution. Splendid idea. The catastrophe was a lesson for the future. Was
Boucot with his innovations going to finish me for ever? We
should see.

We should see because, when I thought about it, the methods he employed were double-edged. The first sight of a comedian who wandered unannounced into the audience, leaned on a box to chat with a pretty woman and smoke the customers' cigars, couldn't be funnier. But it wasn't so funny the second time round, and what about the third? And there was next season to consider too, when he would have to improve upon this year with something similar, only more so. Where on earth could it end? And what happened if he picked on some irritable spectator who just didn't fancy Boucot's joking with his wife, who raised objections or even slapped his face? Then he was in for trouble. Not that one wished him any harm, naturally, but it was logical to suppose he had embarked upon a perilous course and that his easy and enormous success depended on methods he could not use indefinitely. And with the passing of years this theory was justified. Boucot was a sound music-hall comic, he had a fine career, but he was never again to touch the heights he reached with his novel act between 1908 and 1910. He himself must have sensed a change of atmosphere, for he gradually stopped mingling with his audience and left that sort of thing to those who adopted and adapted his gimmicks. They could always make a cheap sensation, going down into the stalls, sitting on people's knees, planting lipsticky kisses on the top of somebody's head, trying on the women's hats. It was all good for a laugh, but it was far too easy. Far too easy, and too difficult to follow up when you remember that an artist must move forward all the time if he is to survive. Nor can he mess about like that for ever. The public, like a wild beast, is never tamed completely. It can turn and rend him at a second's notice. In my opinion, for what it is worth, the singer should stay in his proper place, which is up there on the stage.

PROGRESS, AND PEOPLE

To follow the summer season that ended with my getting the sack from the Ambassadeurs I did a provincial tour of the number-one towns, where I was now a big attraction. Whether I was suffering from shock, however, or whether it was just the way things go, I found the work was harder. I drew good houses, but I could 'get' an audience only with agonizing efforts. My nerves were in such a state that my voice became a croak after three or four songs and by the time I finished my throat was on fire. I began to be aware of the burdens that go with topping the bill and, prone to depression as I was, to imagine I was losing my grip. As though to confirm these melancholy notions, my scenes in that winter's Folies revue were not as good as usual. Everything, in fact, seemed to have taken a turn for the worse. We now had two clowns, for instance: Antonet and Grock, who came to us from the Cirque Médrano where they had been earning a modest 1,000 francs a month, and I think this was about the first time that clowns were seen in a lush revue, on a stage instead of in the ring. The public adored them and their success affected every comic in the company, me most of all.

I worried solidly all that year. People were losing interest in me. Mistinguett still felt the same but, when I saw the way my career was going, I decided this was partly because she was sorry for me. Also, falling more and more in love with her as the weeks went by, I was jealous as hell and of course an awful bore.

One season only remained at the Folies-Bergère before my contract ran out. It was about time, too, for the alternating round of revue and touring with my own act meant that I was making no headway in either. Mistinguett starred as before in this last show, but, try as we might, our scenes together weren't a patch on the original ones. And the management, encouraged by their good fortune with Grock, were importing variety stars from England who put our dance routines to shame with their international polish and their perfect performances. Mistinguett, being Mistinguett, survived by virtue of sheer femininity and sexual magnetism but I, and the rest of the men, were relegated to the back seats.

I could not shake off my despondency. And what was I *doing* at the Folies-Bergère, submerged in a whirl of glamorous women and extravagant décor? I should probably have been wiser to keep out of it all and go on touring the provinces with a few weeks in the capital every year as Mayol had always done. The season came to an end and, as I expected, they did not renew my contract.

So there I was, unemployed again. But though my last twelve

months had not been exactly brilliant and there was no great rush for my services, I was the leading name among the younger singers and in the world of the *café-concert* every door was open to me. Luckily a show was just being fixed at the Cigale in which Régina Badet, the famous and beautiful dancer from the Opéra-Comique, was to make her acting début. With the dearth of young revue-artists they offered me the male lead with top billing and, a day or two before rehearsals began, I accepted, thankfully, as a drowning man accepts a place on the life-raft.

It was a huge success. For months the fashionable audiences flocked to the Cigale and I came bouncing back like a tennis-ball. All my sketches went marvellously and the final number, a parody of the quarter from *Rigoletto* in which Raimu and I took part, was one of the funniest things that was ever seen in Paris. Raimu also played Rodin in a scene with the leading lady and gave promise of the great actor he was to become. As for me, I couldn't go wrong in that revue. Everything I said or sang or danced seemed absolutely right. I was a 'revelation' once again, having apparently remained invisible to all for the last four years at the Folies-Bergère. But now, more than ever, I was on top of the world. An acknowledged part of Mistinguett's life, securely back in favour with the Parisian public, I had a few months which really and truly evened the score.

The one dark spot was the prospect of my military service, due in 1908, but which I had so far managed to postpone. In another twelve months I should have to go like everyone else, and that meant two years away from La Louque and Mistinguett and my enjoyable profession. Still, it happened whoever you were. No use worrying beforehand; time enough for that when the day came.

Meanwhile I drifted happily along on my cloud of well-being. Even Nozière himself, the eminent critic who had nearly discouraged me for life when I opened at the Folies-Bergère, was being nice to me now. To his own great surprise, he said, he 'had to admit' that I had this and I had that; that my talent was 'novel and fresh'; and who, he finally inquired, could resist me? True, he would then go on to point out that my material was basically street-songs, but would add that at least I was making remarkable use of them. These complimentary notices, however, gave me less pleasure than the savage ones had formerly upset me, for I had realized by now that theatre-folk are accountable to two overlords only, public and producer.

I had at this period a variable sort of friendship with Raimu. For weeks he was the perfect companion and we spent all our time to-gether, and then without warning some little thing, a mere word perhaps, would unleash a hurricane of bad temper that often nearly brought us to blows. After all my scrapping and boxing I suppose I could have beaten him quite easily but I usually let him have the last word, for I had a genuine admiration for his scrupulous gifts and a kind of affectionate comprehension of his difficult character. I retained them always. Our paths in the theatre seldom crossed, so this may have been partly because we had so few occasions for getting on each other's nerves; but I had known him from childhood almost, and am glad that nothing ever happened to spoil my recollections of him.

EYE-OPENER

Mist and I, with a few days free, decided to take a week's holiday in London and see as many shows there as we could crowd in. *Hullo Ragtime!* was then packing the Hippodrome. Ethel Levey, the star, was an American of tremendous personality, tall, so skinny she was almost angular and no beauty by any standards. She lacked all the feminine allurements of a Parisian actress, but her face had light behind it. She sang with relentless rhythm, in a mannish voice, and was a marvellous dancer. We sat in the stalls and gaped at her. As for the comedians, they left me feeling very sorry for myself, and my not being able to follow a word they said made them all the more impressive. The least of the dancers apparently understood his business better than I did and I regarded the whole thing as a lesson to me.

They did a number called 'The Wedding Glide', a big set-piece ceremony in ragtime with the full company of dancers and chorus. The bridegroom, gyrating gracefully with the star, was played by Gerald Kirby all in white – suit of smart white flannel, shoes, gloves and bowler hat to match. The effect was so fresh, so youthful and attractive, that for the first time in my career I longed to break away from the red-nosed comic stuff I had done so far. I resolved to suggest something similar for the last revue of my contract, with my partner, Régine Flory, dressed in white and me got up like Gerald Kirby. The more I thought of this idea the better it seemed. Did not my friend Polaire spend hours persuading me not to daub my face with layers of red and white grease-paint? You're young, she used to say, you're no worse-looking than the next man, so why not show them your face as it really is? They might like it. Take the plunge, you're quite capable of amusing them without all this costume and make-up. Pointless buffoonery, she called it.

It was the sight of some of the leading English comedians, men like George Robey, George Grossmith and Wilkie Bard, that made me realize what was so very new and different about the work of Max Dearly. Dearly had borrowed from the English music-hall and clothed his Parisian wit in a good solid layer of Anglo-Saxon humour. That was why his audience sat bewitched, enthralled by a technique they had never seen before. Dearly gave them a mixture of Marseilles-type mime, native French sparkle and this typically English way of being funny. In my receptive state it was all slowly beginning to make sense, and the London trip opened my eyes to the distinct possibility of an international music-hall. Others saw it too, though France was not to know it as a normal part of everyday life until the talkies came, much later on. I also thought of a duet with Régine Flory in the next Cigale revue in which I took a completely new step, abandoned my clown's accoutrements and appeared as my natural self. And this went over so well that I decided, when my *service* was over, I should for the future always include one elegant straight item as a contrast to the low comedy.

It was during this run, as I left the Cigale one night, that I heard a diffident murmur of *Bonjour, Maurice,* from among the cluster of people at the stage-door and recognized my father. It was a shock, seeing him for the first time since I was a child. We went to a place off the Boulevard de Clichy that was almost deserted at that hour, and I looked at him again. A smallish, thickset man with a rather nice face and a fatalistic expression you couldn't quite define. I was moved, and asked why he had come.

'Well, I heard you were off to the army, and I wanted to see you, talk to you a bit, before you went. You really have done well. I've often been up in the gallery, you know. Funny, the way it makes me cry when everybody else is laughing.'

I cut him short.

'Are you all right for money?'

'Oh, I get along, thanks. No, I just came to have a look at you. I should like to think there were no hard feelings, after what I did.'

In a flash the words brought back the memory of what my mother had endured. Vividly I pictured all she had gone through, mentally and physically, and all the struggles we had, without a single word from him, either then or later. Obviously he had turned up now because I was successful, and the thought pulled me up sharply.

'You needn't worry about hard feelings, papa. I've known for years what it was all about, but your name's never been mentioned since. You'd best not come and see me again. It's too late now. We've forgotten you. If you want anything write to me at the theatre, but don't come round any more. And I shan't say I've seen you now. It's better that way. *Au revoir*, papa.'

He hesitated. His eyes brimmed with tears and he shook his head, repeating yes, yes, as though what I said took a long time to sink in. Then he pulled himself together and held out his hand. For what seemed minutes we stood there and when he left I didn't move but watched his bandy-legged figure melt into the darkness. He never attempted to see me again and never asked me for a sou. Later I tried to discover where he lived, and had inquiries made all over Paris, but he wasn't to be found. He made a noble atonement, I think, and it is one of my greatest regrets (if, indeed, remorse were not too strong a word) that I could not, quietly, provide for his old age.

LONG INTERVAL

On 1 December 1913, I went into the army, in good time for the war. We need not linger over that familiar story. I fought, like everybody else. And one day I sheltered in a church, heard a noise like a thunderclap, felt a quick, burning sensation through my

F

knapsack and fell to the ground. Two medical orderlies picked me up and we ran for it as best we could, down the road to Cons-la-Grand-Ville, the bullets swarming round us like mosquitoes, and gained the temporary cover of a slope at last. In the Red Cross hospital at the château they examined and dressed my wound and put me to bed. Never in all my life have I revelled in such sleep. I was too exhausted to bother how, when, or even whether, I was going to wake up, and it didn't seem to matter much. The place was being shelled and shrapnel came through the window and lodged in the opposite wall. There were twenty other people in the room, but I slept for ten hours without a tremor.

Little by little, consciousness returned with a sound of hobnailed boots approaching as the gunfire died away. Unfamiliar songs were heard in guttural chorus, and the occasional remainder explosion of a shell. Then the ward was full of German officers, waving revolvers and making sure that we were truly wounded and weaponless. Prisoners of war.

I was sent to the prison-camp at Alten-Grabow, where the company was excellent. People told their news, and I told mine, and the doctors who had been looking after me trained me as a male nurse, which meant I could be useful and active. My morning job was tending the less serious cases in the barrack huts, and I passed freely to wherever I was needed: I was allowed more or less anywhere with my big bag of paraphernalia. This done, I returned to the hospital where I would take temperatures, see – if nobody minds my mentioning it – to the urine tests and await the daily visit of the two doctors, the German doctor-in-charge and our own French medico, Raymond de Butler.

From bed to bed I followed them, and our man, to give the German a favourable impression of my talents, would gravely inquire,

'*Infirmier* Chevalier, have you done a test for Number 12?'

'Traces of albumen, doctor.'

'Enema for Number 6, *Infirmier* Chevalier?'

'Yes, doctor. Fever's down by two degrees.'

'Very good, thank you', he would reply, without a flicker of a smile, and the round was over.

But I hadn't finished yet, for twice a week, from eleven o'clock to midday, I had to pump injections into the syphilis patients, and they all assured me that I was much gentler than those who treated them before I came. And I was indeed careful and, let me add, compassionate. It could be a painful process, but my method was to rub their backsides with alcohol, then give them a sharp slap as I injected. The heat of the spirit, partially anaesthetizing the skin, combined with the slight shock of the blow to prevent their feeling a thing. (I am telling you all this to show you what a conscientious nurse I was.)

My free time in the afternoon I employed in learning English. Yes, I had suddenly decided to learn the tongue of Albion with no loftier purpose, I must admit, than that of chatting to the chorus-girls when freedom came and I was back in the music-hall. I liked to picture the astonishment of friends as I indulged in these chats before their very eyes. It would also be helpful when I went over to see what was happening on the London stage and the self-imposed task was some defence meanwhile, against the terrible depression that attacked us all in turn. I was thinking no further ahead than that. It certainly never occurred to me that here, one day, might be my passport to work in England or America. Those countries had accomplished variety artists of their own and I scarcely considered myself up to trying my fortunes there. I was delighted simply to be learning something every day and, without delving very deeply or trying very hard, I managed to get through quite a lot of reading, too. Chiefly I needed to avoid inactivity, which gave me the horrors and thrust me into the depths for hours together.

My English teacher was a patient sergeant called Ronald Kennedy. Under his guidance my progress was rapid and rewarding, and working as I did in the hospital I could repay him with a small favour now and then. Our circumstances got worse and worse as time went on, but because of this job I was certainly better placed than most. They couldn't cart me off as a hostage, for one thing. For another, there were concerts every Sunday, and occasionally on Saturdays too, which served to keep my hand in; and I was learning English. All of this, save when a really awful fit of depression overwhelmed me, acted as a safety-valve.

Summer, 1915, was nearly over but the war was evidently going on for ages yet. Dejection like a chronic fever, now up, now down, settled upon us and our second winter began without the hope that had sustained us through the first. Who said this wasn't a ten-year programme? Or twenty, even? What about the Thirty Years War? Fine figures we should be at the end of that lot, if we survived at all! Then we had a violent epidemic of typhoid. The hospital was crammed for weeks on end and owing to the risk of infection nursing was a cushy job no longer. Joe Bridge, the other nurse, and I were run off our feet, but we saved the lives of a good many patients.

Yet I saw a good many die, nevertheless, and always tried to guard them from the knowledge they were dying. It was a bit like being a father-confessor, as I sat on their beds and talked of their mothers and wives. 'Oh, this won't be for much longer. They'll be sending you home, I'm sure, as soon as you're fit. And won't your wife be glad to see you! You'll just about hug her to pieces, I should think. And your mother, too!' And so on and so forth. And the dying man would listen and smile and look into the day-after-tomorrow, when the war and the prison-camp, and having typhoid, would be nothing but nightmare memories. I have seen men die happy and hopeful thanks to this patter of mine. Of all my parts, that will always be the best I played.

Then at last, one splendid day in 1916, the Red Cross organized a prisoner-of-war exchange. By a quite unexpected stroke of luck I was included in it and found myself home in Paris with three months' leave, enough time to think of my career again. Better get going on it, I told myself. No use fretting or hanging about. You've had a basinful, admittedly, but the war is the war, and you can't alter the fact. And you're out of it for three months, so off we go, show 'em what you can do. Get back to singing, get up on a stage and see what happens with an audience that's more or less forgotten you after three years. And do you know what? You're going to start with the Casino Montparnasse, in that friendly old Rue de la Gaîté. Genuine sort of place, popular, and you'll find out in ten minutes what they're wanting nowadays. And after that a few of the big towns, like Lyons and Grenoble. A month's work altogether, to put you back on form, and then we'll see. You should be getting the hang of things by then. Work has seen you through before now, many a time, and it'll do so again, I shouldn't wonder. 'Ready, Maurice?' The call-boy's knock. 'You're on.'

It was a full house and a rowdy Montparnasse audience. I was billed as 'Wounded on Active Service, Returned Prisoner-of-War', so nobody should think I was dodging the column. That was a matter of pride. Nobody wants to be taken for one of those, and they were many, who step in to make ill-merited reputations for themselves while others are away at the front. Better make it quite clear that one had done one's duty as a loyal Frenchman.

I was doing seven or eight songs, a few from the old days and some newer ones I had sung in the prison-camp, and wore my grotesque costume, though with very little make-up on. Stage, galleries and boxes were a disconcerting change from the huts. It seemed I should have to go back to the beginning and learn all over again.

I had been a favourite in this district before I went into the army; they gave me a wonderful reception, then settled down to enjoy a good laugh. And I could not make contact. Men, women and young people, they just didn't react like a roomful of soldiers. I wasn't hitting the nail on the head any more. My jokes jarred slightly and raised a barrier between us. I was not the performer they remembered, the one they had come to see. In nothing, in style, voice or material, was I at one with them and I felt completely at sea. Then I forgot my words, and that really panicked me. I broke into a sweat and my voice faltered. Surely I wasn't going to keel over where I stood?

There was polite applause when I had finished and the singing star who gets polite applause had better start wondering where he went wrong. I made my exit feeling awful and so low that the kind things people felt obliged to say reduced me to the verge of despair. The frightening thought had come to me on the stage that I was perhaps not strong enough any more. I didn't see how anyone could carol cheerful ditties while trying not to pass out at every verse-end, or dominate the house when half expecting to fall flat on the floor at any minute.

It was the same, if not worse, on the short tour that followed: and the provinces are less tolerant of failure than the capital itself. Then came the Olympia in Paris. There the manager was Léon Volterra, a man of my own age, 28, who began life as a programme-seller. A remarkable type, pale and plump, dealing with a mountain of work and an amazing number of problems in a day. He was popularly supposed to be unable to read or write but to rely on a prodigious memory and keep all his accounts in his head. He made himself extremely agreeable to everybody and engaged his artists, rather as a bookmaker might take bets, over a café table. His word, once given, was his bond, but in the course of time he had learnt every trick there was to get the best of a bargain. On Mistinguett's recommendation he booked me for a fortnight.

My material had improved, but I was still physically weak, and liable to dizzy fits on the stage. Seriously, I began to face the possibility of having to give it all up. But what in the world was I supposed to do then? My pre-war savings had kept my mother going and repaid what Mist had lent me, but I had no more money left and singing was the only trade I knew. I was nearly out of my mind. Then, just as I felt the ship was really on the rocks, the most marvellous thing happened. One day, in the middle of a meal, my appetite returned for the first time since I got home. I had begun to eat mechanically as usual, but that luncheon included a superb camembert over which I regained the relish, the wonderful relish, for food. It may seem a prosaic enough memory to dwell on, but the mere recollection is a pleasure. I did not attempt to resist that most congenial cheese. I ate the lot, happy to know that I was beginning again, that my appetite was back and strength would follow. I was ticking over. Not perfectly yet, but, it was fair to say, I was going to be all right.

SHAKY START

I was invalided out, recovered little by little and Mistinguett and I were undertaking engagements. I really began to think that all would be well, and when the author of the musical play, *Gobette of Paris*, discerned in me the makings of an actor we decided to reveal these gifts to the public in a specially written scene for the pair of us. We were going to be sincere and simple, in striking contrast to our usual capricious and eccentric selves.

I was delighted. For years I had longed to touch the soft side of an audience, but hadn't proved very good at it so far. This time it was going to work. The author, who had been an actor himself, was producing and he taught us the whole romantic technique from A to z, and the most telling way to pronounce the words, 'I love you'. And at the end of this scene, when I had told Gobette I loved her and pressed her lips to mine, all the lights were supposed to go out, by a contrivance I will now explain.

We were seated side by side on a sofa, apparently being stared at by a large china dog opposite, with spotlights behind his eyes. The stage, apart from him, was dark and the switch to extinguish him was hidden in the cushion I was sitting on. Mistinguett was to let me kiss her and then, overcome by embarrassment at the dog's-eye beam, grab a siphon of soda-water from an occasional table and squirt it at him. At the same time, kissing her enthusiastically, I switched him off with my left hand and blacked us out, with dramatic effect. Or so we hoped.

For, sad to say, my first-ever love-scene foundered idiotically. The opening night was going splendidly and we seemed all set for a big success. We played our scene, when we came to it, simply and sincerely as planned, to hushed appreciation. All, so far as we could see, was fine. In the middle of my last speech I unobtrusively checked the switch, in preparation for the famous final effect, and the switch wasn't there. Nearing the end of my fervent protestations, I rummaged feverishly among the upholstery behind me. Speculative murmurs arose. What, on that sofa, in those circumstances, could I possibly be doing? And with the words, 'Gobette, I love you!' I discovered to my horror that the thing had shifted and I was seated right on top of it. Pouring my heart out, I was, to all appearances, scratching my bottom as I did so. The audience collapsed into hysterics and my ambitions as a dramatic actor collapsed with them. It may sound ridiculous, but I was so upset that I cried like a child for hours in my dressing-room, beyond consolation by Mistinguett or anyone else.

Mistinguett. . . . Had the prison-camps, perhaps, changed me, or was I more grown-up these days? I don't know, but the fact remained that I was finding her whims and caprices less easy to bear. Our lives, private and professional, were the same as before, but we seemed to have lost our mental bond. Before the war, all she said and did was perfect, fascinating. Now, to my own astonishment, I found myself disagreeing with her actions and attitudes and the way she went about her work. I was no longer swept passively along in the wake of that irrepressible temperament. I baulked. Often.

As our relationship grew less and less harmonious, so did the hangers-on make their covert disapproval felt. Who did that rotten actor think he was, putting on airs? Ought to think himself damn lucky, all fixed up with a marvellous woman like that. What did he expect, for God's sake? People came to see her, not him, surely he realized that much? Bloody bore, too, moaning and groaning and slouching about.

There came a morning when the whole thing exploded. I sent off a telegram to London, to the American singer Elsie Janis, whom I had met on one of her visits to Paris, and suggested that I come over. The answer was there by return: *Maurice Chevalier, Casino de Paris. All right, come over. Will start in four weeks in show with Elsie Janis. One hundred pounds weekly. Sincerely, Sir Alfred Butt, Manager, Palace Theatre, London.*

That same night I informed Léon Volterra and Mistinguett that I was going at the end of the week. This totally unforeseen and independent gesture took the wind out of their sails, but they rallied quickly and Mist turned upon me a basilisk glare.

'Well, you'll have asked for it,' she pronounced.

'You can't possibly win at that game,' said Léon, the gambling man; and continued, with a benign expression, 'but there, it might be a good thing in the end. Teach you a lesson, won't it?'

LONDON, BORDEAUX AND AFTER

I don't know whether it is altogether right to allow one's instincts to dictate like that. You have to be very tough to disentangle yourself entirely from everything – love, life and work, the lot – and go flying off on your own. And where exactly was I flying to? A country where I was just another foreigner trying his luck, a town where all the male stars could make rings round me. During the whole journey, in the train, on the boat, passing through the customs, I felt so lost and terrified in my new-found freedom that I hardly dared look round to see who was going in the same direction.

I went to see Elsie Janis in her show, and that was like being hit over the head with a sledge-hammer. She was beyond belief. I appeared in her dressing-room dazed with admiration, doubtless looking like anybody's country cousin, and she roared with laughter. I owned that I should never have suggested going on the same stage with her had I realized how very good she was. I was thrilled to be here, but at the same time dreadfully upset. They were obviously expecting more than I could offer and I had best not even bother to unpack, but catch the boat back home tomorrow. At my words the laughter faded and her face became severe. Such a proceeding was out of the question. The arrangement was made, rehearsals started in the morning; if I were not a London sensation her name was not Elsie Janis; and so, dear Maurice, good night.

The 'London Sensation' passed a very poor night, however, with a cloud of unsolved questions hanging in the air above him. She had me reeling. And sure enough, next morning there we were at the first rehearsal. She had insisted on our working alone for a day or so, and thank God she did. It is one thing for a Frenchman to chatter on in English, quite another to play comedy in that language. Had I spoken my brand of English on the stage no one would have understood a word I said. My intonation was all wrong; I raised my voice at the end of a word when I should have dropped it. With angelic patience Elsie took me through that script as though instructing a child. Acting was out; I was going to be a parrot. I repeated what she said to me, exactly as she said it, and it was the same thing with the dances. Excellent teacher that she was, she showed me every step and I learnt them easily enough, but not until I came to the boxing sketch, which was practically all pantomime, could I more or less let myself go and relax a little. This was a blessing, for in the process of driving all this work into my head and, as it were, nailing it there, I had lost the easy touch I had in French. I was tense and wound-up, trying to make sure the lines emerged as I had been told to speak them: stiff as a poker, trying to do my party-piece.

We opened on a Monday afternoon and I was in a flat spin. Waiting to go on, I almost wept at Sir Alfred: 'I shan't insist on my contract if we flop, I've got one foot on the stage and one on the boat, you know.'

The idea of gibbering away in a foreign tongue to an audience that didn't know the first thing about me; of waltzing round with the chorus-girls when I had never done this kind of waltz in my life before; of being unable to improvise on the spur of the moment because I had to think so carefully before I opened my mouth; and, finally, of seeing my career at the mercy of yet another woman at the end of it all – the whole situation suddenly hit me and filled me with dismay. It would never do. Visions ran through my head of provincial dates in France, of small Paris theatres where I might have been singing, simply singing, for people I understood, without any of this nonsense. I went on to a round of courteous applause and sang one verse and a chorus of *On the Level, You're a Little Devil* by a new composer named Cole Porter, attempted to be dashing and devil-may-care to match, did a fast tap-dance and off. It didn't exactly stop the show. The errand-boys here could tap-dance better than that and my voice, I was well aware, hadn't a note of music in it. What, then? Exit, keeping cool, and concentrate on the scene with Elsie.

Before every cue, while bearing myself with careless ease, I was mulling over what I had to say next and my expression as a result was preoccupied and far from suitable. Elsie was a good trouper and kept jogging me in the right direction, but I must have looked forlorn to a degree and felt so wobbly that when we danced it was she, not I, who took the lead. Yet I hadn't been off the stage two minutes before her mother, who was in the wings, was all over me with: 'Maurice, you're fine – cheer up, that's marvellous!'

Marvellous. Thank you for nothing. Bloody awful was nearer the mark.

I had hoped to go over better with my boxing sketch, but the house was clearly fed up with me and the response was pretty feeble. I still had a couple of bits before the finale, but by now all was lost.

Back to France tomorrow and they'd laugh their heads off at the Casino. Well, let them. I'd do my old one-man turn again somewhere else. Just so long as it was somewhere in France. Volterra had been right, I needed a lesson and a lesson I had got. I had bitten off more than I could possibly chew, and should have known. With these thoughts revolving in my head, I went up to my dressing-room and found a crowd of people there with their congratulations – Elsie, and Elsie's mother, Sir Alfred, members of the company. I could stand no more.

Dolefully, I asked them all to shut up and stop pretending. The truth was staring me in the face and I wasn't such a fool that I couldn't tell success from failure. I should like to be released forthwith, I'd had enough and I wanted to go home. Immediately the faces changed. I was engaged for three months, and for three months I should work. A contract was a contract, stated Sir Alfred with a steely smile, and he had my signature on the dotted line. Elsie, more sympathetic, gave a longer explanation.

'No,' she agreed, 'you didn't get a lot of applause and you didn't get many laughs, but they liked you all the same. They liked your personality. It's the coldest house of the week, a Monday matinée. But when they went out they were saying: "That French boy's all right." Now, don't be so temperamental. Tonight it will be splendid.'

And fortunately it was indeed much better in the evening and, although everything about this kind of show was new to me, I gradually got used to it. We ran for three months and then Butt decided to put on a revue in Paris, at the Mogador, and I was home again.

'Well, Maurice, and when are you returning to the fold?' inquired Volterra one day.

'Can't tell you yet,' I said, wishing to convey an impression of disinterest. 'I've a booking to do in Bordeaux. We can talk about it when I get back, if you like.'

I had taken the ten days in Bordeaux in order to try out a version of my act I did once at Belfort during my military service, but had never dared repeat when I resumed my career after the prison-camp. I was planning to appear in brown tail-coat, trousers in a small beige check, light spats and gloves to match, wear a top hat and carry a cane. In case I lost my nerve at the last moment I didn't even take my old eccentric costume with me. They'd have to accept me looking smart or not at all, and if they didn't, I warned the manager, I should have to pack up, and that was that. It was a risk he'd have to take and I was coming only on those terms.

And so, one night, I went on to the stage of the Trianon at Bordeaux, dressed as an English man-about-town, to do the songs, the acrobatic dancing and the comic business for which, before, I used to get myself up like a clown; and success was never in doubt. From the first song, *Oh, Maurice,* to the last dance, they loved it.

And in Marseilles, Lyons and Nice they loved it too. What I was doing was completely new in the French music-hall. I was getting laughs and being elegant, mingling grotesquerie and charm, eccentric dancing and sophisticated songs: the mixture as never before. And somehow I seemed to typify all the sporty young things of the time.

With regard to the songs, people have complained that I don't say enough about them, but the fact is, I never analysed them much. And in any case a real comic effect, the real, ringing burst of generous laughter that greets a song – and I mean a good, honest belly-laugh, and French at that, with nothing coarse or cruel or low in it – is a rare and precious thing. It doesn't transplant easily and should be valued for its rarity. Natural, unforced laughter is good, and it's good for you – don't you agree? Let me tell you about a man I met on one of my pilgrimages to Ménilmontant.

A kind of need for the place would seize me from time to time; I used to go back for a wander-round, and it was on one of these occasions that this man collared me. He was sitting in a bistro, happily ensuring that his nose turned finally and utterly purple. When he saw me pass, he emerged and in hoarse tones addressed me.

'What the hell are you doing here, then? Sight for sore eyes, you are! Hey, everybody, look who's here. Maurice! Maurice Chevalier! Well, if anybody'd ever told me I should find you here, in Ménil-muche! Come and have a drink, cock. Come on, come on – I've got to tell you something. You're the man who saved my life. Didn't know that, did you? *Patron*, glass of the best stuff in the house for Maurice here. Yes, I know, mate, you're a busy man, can't spend all day with everyone who bangs you on the back and says "Hullo", but I'm a special case. It's every word true, and I owe it all to you if I'm here to go on about it. D'you know that, cock? Owe it all to you.

'It was a long time ago, 1909, I should think, when you were at the Ambassadeurs – ages ago. Well, I'd had a load of bad luck, women and so forth, and I was just about fed to the back teeth. You know – got to the bloody end. They could stick it – life, and women, and earning your daily bread and the bloody lot. And I was so fed up I decided to chuck it all in. Know what I mean? Oh yes, I did, and I'd got it all planned. I just wanted to drop the whole damned crew of them; silly cows, not an ounce of spirit in 'em. So I went out and I got drunk – farewell party on my last night. It was running out of my ears when I went down the Champs Élysées. Next stop, Place de la Concorde. Last stop, the river. Concorde; the bridge; gurgle, gurgle. That was my plan.

'All the lights were dancing up and down, I was so drunk. Crazy city. It certainly looked gorgeous on my last night. Then, going past the Ambassadeurs, I heard the music. It pulled me up for a second and I thought I might as well have a bit of music, too, before I carried on. See a few legs and a few tits and hear a song or two. Sort of last cigarette, like when they cut your head off.

'I felt in my pockets and I had just enough money to get in. So I bought a ticket and pushed right to the front with all the smart lot and posh tarts, but it was all nonsense as far as I could see. Dancers and singers and folk rolling their eyes about and turning cartwheels – no, thank you. I was off to jump into the drink. Then you came dashing on. I'd never seen you in my life before, never even heard of you, but now, I thought, who's this? He's a bit different, he is, with his gear too tight and his arse sticking up in the air. Twisting and turning all over the place, too, not a bit like the rest of them. I've got to watch this before I bugger off, I thought. Truly, Maurice, without a word of a lie; on my mother's life, that's exactly what I thought. And there you were, singing like mad, babbling all that nonsense and prancing about on those long legs of yours. Shooting your neck and your bottom in and out and pulling faces. By the time you finished I clean forgot about doing myself in. Never gave it another thought, just sat and goggled at you. All churned up I was, and before I knew it I was shouting at the people sitting by me, all screwing their noses up as if I smelt of shit, or something: "Let me enjoy myself, can't you? Let me enjoy myself!"

'And that was it, really. I was round the corner then. "Let me enjoy myself!" I kept yelling, as if they were trying to stop me. I wanted to wait and see you afterwards, shake hands and say thank you; it was quite a thing you'd done for me. But then I didn't like to, in case it was a nuisance. Still, I was back on my feet again. Crisis over.

'Well, that's it, *mon vieux Momo*. All these years I've been wanting to thank you and never had the chance. So when I spotted you just now I had to grab you straightaway. And now, you get on and do anything you want – poke round all these old alleyways and stick your head in all the old houses. And keep out of his *way*, everybody. Can't you see he wants to be left alone?'

To go back to the songs. I believe that any artist, if he is honest and of average intelligence, cannot choose but improve, fractionally, with every performance and that, as he gains in tact and decency, and learns what quality is, he is sure to weary of the vulgar way. One need not be in the very first flight to appreciate the difference between getting a clean, unlaboured laugh and descending to the depths of obscenity for the sake of a cheap one. It is a matter of artistic instinct. In his own thoughts and feelings and way of doing things, an actor is worth nothing, or he is worth something. If he is worth something, then he will try to be worth something more, as is only normal in anyone who wants to get on. I can think of no other way to explain artistic development. A career resembles a piece of music set in harmony, and the nature of a man's imagination dictates the melody. If God's good, your imagination will take form in satisfactory work. If not, you have a lot of effort and energy for little or no result.

It all boils down to instinct, good or bad. Artistic creation must be spontaneous. It comes from the heart; it has to pass through the brain; and still one needs the guts, and good old, indispensable technique, to bring it to the light of day. That, at least, is how I see the process, not that I have ever been able to pin it down very exactly in my own case. You hear a voice inside. You obey it, and produce whatever it told you to produce; and then you wait and see. And oh! the trouble you're in for!

Where had we got to? In the course of 1921 I had replaced the star in three consecutive revues, and this so reassured Léon Volterra that he gave me the lead once more in a summer show called *Dans un Fauteuil* at the Casino and here, for the first time, I did my speciality number in a dinner-jacket. The problem, a very tricky one, was to find a suitable hat. An English top hat? Wrong on the Paris stage. A soft black hat, perhaps? Too sombre. An opera hat? Same as the topper. Then I suddenly thought, why not a straw? It would go perfectly well, and light up my face into the bargain. So I bought one and in it sang '*Je n'peux pas vivre sans amour*', and '*Quand y a une femme dans un coin*', with such satisfactory results that ever afterwards a straw hat meant me. I had found my personal trade-mark.

DÉDÉ

By now I had a reputation as 'good box-office' and as a result was offered the lead in a show called *Dédé*. This was a great change from simple sketches and monologues, for the rhythm and pitch of a ten-minute revue-sketch are nothing like the sustained tone needed for a three-hour play. When, in my campaign for independence, I rather hastily took it upon myself to try a modern operetta, I feared the difficulties might be more than I could cope with. I should be bringing my own touch of novelty to the Bouffes-Parisiens as far as the songs were concerned, but that awful inferiority complex of mine made me dread the long speeches. I thought I should look anything but natural as I listened and replied to other people on the stage.

Came the dress-rehearsal. As I waited in the wings I could hear that the accomplished and delightful actor playing Urban couldn't raise a glimmer from an obviously difficult house. The omens indicated failure. Two more lines, and I was due to saunter across the backcloth, as though outside a shoe-shop, look in through the window, see him, enter – and try my luck.

He gave me the cue. This was it! A slight stir in front sounded, from where I was, like the murmur of a crowd. Once on, the applause I received was less noticeable than the wave of excitement that ran from stalls to gallery like a charge of electricity through the lovely old theatre. Urban and I, beginning our dialogue, managed to get laughs for the least little thing and a response to lines I thought would go for nothing. My first song and dance – and that day angels, it seemed, could not have danced better – had a reception that left me breathless. The audience went mad and stayed that way for the whole three acts. We were a huge, magnificent hit.

The news spread like wildfire and *Dédé* ran for two years to full houses, always booked up for days ahead. Volterra and Mistinguett just had to accept the fact and find somebody else to take my place, for good and all, at the Casino.

TWO MEMORIES

Around 1922 Paris suddenly adopted a new favourite, a young comedian named Fortugé. He was new and he was good and he sprang apparently from nowhere, to be hailed and cried up by the discerning public and the critics alike. They exalted and idolized him. He was everybody's darling. He had an excellent repertoire and a light tenor voice. Why, they asked, didn't he sing at the Opéra, with a voice like that? He was a charmer, he was adorable.

But Fortugé was no surprise to us. He had been knocking around the provinces for fifteen years at least and we in his own world knew how he worked. We knew that he had come up the hard way and got a thorough grounding; never grumbling, never trying to walk before he could run, slightly improving his talent with every engagement, enlisting a few more friends wherever he went. He was a true professional who had as yet done nothing startling but was making progress all the time.

He was on the small side, very dark, and his appearance seemed to

5. A scene from a performance at the Ambassadeurs in 1908, aged 20

Ambassadeurs 190?

In 1910, aged 22

6. Aged 22 and 23

please people. He had compounded a style for himself, borrowing ideas for costume and make-up from one, vocal effects from another, patter and comic business from me. He had a run of good songs and the famous voice did well on records. A Fortugé fan-movement arose with accompanying flutter and agitation, but it left him personally unmoved. He remained his own genuine self, a sensible little chap who didn't get carried away as his stock went rocketing skywards. Then, stupidly, tragically, he had to die of some peculiar disease which crumbled his internal organs into powder, like dried-up tissue-paper.

He was only 35 or so, poor man, and newly reaping the harvest of success. Everything was coming his way – popularity, big fees, and all the lovely feminine attention that follows in the train of big fees and popularity. And, because of this unfairly sudden exit, all he got out of it was a legend. Still, unlike many people, he at least did nothing to spoil that exit. The public came to know him, took him to its heart, adored him, and then abruptly, it was time to say good-bye and he was gone, leaving an unalterable memory behind. One could almost envy him.

Could Fortugé have lasted? How would he have stood up to changing tastes and changing critical standards, to other performers and different audiences? As it was, he appeared, bewitched them all, and went. It was symmetrical. One does tend to ruin everything by going on too long.

My second tale begins when I read an article by some distinguished journalist on the execution of a murderer named Moyse in the Santé prison on the Boulevard Arago. Its concluding words, 'the most cowardly death ever seen in the Boulevard Arago', reminded me vividly of a true experience.

It all started a long time ago, when I was about 14 and living with my mother in one cramped room in the Faubourg Saint-Martin. I was a professional singer already, though not a very successful one, earning five or six francs a day when things were good. I say 'when things were good' because there were so many weeks when they were non-existent. These were weeks we dreaded but through which I continued to swagger round with my hat at a rakish angle, trying to look as though all I had to do was take my choice of offers. This putting a brave face on poverty was nothing new in a locality where the *café-concert* artists met and mingled. And they met and mingled with the underworld as well, for our district was at that time a favourite haunt of pimps.

On a lean day, then, I was jaunting along as usual when one of these pimps – you got to know them all by sight – came up and spoke to me. He was a big man, broad-built, with an uncommonly direct and honest aspect.

'Hi!' he said. 'I heard you last week at the Persan (this was a low dive on the Boulevard Sébastopol). Made me laugh, I can tell you, those stories of yours.'

He paused, and eyed my clean but shabby garments.

'Working now, are you?'

'Not at the moment, no, but I shall be soon. Just waiting for the contract.' (This was a lie.)

'Anything you need?'

'Lord, no. Thanks.'

He smiled amiably. 'Oh, that's all right then; pleased to hear it. I thought you seemed a decent lad.'

He never addressed me again, but we nodded when we met and there was always kindness and understanding in his look. Mine, per-haps, conveyed alarm, but for all that I truly admired his strength and was grateful for the proffered help. I may have been slightly ashamed of the fact, but I felt he was my friend.

Well, in time I moved away from that part of Paris. Then I was busy working, and the war came, and life went on, as it does, until after my various freaks of fortune, I was playing in *Dédé* and a re-porter of my acquaintance said to me one day,

'Tell me – you're acting Dédé in this show. There's a fellow called Dédé being guillotined tonight. How about coming along?'

'Now that I've never seen,' I replied, without really thinking. 'Yes, I'll come.'

I regretted the words before they were out of my mouth, but I am unhappily too stupid to say No once I have said Yes. And it meant staying up all night and I was furious at having let myself in for it.

So we sat about, whiling the hours away until it was time to leave, and I learnt that the Dédé in question was a ponce who, in the course of paying off some private score, had murdered another of the same calling. Once in the Boulevard Arago we ran into a barrage of policemen who examined our permits and let us pass. There were more policemen farther on. Then, suddenly, it came into view, The Widow, Madame Guillotine. I fought down my revulsion and kept walking as though I were used to the sight, my expression unmoved and my legs buckling under me. There were some fifty spectators, I suppose, police and pressmen, with that dreadful contraption all complete about three yards away – the board, the blade, and a solemn, lugubrious man who ran it up and down a time or two. To the right a basket, waiting for body and head.

I was sweating despite the cold morning air and terribly tense. Deibler, the executioner, chatted calmly with his assistants and kept glancing at his watch, as though he had a train to catch. Then, with a sudden noise of hoofs and tyreless wheels clattering on the *pavé*, a cart came up at a gallop and stopped just by the guillotine. Someone let the tailboard down and placed the steps. It might have been a film, it happened so fast.

A priest backed out, holding up a crucifix, followed by a man in shirtsleeves, hands bound behind his back. I almost cried aloud. This Dédé, to be killed in a moment, was the man who had offered his help in the Faubourg Saint-Martin when I was a boy, the man who wished me well.

The rest I did not see clearly, though I stood there gaping, stunned and rigid. As for him, he was strong, serene, dominating. Mildly he thanked the priest with a look that seemed to say: 'Surely you don't imagine that I'm going to collapse, by any chance?' Mild and unhurried, he glanced round him with a slightly mocking air, and neither shouted nor swore. He went himself to his place in front of the board, as if telling Deibler: 'This is your job, get on with it.' They got on with it. And though I was shaking all over, I could yet feel a certain inner pride, as at the creditable conduct of a friend. This was what came back to me when I read of Moyse dying like a coward. I, at least, could think of someone who had put up the best of all possible performances in the Boulevard Arago.

SHOCKS

The day after *Dédé* opened, the manager of the Bouffes-Parisiens did something I have never heard of anyone doing in the world of the theatre since – he came round to see me, took my contract away and gave me another. I was earning 600 francs a night and this he promptly raised to 1,000 for the first twelve months of the show and half as much again for the second. I was incredulous, though thrilled, but he seemed to have got it all worked out.

'Mainly thanks to you,' he said, 'we have a success on our hands. We shall probably run for ages and it's you they'll come to see. Other managements will be after you next season with higher offers, and I'm simply getting in first. I want you to have your proper share, too, and if you have a fair deal you'll presumably be happy about it. And that's good for your work, so you're a bigger draw than ever. See?'

Alas, I have learnt since that managers who tear your contract up and hand out a better one of their own accord are sadly, sadly rare.

That season sped by on a magic carpet. I fixed to play an English version of *Dédé* in America after the Paris run, and in preparation decided to spend my holiday over there. Mistinguett and her current partner, Earl Leslie, came too. We had heard reports of a Negro revue then running in New York and the first evening I went by myself to see it. The curtain hadn't been up five minutes before I was aware of a new artistic rhythm, something I had never met before. Neither at home nor in London was there anything like this. It never stopped. It was incessant, vibrant, dynamic, beating on without leaving the company time even to acknowledge applause between one number and the next. It just kept coming, like a dervish dance. Among the coloured chorus-girls I noticed one especially, nearly naked, beautiful in an outlandish sort of way, pulling wild, contorted faces that would melt suddenly into ravishing softness. Josephine Baker was listed on the programme – a name with many others; but within a few years she had conquered Paris with the qualities that drew my attention among that dark-skinned bevy in New York.

The Negro song-and-dance comedians had the latest American technique of the off-beat, violent, unexpected laugh. I saw dance routines that brought the house down at the end of every chorus. It was like being transported as I sat there to some foreign planet where things in my profession went at three times their normal speed. Obviously, one had to keep up with all this, or else drop out.

After that impressive evening I determined to revise my methods. The entire music-hall was in for a change, judging by these Negroes and their performance. They had an attack, a frenzy and a knock-out physical force against which nothing literary or intellectual could possibly stand up any more. It was all Load! Present! Fire! and rather like a punch on the nose.

This trip, too, marked the end of the road for Mist and me. After it we went our separate ways. I retain only the most kindly memories of her, but I could easily enumerate the shows which, one by one, served to drive us apart. Two successful artists can sometimes make a career together, if they have complementary or matching talents. But Mistinguett and I had the same alleycat appeal in those big Casino shows. It was born in both of us. We were both, so to speak, serving the same drinks, and positively shouldered each other out of the way in genuine anxiety to get at the customers first. Two dogs, if you like, baring their teeth over the same bone. And Mist, you know, had the sharpest, prettiest teeth in the world ...

That was the underlying trouble, and nothing could alter it. Everything we did became a competition: songs, sketches, dances, ideas, everything. The theatre is a drug that can affect the heart and brain, and take over the dedicated artist's private life. (And when it does, of course, you have the ideal arrangement.) The theatre lets you have a love-life only if that does not get in the theatre's way, and its vengeance isn't funny. Step out of line, and retribution falls like a blow from a blunt instrument.

You can count on the fingers of one hand the theatrical couples who have been granted happy lives: and I mean happy, not just happy on the surface. I have known many husband-and-wife teams, including some of the most famous in the world, and been the unwilling witness of some monumental rows. It is hard to picture the full horror of it. Imagine two people, in love, who act together in a theatre every night. And those two people run into trouble, grow apart, and jar and clash. They end up loathing and detesting each other and still – a contract is a contract – are shackled to the nightly love-scene on the stage. They play it in a nightmare. There is nothing worse than sleeping, or trying to sleep, beside a hostile woman with a look at the back of her eyes that makes nonsense of every loving word she says. In that ghoulish masquerade the very stage you stand on seems to come alive and mock you, a vindictive, personal witch. No, there is no getting away from the fact that our adored theatre is often very far from kind, the joys she graciously allows us can be very dearly bought. How many stage marriages can you think of where one partner doesn't take a back seat? Go on – how many? I *could* quite happily have left our front seat to Mistinguett; I am sure she *could* have done the same for me. But there it was. We were ruled, as dancers, by our dancing feet; our hearts were forced to follow them. And as dancers, we were unfortunately doing the splits.

ALL WASHED UP?

Before the theatre re-opened in Paris I had an engagement in Bordeaux which saw the beginning of a new love-affair and so, when I came back to playing Dédé to packed houses at the Bouffes-Parisiens, it was with a companion I adored. My love was very fond of night-life and champagne, so we were always going out. What with this, and all the activity when we got home in the small hours of the morning, and a three-hour stint at the theatre – six on matinée days – I began to suffer from fatigue. It was nothing much to worry about, but I had rather too many small lapses of memory on the stage. All at once, instead of enjoying my work as I had always done, I found I was counting how many songs I had to sing, how many scenes to get through. I was labouring before the show was over. I thought it was temporary exhaustion and dismissed it from my mind, and rest was out of the question in any case. I was doing four films (silents, of course) for Henri Diamant-Berger and, on top of Dédé, was out at Vincennes shooting from morning to evening except when I had an afternoon show. Three of these pictures were finished and in the short interval of comparative peace and quiet before we set about the last one I decided to have a luncheon party in the Rue de la Bienfaisance, where I was living at the time – Max Dearly, Raimu, Martel, Milton and one or two more.

Martel, Marseilles-born and a talented man in the kitchen, made us a notable *bouillabaisse*, generously laced with saffron. The other courses were in the loving hands of my own cook, and the best wines and spirits I could find in the district bedewed our friendly gathering. Chablis first, then a 1906 Hautbrion, then champagne; and glass after glass of brandy to end up with.

In this convivial atmosphere of professionals together, swopping anecdotes and shop, the party, which sat down at one, went on until nearly six o'clock. It had all been perfect. A gratified host, I wrung the hand of my last departing guest, and was suddenly aware, when he had gone, of having had too much to drink. My face was flushed, I couldn't walk straight, my head was going round and I had a show to do that night. Still, it was only six o'clock. Best get to bed at once and take a nice long nap. A cold shower afterwards and I should be as good as new. I leapt into bed and immediately had the sensation that angels had arrived and were bearing my brains away skywards, leaving the rest of me here below in the Rue de la Bien-faisance. My head was singing like a kettle that wouldn't stop, but I fell dead asleep and never stirred until the maid woke me up at eight to go to the Bouffes-Parisiens.

God! What the hell was the matter? Then I remembered the lunch and all we had to drink. Good thing I'd had that two-hour nap, it would have given the alcohol a chance to evaporate. It hadn't, though. My head was thrumming as badly as when I lay down; my brains might have been jumping out, or my blood running the wrong way round. It was a very odd sensation indeed. But I was due to sing and act quite soon and how was I going to do so? I stood up and couldn't feel the floor. An ice-cold shower made no difference and I began to panic. The car came round and I was driven to the theatre. Were my nerves affected, or what? My face, when I looked in the glass to make up, swam towards me, then away again. My hand was full of cold cream but I couldn't lift it up. What *could* it be? I insisted on seeing a doctor before I went on and told him all the symptoms and what I had to drink in the afternoon. He thought the excess of saffron in the *bouillabaisse*, together with all the wines and the liqueurs, had set up poisoning, and that explained the boiling sensation in my head. He sent out for a powder of some kind, which I took in a glass of water.

The callboy knocked. As if from outer space, I heard the others speaking their lines on the stage and left my dressing-room, still with the feeling that my feet were not touching the floor, and that my head was stuffed with cottonwool. My cue came. I stepped in front of the backcloth, not knowing how to stand upright, and made my entrance to laughter and applause. Urban gave me the first line of our dialogue. Completely at sea, I replied with one from the third act. He did a slight double-take, went on to his next line and got a jumble of phrases from the last act. Heads bobbed up from the orchestra-pit. What's happening to Chevalier tonight – Lost himself? Lost his memory?

It was a disaster. I was no longer drunk, I had stopped staggering, and yet my brain wouldn't work. It seemed to be blocked at the vital point and the only words it would release were the wrong ones. We couldn't go on like this. Ordinarily no one pays much attention to the text of a musical but the audience, aware of something strained and wrong, was restless like a wild animal scenting blood.

Urban loyally produced a burst of laughter by way of distraction, turned upstage and whispered the words I needed. I seized upon them like a drowning man and recited the line he gave me. He repeated the process and I stammered the words after him. I clenched my fists so tightly, trying to dredge up such fragments as I could, that I drove my nails through the skin. Sentence by painful sentence, he managed to get me back on course and safely through that first act. I was bathed in sweat and trembling like a leaf. The company flocked round for details of my stupid lunch-time session and of how ill I felt. Oh, poor Maurice! But it's passing off? Good, that's the main thing. Louis Verneuil, the author, came round to see me. He had noticed nothing wrong, thought the show was most amusing, offered his congratulations and left. I was feverish, still jittery from my narrow escape, and there were two acts still before us. They seemed to stretch ahead for ever. I was afraid I should have another attack and was terrified of forgetting my lines.

The second act was an ordeal. Before every cue I was going over the answer in my mind, morbidly tense and taxing my memory three times as much as I need have done. As a result I stumbled over certain words and grew more frantic than ever. The cold sweat remained, I was dizzy and unable to enunciate properly, while all the time my head rang with that peculiar confusing noise, as of a kettle boiling. It was over at last and I went home, armed with everybody's assorted advice and nearly out of my mind. I couldn't stop shaking and was already dreading the next night's performance. I found myself endlessly going over my scenes before I slept, running through my songs, and running through them again. A bit from Act Two, a scene from Act One, lines and verses jumbled up and whirling round. Finally, I dropped off, worn out, trusting it would all seem like a nightmare in the morning. Well-known Music hall Star in Fine State, I thought.

I slept fitfully and the whole thing came back to me the minute I awoke. The strange noise continued in my head and I knew I should forget my lines. Tonight, I knew, I should dry up. I passed a dreadful day and got to the theatre exhausted, haggard and pale. I didn't dry up, but I hesitated over every syllable for three acts of purgatory.

Thinking I must have contracted some sort of nervous disease, I consulted various leading specialists. They gave me gland-injections and electrical massage. I went on a diet and stopped smoking. I stopped drinking. None of it had any effect at all, or helped to conquer the conviction that my head and my memory were going to let me down. The hours on the stage, that had always been a joy and recreation, became a torture to me. I was in more than a fine state, I was in agony, undermined by ineradicable fears, struggling to look normal. I rose one morning with a fresh solution altogether. I would kill myself.

My career, I felt, was finished, past redemption. Something was going to snap soon. One night or another I should go to pieces beyond hope of rescue. My life was a failure and I had best summon up the second's necessary courage and get out. Yes, that was certainly what I'd do. But how to arrange it all? And what about my mother, who was with me in the Rue de la Bienfaisance? (Thirty-three, if you please, and still living with my mother!) Desperation suggested the answer to that problem. After making a will in due form I should ask the doctor to tell her that Paris was really getting too much for her and she ought to move to the country. Once my beloved La Louque was out of the house I could get on with the job any afternoon I chose.

And how about the method? A revolver, I thought. Dignified. Clean. I was obsessed by the plan and mentally rehearsed it time and time again. I was absolutely determined.

Then one day I broke down all over the doctor and confessed the whole thing. He had not taken my ailments very seriously before, but now he looked somewhat shaken and said I must stop working as soon as possible and go into a country nursing-home for several weeks at least. He would be back next day with another doctor for further consultation.

They discovered I had chronic appendicitis and decided to operate when the play came off and before I left Paris. It was just feasible that a grumbling appendix was at the root of my ills and I agreed eagerly to the operation in hope of recovery. I informed the management of the Bouffes-Parisiens that I should take advantage of the clause in my contract that allowed me to leave after the hundredth performance of our current play, *Là-Haut*.

The hundredth performance came and went and I had the operation two days later, only to realize, despairingly, that it had not made the slightest difference. My nerves were as bad as ever, my depression even worse. The doctor advised immediate admission to Dr Dubois' clinic for nervous disorders, at Saujon, and Yvonne Vallée drove me there one morning. She had to leave me and get back to her work at the Bouffes, where somebody had taken over my part.

Dr Dubois, whose father had created this oasis for overworked and overdriven people, was a most kindly and intelligent man. He had my notes from his colleague in Paris and knew all about me, but he made me go through it all with him again. I did so in great detail, trying to remember anything that could help.

There was no elaborate treatment. He put me on a not very severe diet and himself gave me a hydropathic showerbath every day and two sessions of conversation every week. Apart from that it was rest, and long country walks. I thought I was beyond deriving benefit from any such placid routine, fell once more into despair and contemplated suicide. I got as near to it as anyone possibly could, and had to acknowledge that when it came to the point I simply wasn't brave enough. I knew, too, that I never should be brave enough, and so I didn't have to think of it again, though I was left with a load of sadness I cannot describe, and measureless despondency.

Then Dubois said: Would I sing a day or two later at an entertainment in the local hall? The suggestion upset me terribly. How could he expect me to sing? It wasn't on. I couldn't sing ever again. All that was over and done with.

But, 'You can and you must,' said that admirable man. 'I am ordering you to sing, just to prove you can do so perfectly well, and you'll see that I am right.'

I practised my songs for a week, like an amateur making his début, and arranged two numbers with Yvonne, as though I needed her by me in case I went to pieces. And when the evening came I, who had held the ultra-sophisticates of Paris in the palm of my hand for years, arrived shaking like a jelly to play at that tiny hall for a homespun handful in an out-of-the-way village.

Professionalism took over, sure enough, as soon as I was on the stage. Every word was anxious work, but nothing went wrong, and they obviously appreciated having a real live actor on their private programme. But my old confidence had not come back. That I never regained, either then or later. What I did regain was courage, and from that moment I determined to take up my work once more. To work, that is, until what had haunted me since the appalling night at the Bouffes-Parisiens finally came true and disaster really struck. To carry on, in other words, until I finally collapsed. No nerves or terrors were going to keep me from it any longer. Until . . . until . . . For I have never given a performance since without wondering whether it would bring the fatal moment with it.

At last Dubois told me I must make a start and I rehearsed a song and dance routine with Yvonne. The next question was: where should the start be made? Not in Paris, I was far too frightened. What we wanted was somewhere small and quiet, where nobody who mattered would dream of finding me. From the days of my military service I remembered Melun and there discovered a tiny picture-house. I called on its manager and proposed myself for a week-end there. Friday to Sunday. The poor man thought at first that I was joking, but I put it to him that I could try out some new songs and wasn't bothered about salary. He saw I was serious and we fixed the thing for a nominal fee.

I will pass over what I went through in that obscure theatre before the curtain rose. Just as at Saujon, however, and despite my fears, I did not forget a single word and our programme went over very well on all three nights. You might think this would reassure me, but it did nothing of the kind. I was still painfully, unbearably convinced that I was going downhill, and yet I returned to the theatre and I battled on, playing town after town until a triumph at the Alcazar at Marseilles finally put my mind at rest. And at last I was in Paris, opening at the new Empire Music Hall on the Avenue de Wagram.

And there, as I went into my first song, a sort of miracle happened and gave me power I didn't know I had. Half-way through the first verse it dawned on me that the huge, packed auditorium had the most incredible acoustics. I could hear my voice, which was never very strong, penetrating to the very back of the circles and gallery. My diction seemed to go slicing through their solid, rapt attention like a hot knife through butter and a current was generated which everyone, they and I, could feel. My come-back was a resounding, one-hundred-per-cent success.

'Never seen Maurice in better form,' they said.

'For a man on his last legs he's certainly done all right tonight.'

'Just shows how stupid people can be, though, and the way that rumours get around. I even heard he'd lost his memory, gone off his head, or something.'

After that I was working all the time.

SUCCESS IS ONE THING, HAPPINESS ANOTHER

I seemed to be borne along on a wave of almost unreasonable and scarcely-deserved success, owing, I think, to a dearth of serious male competition in the French music-hall. Apart from the older generation, most of the men were modelling themselves on me in any case, for by now my imitators were legion. I was the Golden Boy and everything I sang or danced was a pattern they all fell on enthusiastically.

Was I happy though? I was successful, certainly. I was living a temperate and agreeable life with Yvonne in a perfectly charming villa at Vaucresson which we had christened '*Quand on est Deux*', 'The Two of Us', after a song of mine, and the humdrum, regular existence appeared to suit my nerves and my head. Most nights we drove home to Vaucresson as soon as we had finished at the Casino, and went into Paris as little as possible during the day. My fears and anxieties gave me an occasional twinge, just to remind me that they still existed, but I was no longer at their mercy. And I could earn as much as 10,000 francs for an evening's work.

Yet, where did the happiness come in? Well, I was, obviously, less unhappy than at the time of my collapse, for I had been able to get to grips with my job again. With what seemed ridiculous ease, in view of the state I had been in, I scaled the ladder of popularity as though nothing on earth could stop me. My energy had mastered my illness, which was comforting. But . . . was I happy?

Had I possessed a physique that allowed me to work as hard as I could and live life to the full at the same time, then I should have been happy. As it was, in spite of all the cosseting I got at home, I was irked at having to be reasonable. My trouble is that my instincts demand a great deal more than what I know is reasonable. I am a very curious mixture, with a passionate nature inherited, I suppose, from my father, and my mother's common sense. I am perpetually teetering on the edge of some precipice or another and yet always – touch wood – it is the common sense that marginally prevails to prevent my actually falling in.

Well, however that may be, during a tour in the south of France

I bought a farm and some land at La Bocca, near Cannes, I thought it would be fine for summer holidays and I called the house 'La Louque'.

For some unfathomable reason the actor is not born who, once he is earning decent money, can wait to complicate his existence by buying or building something many inconvenient miles from where he has to work. If you sing or play in Paris, then get a house not too far out, and very sensible too. What is fatal is to do as I and many others have done and buy one on the Riviera. You may see yourself spending months at a time down there, but that isn't what happens at all. You are off on tour in the summer when the Paris theatres shut, or you need a cure and go somewhere to take the waters. In the end it works out at a couple of weeks a year on a property which causes you untold worry and runs away with a fortune. Theatre people ought to live in Paris and follow their fancy when it comes to holidays. France is full of glorious places, beauty-spots, and inns and hotels with marvellous food. All you need is a dependable small car, light luggage and some money to spend, and you are as free as a bird. And what is to stop you going abroad, if you can afford to? The whole wide world is there to choose from, so what is the point of tying yourself down to the same old destination year in, year out, because you own a house which costs so much to keep up that you feel you simply have to use it? These truths, of course, become evident far too late, when you have lived long enough to learn that people are happier with rather too little money than with rather too much. If I were to begin my career all over again I do not think I should strive to reach the very top; I should just try not to stay at the very bottom.

So ends my lecture on 'House-hunting for Actors', due to an excess of common sense which came over me as I wrote. But common sense and inclination often pull in opposite directions, and as this book went to press I took an opposite direction and decided to hang on to the house at La Bocca in spite of all these neatly balanced arguments and all the lessons I should have learnt by now. My reasoning was as follows.

I am a gambling man, but I seldom or never bet, which argues a degree of self-mastery. I am a drinking man, and I seldom or never drink; self-mastery again. I master, too, the masterful instincts that impel me so strongly towards the glamorous and interesting ladies whom I meet. My life is passed in careful conduct, I battle with a host of temptations. I get excited about something, and argue myself out of it; rush forward, and then take two steps back. But by and large, until and unless I get knocked right off balance, I have achieved a kind of equilibrium which has, so far, allowed me to steer safely between a considerable number of dangerous reefs, and to avoid numerous sea-monsters open-mouthed and ready to devour me. I have no devastating vices, never having let any one vice gain control, and I propose therefore to have the Riviera house instead. It can be my darling paradise, a private haven of my own, and I can even produce deep-seated emotional reasons why this should be so. For one thing, La Louque was a pet-name we coined in childhood for a mother we adored, and how can anyone get rid of a house with a name like that? No, one does the exact opposite and turns it into a shrine, a kind of memory-house, with every detail designed and thought out to make the meaning clear. It is a nest, lined like a nest with one's dearest recollections, a love-token, a way of saying thank you. Bring on the architect, therefore, send for the interior decorator. I want to spend my money on that house. I want to feel proud of it and its beautiful fittings and furniture. The house can be in fact, my vice. I want to invite my friends there, as I once brought them home to my mother, and for this La Louque, too, their visits will be a distraction and a compliment. I shall make my mother's house lovelier than ever.

VIVE LE ROI!

I must find a corner in this book for a King, of all Kings the one who seemed to me to be the sort of ordinary man that I can understand. I therefore beg his leave to bring him forward, stand proudly to attention and announce my friend Alfonso XIII, King of Spain.

I first danced before him and the Queen with Mistinguett at an evening party at the Ritz where the élite of Paris society mingled with the élite of Spain. Sacha Guitry and Yvonne Printemps were there as well, acting in some sketch specially written for the occasion, and I remember approaching Sacha on the quiet, for a little guidance.

'Monsieur Sacha, is it true the King and Queen always send for the artists and congratulate them after the show? What do we do? What do we say to them? And how do we say it?'

My mentor thereupon disclosed that the Third Person was the correct form of address, and was kind enough to give a lesson, too. 'I offer Your Majesty my humble thanks'; 'Oh yes, Your Majesty' and 'Certainly, Your Majesty'; and Your Majesty this and Your Majesty that, all over the place. Uttered in his solemn, booming voice, it was impressive to a degree and devoutly I heard his long list of exemplary Majesties through to the end. Gravely, he concluded. I thanked him and with a calm and serious bearing anticipated the experience to come.

At any function before royalty, I had been warned, protocol forbade those present to clap before Majesty had graciously given the signal. Well, it stood to reason that Kings could not be banging their hands and feet and yelling 'Do it again!' like music-hall patrons in Belleville or somewhere. All they could do was assume an air of refined satisfaction and applaud quietly with their finger-tips. Everyone else, as they did so, tapped their fingers very lightly, with a minimum of uproar, so that the rustle of royal approval might be heard in the deafening hush. And indeed, not a laugh rang out, not a note of approbation. It was rather like working to a house of deaf-mutes whose disability had spread to the palms of their hands. It was flattering, I suppose, but I can't say it really kindled you.

Having done our best in this somewhat chilly atmosphere we awaited our summons to the presence. Over and over again I repeated to myself sentences in the Third Person on a vast variety of topics. Hardly had I polished one than I set about composing another, up to my neck in a right royal mess. It was no good trying to look carefree, either; I should never get my tongue round this head-waiter's language. But whether I should or whether I shouldn't, here came the Spanish ambassador, and pray would we follow him, Their Majesties wished to see us.

7. On mobilization in 1913

Performer in the French Army Theatre

8. Prisoner of war

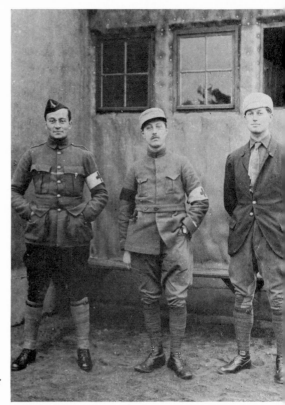

Male nurse in a prisoner of war camp

Sacha and Yvonne were presented first and appeared to be thoroughly on home ground. I even had a fleeting second of slight optical delusion, for Sacha, still in his greasepaint, looked so very lordly and the real monarch so very unaffected that the one in make-up might easily have been the Majesty of Spain. I dismissed the vision quickly, which was just as well, as it was now my turn to step forward, with Mistinguett.

And how incredibly relaxed she was, with that innate chic of hers! Where in heaven's name had she learnt to behave like this, I asked myself; had she been popping off to court circles, visiting the Comte de Paris, or something? Now for it, here he is. Oh, dear, he's said something to me. My knees begin to shake and I have a wild impulse to ask him for a chair. No, that wouldn't do at all, sitting down while H.M. talks to me standing up. Perish the thought.

'A beautiful performance, Monsieur Chevalier.'

'Your Maj ...' I got stuck and had to clear my throat. 'Your Majesty ...' It occurred to me how silly I must look and I wanted to giggle. 'Your Majesty is too kind.' (And *trop bon* (too kind) damn nearly came out as 'trombone', I may say.)

'It must be most difficult, Monsieur Chevalier, most taxing, and you made it seem so easy.'

'Your ...' Another lump. I hadn't got it yet. 'Majesty', I added. And oh dear, Your Majesty, my mind is so entirely concentrated on this proper form and its various appropriate constructions that this is as far as I go. I dried up completely. 'Your Majesty is too ...' Even the trombone failed me. Then the word came: 'too indulgent.'

Was I dreaming, or did he catch my eye with a gleam of amusement? Did he see that I was about as much at my ease as a fish out of water? Why, he was a nice type, this! And I smiled back, feeling more sympathy in the exchange of glances than in all the convention and formality around us.

The smile acted as a release. Whether or not I kept to the required grammar after that I do not know; I cannot swear to it. But as our conversation went on he remained so natural that I forgot everything, where we were, who he was, and who I was. I produced a spasmodic 'Majesty' at intervals, only to forget a second later. I recovered myself at the finish, however, and, all tensed up as though poised for a somersault, managed: 'Your Majesty makes me very proud.'

And I cannot have made so bad an impression on him, either, for in 1925, just after I had launched my song '*Valentine*' at the Casino de Paris, the same ambassador, Señor Quinones de Léon, appeared once more with an invitation to perform my newest numbers at his embassy. This time the company would include, as well as his Sovereigns, all the big political guns of the day – Poincaré, Briand and, last but not least, Edouard Herriot, Prime Minister of France.

I warned him that there were aspects of my newest numbers, '*Dites-Moi M'sieur Chevalier*', for instance, sung with Yvonne Vallée, and, of course, '*Valentine*', which might be considered less than suitable for royal ears. Breasts, he ought to realize, for one thing, were mentioned in the lyrics, the *tétons* of Valentine. Hopeless to deny it.

'Oh,' cried His Excellency, 'don't give it a thought! Absolutely not, he'll adore it. *Tétons*, what a nice word. Really French: slangy. Their Majesties will simply love it.'

And so the evening arrived, with the silent laudations that were, we knew, in order. The applause for '*Dites-Moi*' was about what we should have evoked if we had sung it on top of the Eiffel Tower at five o'clock on a mid-winter morning, though, certainly, the King and Queen smiled. And next came '*Valentine*'.

Never, while memory lasts, shall I forget doing that song, First verse: the abiding memory of one's first mistress; the rainy day we met and got on so very well together; how we could always meet in the Rue Custine and how I took her hand to begin with and the rest of her afterwards. And then the disastrous refrain with the attributes of Valentine.

> *Elle avait de tout petits tétons*
> *Valentine, Valentine,*
> *Elle avait de tout petits tétons*
> *Que je tâtais a tâtons.* . . .

As I sang these lines my eye was drawn to where Edouard Herriot sat, huddled in his chair the picture of agitation. I was terrified of the fatal word in any case, terrified of upsetting everyone, of doing the wrong thing and being vulgar, and I got agitated too. Judging by the Prime-Minister's reaction, I had rung my death-knell. As I continued the chorus, an unending prospect of disaster stretched ahead.

Elle avait un tout petit menton,

(If Herriot was as shocked as that I must have made one of those blunders that finish an artist off for ever. Treason, I shouldn't be surprised.)

Valentine, Valentine,

(I knew it, I knew it. Why didn't the ambassador listen to me when I told him? Now they'll sack him too. That ought to do his career a lot of good.)

Outre ses petits pétons ses p'tits tétons
Son p'tit menton

(And this is just what I needed, too, getting into a hole like this. Kings should stick with Kings, and ordinary folk with ordinary folk. Promenade and gallery, that's all this stuff's fit for. My brain was racing. The gallery never made a fuss about a couple of innocent *tétons*.)

Elle était frisée comme un mouton.

All through the second verse and chorus the cold sweat poured off me. I could feel it dripping into my ears and off my eyelids. My past existence and all its struggles unrolled before me like that of a drowning man. What in God's name had possessed me to get involved with this lot, anyway? Look what it had led to. This should teach me to shut up about *tétons* for the future. Desperately I scanned the famous and distinguished faces for signs of disapproval to match those shown by Monsieur Herriot, who was by now cowering down as if to say: 'How *dare* he? The *monstrous* man has taken leave of his senses, trotting out all these *tétons*, with the Queen here!'

The Queen. The King. I dare not even glance in their direction. The outraged royal stare, I thought, would freeze me solid where I stood. I embarked on the third verse in a sightless sort of way, concentrating three feet or so in the air above the heads of my celebrated listeners, though a masochistic desire to make a meal of it attracted me continually to the corner where the Prime Minister seemed, by his presence, to confer upon me First Prize for National Stupidity. The minute it was over I fled from the scene of the catastrophe. Still hot and cold with shame I made for home with Yvonne in a state of fevered alarm, as though the whole Spanish police force were waving warrants on our track. Our lonely supper would have made a marvellous subject for a gloomy still-life. *Nature morte* with a vengeance.

For several days I heard no more, though fully expecting the scandalous tale to hit me in every morning's paper. There it would be, in enormous headlines: 'Maurice Chevalier: Insult to Royalty'. Then, one night, the Spanish ambassador was announced in my dressing-room. Oh, well, I thought, looking on the bright side, they haven't actually carted him off to prison yet, that's some comfort, I suppose. But now he's come to tell me he's got to find another job and it's all my fault. That or something else, but something horrid, anyway.

In he came, quite calm; calm as a calm Spaniard can be when he has no reason to be otherwise; and, smiling, handed me a small parcel.

'With His Majesty's compliments,' he said.

He continued calm under my glance of inquiry and the parcel, I found, contained a quite beautiful cigarette-case, engraved inside with the royal signature. After a moment or two, when I had taken this in, I ventured.

'Then Their Majesties were not annoyed, *Monsieur l'ambassadeur*?'

'Annoyed?' he said. 'Whatever for?'

'Oh, singing "*Valentine*", upsetting them with the *tétons*. And you said it would be all right, remember?'

'No, no, Monsieur Chevalier; absolutely not. Believe me, everybody loved it – the guests, the Queen. As for H.M. (he lowered his voice, as though to impart some secret of state), H.M. told me afterwards he'd very much like a copy. Wants to learn it himself.'

All the same, I wanted further details.

'But why did Monsieur Herriot clutch his head like that as soon as he heard the word?'

'Did he? Nobody noticed, I assure you. Heavens, you're imagining things, Monsieur Chevalier. Monsieur Herriot hasn't the least objection to Valentine's anatomy. Goodness, no. Pure imagination on your part – bit fatigued, I shouldn't wonder.'

With a cordial handshake he was gone, leaving me in stunned confusion, and it was the best part of a week before I got back to normal. I am like that, though. Such disturbances overcome me, and I stay overcome for an indefinite period, until I wake up one morning having absorbed that particular shock, all ready for the next.

I saw him again – rather, I saw His Majesty again in December 1940, when I was appearing in Lausanne. He sent for me as soon as I got there, took me out to a restaurant and talked to me simply, man to man. He said how much he loved France, how firm was his faith in her destiny. It was wonderful, just then, to hear such things about my country and I left him with a full heart, moved and grateful. In the evening he came to the popular music-hall where I was playing, and there he sat, with the ordinary tradespeople and artisans, as natural and as much at his ease as in his own embassy in Paris among the sort of people he was used to. We exchanged a look now and then and that comradely expression of his could have spurred one to the performance of a life-time. Next day, after my morning walk, I ran into him again, coming out of the Beau Rivage Hotel. The girl with him was very young and very beautiful.

He hailed me by the familiar *tu*. 'Maurice,' he said, 'you were marvellous last night! You're at the top of your form. Top of your form!'

The tall figure, the open, manly face and friendly voice – and the pretty companion too. The rejoinder was on the tip of my tongue: '*Dis-donc, Alphonse*, you're not doing so badly, either.' No I didn't say so, but it was a great temptation.

Unbelievably, news of his death was in the paper two months afterwards; and I doubt whether many of his own subjects felt the blow more than did a certain *caballero* of distinctly non-Spanish appearance, born and bred in the twentieth *arrondissement* of Paris.

For, despite this talk of Kings, you know, I come from the back-streets, and brats from back-streets never blend properly with what is called 'society', whose members are too blasé, too sure by a long chalk of what they really want and what they really like. They will concede a little, certainly, open the door an inch or two, but none of it means very much. They do not understand what goes on inside someone in the throes of creation. Their judgements are un-complicated, like those of a literary critic who has never written a book; superior judgements, for they take a lofty attitude. Actors artists, singers – we are there, paid puppets, for their entertainment, after all. Welcome us in or say 'no thank you' – it couldn't matter less.

HOLLYWOOD BOUND

Yvonne and I had got married in 1926. Marrying her had seemed the right and proper thing to do, but after a while I recognized that it wasn't going to work out as I had hoped. I don't know whose fault it was. Hers? Mine? Or it may have been simply the fault of my profession. Whatever the reason, our life was turning into hell and I was only happy working. It was a half-and-half existence. I was still faithful to her but I could never make her trust me, and without trust what marriage can survive? Heaven had granted me a successful career all right, but not domestic harmony.

As usual, I was inclined to blame myself. She was suspicious by nature and perhaps I didn't know how to reassure her properly. Per-haps, too, I was unduly irritable, in normal male reaction against the watch and ward she kept on all my movements. It is Plato, I believe, who says that every man and woman is the separated half of what was once one body, searching for the other through eter-nity, and that when two such halves meet you have the perfect love, a marriage made in heaven. I can only think that Yvonne and I rushed into each other's arms without looking to see if we matched at all, on a dark and cloudy day with a bad weather forecast. And yet I had expected so much of our union. I so longed for and needed the solace of shared affection. Everyone thought us a delightful couple, too, and so well-suited. In public, as at home, there seemed nothing for it but to go on pretending.

I was the most envied figure on the variety stage and a profoundly unhappy man. I didn't know what to do. The moment for getting a divorce had passed, yet it was too awful to contemplate going on as we were. I think what really made me hesitate was an unreasonable fear of being alone again. The suffocating fuss of stardom that was the breath of life to Yvonne, left me terrified of another breakdown if I had to face it unsupported. Night after night, I have no doubt, I played to theatres full of people who envied me like mad. Smiling, carefree Chevalier! That optimistic character up there, so obviously master of his fate! Poor devil.

Such, then, was the situation when I was told one night,

'There's a man to see you; says he's a director of Metro-Goldwyn Mayer in Hollywood. Name of Thalberg. Gorgeous female with him, too.'

'Thalberg? I don't know any Thalberg. Still, you can send him in.'

And there appeared in my dressing-room an almost bashful and extremely young man, accompanied by a strikingly beautiful woman.

Why I cannot say, but I just didn't take them seriously. He wanted a film-test and, if I photographed well, was in a position to offer me a Hollywood contract. I replied, somewhat brusquely, that the days were over when I gave auditions; a management either engaged me or it didn't and I considered his suggestion humiliating. The truth was, I thought he was bluffing and not half as important as he claimed to be. Politely, he took his leave and no sooner was he gone than my secretary – I had had a secretary for some time now – burst out,

'Maurice, for heaven's sake – *Irving Thalberg! Norma Shearer!* You've just sat on the most powerful man in American films!'

'What!' I yelled, 'that boy? He's the top man in America? Oh, God, go and catch him! Say I'm sorry, say I'll make a test tomorrow. And tell him, if nothing comes of it, all I want is a print for a memento.'

Out I drove to Vincennes the very next day to one of the studios there. The cameraman was an American whose sole function was to travel with the boss and photograph selected discoveries. I walked about and I sat down; I grinned at him; he shot me full-face and he shot me in profile. And when they showed me the result twenty-four hours later I was pleasurably surprised to see at last that I was quite photogenic, since previous experience had not exactly encouraged dreams of a film-career. However, after all this, we failed to agree on terms and no contract resulted, though I kept the print as we agreed I should.

Then Jesse Lasky of Paramount turned up. Here we go again, I thought. But this time I signed a contract, with less than a day's negotiation; one film to start with and the option of renewal. What brought him to my door was the fact that I could sing in English. Talkies were just beginning and, as he pointed out, my knowledge of that language put me in a strong position. But he, too, wanted a test to begin with.

'You needn't bother,' I said. 'I have one I did about a fortnight ago.'

'Bring it along at eleven tomorrow, then.'

And, thanks to the test shot by the rival concern, the contract was in my pocket by twelve: six weeks, complete with option and return fares paid from Paris to Hollywood for Yvonne and myself. From that day onwards the American publicity machine took charge of me, and Lasky and I were dogged at every step by reporters and photographers. Money was poured out, in true Hollywood fashion, to ensure the maximum ballyhoo for this début in the great world of the cinema. Critics and actors were wined and dined in my honour at the company's expense and leading members of the profession made farewell speeches to me. Paramount Pictures, waving their wand, had turned me into a sensational personality and Paris fell over itself to see me at the Apollo before I left.

For Yvonne and me, in the midst of the whirlwind, it was like being wafted away on a magic carpet, and already I found it all un-real and larger than life.

'*Au revoir*, Maurice!'

'Good luck!'

'Don't forget to come back home!'

We were on our way, among flowers and flashlights, to New York and Hollywood. The Gare Saint-Lazare was black with people. Even at this stage I felt up to my neck in a process that exploited me by means I could neither understand nor approve. And dear God! I thought, the downfall if any of this goes wrong! A deflated home-coming *that* will be. The train pulled out through a sea of faces. Many of my oldest friends were there. (Not my mother, though. I had been to see her beforehand and she was terribly proud of it all, old and weary, but smiling and proud.) On the boat, baskets, bouquets and bunches of flowers spilled round us. There were cards and greetings and good wishes wherever you looked. I thought of my departures on tour, not so long ago: leaving for the station alone, unless a solitary friend might come to see me off; the unap-plauded arrival at Perpignan, or some such place. And now, all of a sudden, this. Everybody off their heads. An enormous crowd of my fellow-countrymen beside themselves because I was bound for America to act in films.

Wait a minute, though, I was bound for America to try to act in films. Nothing was sure or settled about it. Just, we'll see how it goes, we'll have an option; that was all. And if it didn't go, then I could whistle for the florist's shop and the luxurious stateroom. An ordinary cabin would be my lot, without trimmings, and quite good enough, too, for the prize idiot I should look by then, I had no illusions on that score. But the die was cast; one could only await developments and make the best of it.

I said good-bye to my friends at Le Havre and the boat pulled away from the French quayside. Good-bye to France. Georges, I reflected, had been through all this when he went to fight Dempsey in America and at least I preferred my trade to his. The crash wasn't physical in mine, and it didn't hurt so much. Oh, hell, I decided, better stop *brooding* about it.

I put on a dinner-jacket, for I was to dine in magnificence at the Captain's table, there to meet the most distinguished of his passen-gers and, presumably, to enjoy sophisticated conversation. 'Sophis-ticated' and 'sophistication' were words which were to haunt me from now on. We were sophisticates to a man, it seemed, we Latin types from Paris. Actually, the term was double Dutch to me and I had to have it explained, but you couldn't let the public down and for the future, to prevent disappointment, I should certainly have to dispense sophistication by the ton. To do so was foreign to my nature, but by this time much else was going on that was foreign to my nature and I saw no likelihood of ever being able to halt the glamorous, perilous enterprise at all.

Well, we should see what we should see. I could but try, and it would be crazy to refuse an opportunity like this. I could only come a cropper at the worst, in which case I should turn round and go home. They couldn't expect to conjure a genius out of their lamp in three months, could they? And what was the difference, after all? Number 1 in France, or Number 2, or even Number 10, it was still a lot more than ever I hoped for when my greatest aim in life was pulling down ten francs a day. I had everything to gain and nothing to lose, and it was hardly the end of the world if an actor didn't make it. You simply packed your bags and returned to base, and not the first to do so, either. What about so-and-so, poor man, and such-and-such, poor girl, and all the others one could think of? Name after name occurred to me. They hadn't let it put them off their stroke. Far from it. Back they came with their tales of trans-atlantic glory, and in a little while took up the threads in France and nobody any the wiser. Only people in the know would realize that they didn't repeat the American visit because they were never asked to; and if they were never asked to it was because. . . . Well, the reason stared you in the face.

There was a grand dinner at the Waldorf-Astoria to which Paramount bade all the chief figures on the New York scene, producers, players, journalists. I was presented to this galaxy and later, when dessert came round, was supposed to mount the platform and oblige with a song or two.

After the meal the famous French producer, Louis Aubert, rose to his feet. Not that he had ever seemed keen to use my talents at home, but this was apparently the moment to proclaim his confidence in my success this side of the water. I was, he said, the faubourgs of Paris incarnate and they mustn't think of changing me. Oh, no; I must at all costs remain untouched, unspoilt. And it was with deep concern, he told us, that he consigned me to the keeping of America.

Our final speaker was Richard Dix, who had had a fair amount to drink and proceeded to contradict everything that anyone had said so far. I was not to believe the pretty compliments handed out by Paramount, for one thing. Beware the lot of them and never trust a word they said, was his advice to me. In the distinctly awkward pause that followed I leapt to my feet, tendered my thanks as simply as possible and almost ran to the sacrifice, or, rather, to the platform where the pianist sat waiting for me. Best to get it over.

Silence fell. The assembled company lit its cigars and eyed me with more curiosity than friendliness. They had heard all too much about me by now and suspicion had set in. And then some happy instinct prompted me to introduce my French songs in English; my accent would amuse them and they would at least know what they were listening to. That fortunate inspiration, I always thought, laid the foundations of my American success – for success it was from the very beginning. I came to the States with songs they'd never met, sung in a way they never dreamed of. I was *new*. They had Al Jolson and Harry Richman and Georgie Jessel, all splendid variety artists with superb voices and terrific personalities, but nobody who sang in this particular simple, natural way. I sensed as much that evening. It was going to be all right.

So we had more flowers, more speeches and handshaking. We also had the *Marseillaise* performed on a consort of trumpets, which I thought was taking things a bit too far and found embarrassing. Yet what could I do but go along with everything? 'Wonderful!' they said. 'Marvellous!' The French consul from Los Angeles, looking benevolent, watched my dilemma with the hint of conspiritorial smile. Nothing that had happened to me since I got off the boat had been in the least bit like anything I had previously come across in all my days as a singer. I just wasn't prepared for it. Raging inwardly, I smiled until my face ached. I could have wept.

HOLLYWOOD, 1928

We started off at the Beverly Wilshire Hotel, staying there for a few days until we could rent what Hollywood called a bungalow. To reach the hotel, you went through Beverly Hills, an area where every house seemed more attractive than the last, with the Spanish style predominating. The homes of the stars were pointed out to us.

Charlie Chaplin, Douglas Fairbanks (who had sent a telegram of welcome to the boat), Emil Jannings, Lupe Velez, Clara Bow – this really was a different world. Their mere names took me back to the foyers of Paris cinemas where I had marvelled at their photographs; and now I should be seeing them close to and actually talking to them. I was thrilled at the prospect and longed especially to meet Chaplain and Jannings, both of whom I venerated, rather than admired, as an utterly devoted fan.

This I confessed to the people who were looking after us and one of them, a talented young French producer named Harry d'Abadie d'Arrast, immediately said: what about dining that very evening, quietly, just with him and Charlie Chaplin? I stammered and stuttered at him. *What* did he say? And *who* did he say? And could he really work this miracle?

He could and he did, and with no fuss at all. He called for us at the hotel and took us to his charming, unostentatious house where we were joined five minutes later by the wonderful little man to whom the whole world was on its knees. He arrived alone and we were introduced in the tiny sitting-room. He had a broad smile for us both and I couldn't think of a word to say. Aware that I must appear completely idiotic, I stood and goggled at him. Seconds ticked by and the situation grew more idiotic still. I had to say something. At last I mumbled, in a voice I failed to recognize,

'Monsieur Chaplin, I'm not very bright at the best of times and this is so shattering it's made me worse than ever. You'll have to let me get used to the fact it's really you, and I might improve a bit.'

I was babbling in a state of shock, but he took it very well and inquired about my singing and what I was hoping to do in America. Whose idea had it been to bring me over? Had I done any filming in France?

Yes, I said, I had, but only silent pictures, nothing very startling. I had come to Hollywood because the talkies would probably have more to offer me.

And as I said this I was suddenly aware that the thought of the talkies worried him. The great Chaplin knew the cinema had reached a major turning-point. On silent film he was unchallengeable, but sound had brought many gifted comedians to the fore already, and he had to reckon with them. He had never spoken, never sung, and he faced the future, unsure of what he was doing to do. He had to wait and see. To speak or not to speak?

He mentioned nothing of this, of course, but his eyes, and the way he pressed for details, told the tale. He made me think of a general gathering information as to what the enemy was up to.

Chaplin was only 40 then, but already his bushy hair was white. With our host translating from time to time, we talked of screen and theatre stars. He gave the impression of being somehow above it all and could not have been an easy man to know; hard to analyse. But one thing was clear enough: this was not the happy, simple soul the films might lead one to expect. Chaplin was not simple at all. He was a genius, he was anything else you liked to call him, but he was terribly complicated. He was a mass of complexes.

He discussed politics and international relations, subjects on which I was a complete non-starter. I could hold my own when we talked shop, and that was all. For the rest he might as well have been discoursing by himself, to himself, in front of a looking-glass. Also, his private life was in a mess just then; nobody alluded to the fact, but he had recently separated from Lita Grey Chaplin, a beautiful, dark-haired girl whom I had heard singing in New York a week before. We got on well enough, but I felt at the end of the evening that we hadn't much in common. I was too ordinary, he was too extraordinary, for that. We were to see each other often at parties, but I always knew that between us, with our wide, welcoming smiles and our 'Hullo Charlie', 'Hullo Maurice', a great gulf lay.

Work began on my first film. Our story opened on the banks of the Seine, reconstructed for the purpose on the external lot at Paramount. A poverty-stricken woman throws herself into the water with her child in her arms as I, in my character of young rag-and-bone man, come carolling round the corner in time to hear the splash. I peer into the twilight, I see bubbles rising from the water. My God! and in I go. I rescue the child all right, but the mother is drowned. It was, you may gather, a nice cheery start. The child being now alone in the world I adopt him and take him to live in my garret. These details will fill you in on the plot and serve to explain the incident I am about to tell.

At one point in the film this 6-year-old darling was overcome by the thought of his mother and had a good cry, upon which I threw a paternal arm about his neck and did my best to comfort him. I murmured to him gently, but he only cried the more. The sobs were heart-rending, and having tried everything else I could think of, I finally resorted to a hit song called '*Dites-Moi Ma Mère*', 'Tell me, Mummy'. I donned large comic hats, including a helmet, from his soldier-set and brandished a little gun. Watching these antics at first with disbelief, he soon began to smile and at last stopped crying and joined in at the top of his voice. It all ended up with shouts of glee and a piggy-back ride. Not exactly a scene with the Victor Hugo touch (Hollywood, after all, hadn't got around to hiring Victor Hugo then) but, such as it was, it was the average cinema-goer's ideal cup of tea.

The action leading up to this song, then, lay entirely between this near-infant and myself. I laid my arm upon his shoulder, clasped his neck and spoke in tender tones to assuage his piteous grief. We rehearsed it to perfection and then we shot. Take One. 'Again, please', said the director. Take Two, and again there was something not quite right. This worried me and I inquired what the hitch was. Dick Wallace thereupon drew me into a corner and told me the little one was wiping the floor with me.

'What do you mean, wiping the floor?'

'Just what I say. That brat knows you're fairly new to films and he's pulling the old, original Hollywood one-two. He gets himself a couple of inches behind you the whole time, so you have to turn around to talk to him and all the camera sees is the back of your neck. He's right in there full-face, of course. Get the idea?'

'That *child*? A fast one like that on an old hand like me?'

'We'll just make good and sure.'

He called the culprit over and explained that somehow, without realizing it, he seemed to have moved away from the exact spot on which he should be standing for this scene. Would he please take care to keep his right position, as we were having to re-shoot, and all because of him? The cherubic boy was contrite. Why, he hadn't been *thinking*! He was real, real sorry.

Take Three.

And at the same place that imp of Satan began the same manoeuvre, just very gradually up-staging me until I had to turn my head. The exasperated Dick yelled, 'Cut!' and the boy assumed the slightly pained, inquiring air of one who can't think what's got into everybody. Another rehearsal, and he stayed fair and square on his marks. Then we shot the thing.

Duly he wept and sobbed. I took him by the shoulder and poured out the soothing English words. But this time, when he started, the thought of being got at by the little beast lent strength to my arm. He nearly pulled it out of its socket but I forced him to stay put and kept myself in camera, in profile if nothing more. And this covert professional struggle was conducted, to a running accompaniment of almost motherly cooing and tenderness, between a grown man and a child of 6! In Hollywood, it was plain, one learnt to stand up for oneself at a very early age, and the placing of hits below the belt was part of an actor's education.

The film was called *Innocents of Paris* in the English, *La Chanson de Paris* in the French version, and the preview took place at the Paramount cinema in Los Angeles. A stirring occasion, for me more than anyone. Scattered among the typical big-town audience were several of the studio's stars, come to cast an eye over their Gallic recruit, and all the bosses were there as well – Lasky, Zukor, Schulberg. Yvonne and I were in the ordinary seats by ourselves. The film came on. My name on the screen provoked no reaction at all, and I didn't seem to have much personal appeal, either. I broke into a cold sweat sitting there, and at the end of five minutes an American in front of us, a workman by the looks of him, turned to his companion, made a face and let fall the one word, 'Lousy'. (*Vomissable*, I suppose it would have been in French.) But the first song, though they didn't go mad about it, evidently pleased them better, and after that, thank goodness, they began to laugh! Even the churl who said I was lousy softened enough to utter a sudden loud guffaw. Steadily, they were warming up.

The song *Louise* was applauded. Certainly, this was better, and the audience and I were firm friends for the final third of the film. Things tailed off again towards the end, but that was the fault of the story and I had undeniably won the day. The Paramount moguls were lamenting as they left that their picture was unworthy of me. As for me, I scarcely knew whether I was on my head or my heels. I heard Adolphe Menjou saying: 'The film's only fair, Maurice, but never mind that. You'll be the biggest hit a French actor ever has been over here.' I don't know whether I managed a reply, or merely wrung his hand a bit harder than usual. I do remember that I had great difficulty swallowing.

We went home to France for a while, then back to Hollywood, where they cancelled my existing contract and dished out another at three times the salary for the two remaining films. We were made much of, invited everywhere, although I felt at the bottom of my heart that this promotion to Number 1 International Star had happened rather too easily and that I didn't deserve it all. The fore-most actors poured compliments upon me. I was unique, I was this, that and the other thing; whereas I honestly considered them to be more intelligent people and technically much better performers than myself. In every theatre, variety-house, cabaret and cinema in the country some man, woman or child had seized a straw hat and was doing a Maurice Chevalier imitation. The vogue was inexhaustible. I was almost mobbed whenever I showed my face in public. And endlessly they played the *Marseillaise*. Ah, how they played the *Marseillaise*!

Then I had some free time and decided to work on Broadway for a week or so. As well as doing something different from the ordinary variety turn, I also wanted to do something for C. B. Dillingham who had booked me to play Dédé in America in 1924, when I had been ill and had to disappoint him. To appear at one of his theatres would be a splendid way of making up for my defection then. Our choice fell on the Fulton which, with a capacity of 1,300 or so, was not too big.

I wanted a two-part programme with a top-class jazz band for the first half, which would move down to the orchestra pit and accompany me in the second. It was an ambitious and somewhat perilous formula, but I was then unbelievably popular and it seemed a good idea to strike while the iron was hot and demonstrate, by this unconventional show, how solid and real was my transatlantic success.

The question was: which band? We went through them all. The Waring Pennsylvanians? Paul Whiteman? Ted Lewis? Then someone asked whether I had heard Duke Ellington, the coloured jazzman who was drawing all Broadway to the Cotton Club in Harlem, the Negro quarter of New York. Yes, certainly I had heard him, he was terrific. But Harlem was Harlem and Broadway was Broadway. There was a dividing-line and Ellington had never crossed it, never at any time worked on Broadway. He always stayed in Harlem, on home territory. Could he play for an hour in a white theatre, in the middle of Times Square? And what would the effect be if he did? Personally, when I thought about it, I could foresee a sensation, and he was approached, at my suggestion. He was both delighted and petrified at the idea, but the contract was settled, signed and sealed, and Broadway rang with the news – an artistic association of Harlem and Paris, here in the heart of New York: Ellington conducting his own band when I, alone with my straw hat, took the stage for the second half.

Once over the initial surprise at rehearsal, I soon got used to the sight of their faces, the huge white eyes and wide-open mouths, all laughing like children at the succession of incomprehensible French songs. And here was Ellington, looking straight at me with searchlight directness, carrying me along on that strong, muscular rhythm; I felt I was in contact with yet another aspect of America. We had advance bookings for a week and the most influential critics had struck a friendly note ever since the show was announced.

Ellington was having dancers in his half, as well as the tearing, rending music of the brass. There were three of them, one a mere child, and they appeared between two of his blues numbers, 'Hot' was how he described them, and hot they surely were. Interested, if not exactly carried away, the audience applauded warmly though not wildly. They hadn't decided yet. A Negro orchestra, later recognized as one of the greatest in the world, was setting off, almost diffidently, on the road to glory at the Fulton Theatre that night, and the oddest part of the whole thing was that opportunity should have come their way through a stray Parisian whose name was unknown in America a few short months before.

For the second half Duke and his boys were duly installed in the

I

orchestra pit and my introductory music, heard from the wings, was like a gun going off. Those boys – what could their throats be made of? Every crash of syncopation ran through you like a shock, unless it was that every shock you got set up the syncopation. All went well. My hour of songs and stories passed like fifteen minutes, with an ovation at the end. The press next morning was unanimous, we were turning people away every night and there sprang in me the germ of a persistent idea. Why not do a whole evening of my solo programme, just me and the audience; make a little more of my light songs, fine down the more robust ones, and produce something whose style and quality would attract the public as would a good play or a revue? *La Soirée de Maurice Chevalier*, 'An Evening with Maurice Chevalier'. And if this were a bit over-ambitious, the future would tell me where I stood. I do not think you can force public opinion, any more than I think that public will condemn you for ever if you don't deserve it. And anyway I would rather aim too high and get a crick in my neck than have a permanent stoop from aiming low. What will be will be, in any case.

Meanwhile the Americans with one voice declared me the most popular male star in the world. Paramount tore my contract in shreds yet again and upped my pay into the highest Hollywood bracket. I did a week at the San Francisco Motor Show for a sum you wouldn't credit, far above the 2,000 dollars I had been earning in New York a month or so previously. But that's America for you. You become the thing and the dividends of success are magnificent. You roar along. And I was riding a whirlwind of success.

There had been remarkable changes already, in my short time in the States. Richard Dix, Adolphe Menjou and Emil Jannings had left Paramount, contracts expired or contracts terminated. Rumour said that Clara Bow was also due for departure, which was sad. So short a time ago they were all so famous and with such a following. It was indeed a very unsentimental and a very cruel world that grew up in and around the big studios. I myself was safe for the moment, but how long would that be? There was no reason to suppose it would deal with me any more kindly, once I slipped at the box-office.

But now I had to go to Paris for a fortnight at the Châtelet. The press was not too welcoming and the public seemed to have taken the cue. The booking arrangements went wrong. I was on a salary and percentage and the management got into a panic. Two days before we opened I took pity on them and crossed the guaranteed-salary clause out of my contract, leaving myself no more than an agreed percentage of the takings. I can only imagine that stage-fright had impaired my mental processes.

I am possibly being a bore with this perpetual stage-fright of mine, when things almost always turned out all right in the end, but if I am to take you honestly over my road through life it's no use leaving out the bad bits. In our profession, anyone to whom his work means anything suffers from stage-fright, which is incurable. So much can go wrong when you are up behind those footlights that it needs only one little anxiety to glimmer in your subconscious mind for you to see, immediately, a whole army of horrors, similar or far, far worse, all looming up to make everything more dreadful still.

Stage-fright occurs in varying degrees, but it is always there. It lodges in the pit of your stomach, whether you acknowledge it or not. And different terrors lie in wait for all who perform professionally in public. Actors, sportsmen, musicians, politicians, lawyers, priests, you could write a book about them. However, that's enough on the subject for now, and my apologies if I seem to go on about it and repeat myself. But it is in fact the stage-fright which repeats itself, time and time again.

Well, I went back to Hollywood. And thinking about that return, I begin to see why, although I had seven seasons in that spellbound, curious corner of the world, I never really came to terms with the illusory and unstable life I led there. Hollywood is, above all else, a market, based on box-office receipts and has, of deadly necessity, to flatter the great paying public and give it what it wants. For this reason the actor who strives constantly to improve runs into snags at once. There was a Hollywood conception of things, a Hollywood outlook, a Hollywood way of thinking, and in the end you either had to adopt it or escape from the whole poisonous atmosphere. Nothing was, or could be, completely human in that land of make-believe. Success and failure, love-affairs and separations, friendships and feuds and even haircuts – it was conform or get out.

I know for a fact that I shouldn't be the slightest use there now. Which is why, until and unless the perfect offer comes, with part and producer of my choice, the place can stay where it is, among my souvenirs. I know what it's like to be a Hollywood idol. That kind of popularity brought me no happiness and was often a fearful encumbrance. Hollywood is the complete tart and temptress, with whom it is wisest to have nothing to do unless she makes passionate advances of her own accord. If she doesn't, if she merely lets her sultry, not very interested, regard stray in your direction, take off as fast as you can. Really fast, or you're in for something that won't be funny at all.

INTERLUDE: MARCELLE

His name doesn't matter. He was the man who, so the American statistics said, was now established as the screen's Leading Lover, temporary holder of the masculine Sex-Appeal Championship: *Tombeur* Number I. We could call him Heart-Throb Number 1, perhaps, or First Irresistible.

The First Irresistible, then, had been to Europe on holiday and, recalled by pressing cables from the studio, was on his way back to California. He had just emerged, for the umpteenth time, from the regulation ballyhoo attendant on the leave-taking of a great star. A crowd at the station, forewarned by the morning papers, themselves advised by the film company's Paris office; photographers by the dozen. Raise your hat please, *Monsieur Tombeur* Number 1. That's it, that's fine. Smile, please; wave good-bye! 'Click' went the cameras. Thank *you*. Now let's have another, with some flowers. *That*'s it. Now laugh, laugh, LAUGH, let's see those teeth! Click, click. Thanks, that's fine. Meanwhile reporters strove to garner some novel phrase or original pronouncement, no easy task for either side. Is it true he is in love with Miss Joan Gotobed? When's the wedding? What is his next film called? How, in his view, does the American woman differ from the French? To all these questions – the same old questions in any language, anywhere – the First Irresistible had managed to respond politely. Somehow, this side of screaming-point, he had satisfied the horde of journalists worrying and pestering him because some editor wanted an article.

And now the transatlantic liner was leaving for New York. Absently leaning on the rail, he watched the final preparations before the floating city moved. His manager had gone off to look at the cabins and he was alone. The gangway was up and the passengers, sure of 'having him to themselves' for the best part of a week, would display no ill-timed haste; so for the moment he was safe.

He was sad and melancholy as he thought back over the stages of his marvellous career. Over the days, so long behind him now, when he had to scrape and save to keep going; back to all the journeys, opening nights, departures; and then, his coming to Hollywood. Hollywood, where the miracle that sometimes happens, happened; where his first film showed that he photographed 'like a million dollars' and, in the capable hands of the studio bosses, he became overnight the biggest box-office draw and the brightest male star in all that magic firmament. He had retained this position for some time now and though there were signs of a falling-off they didn't amount to much so far. The oracles estimated that his own impetus would keep him up in the top ten for the next two years at least.

It all ran in his head as the huge liner slid through the water. Mobbed by hysterical fans, he had never lost his native common sense. The appalling embarrassment of those everlasting women fainting at the car-doors, gibbering his name as though hypnotized, and clamouring for autographs! He knew perfectly well that the more hysteria there was, the sooner it would pass; that his immeasurable, artificial fame would go sour on him one day.

And had he been for a moment gratified or proud at all the fuss about him, his likes and dislikes and his love-affairs? He certainly had not. How could anyone possibly take seriously such an eruption of worship and publicity? No, this star business had been offered to him on a plate and he had simply accepted it and all that went with it, the triumphs, the glory, the money, the women. He had known the other side of this particular brand of glory, too – threats of blackmail, injuries plotted by people who wanted him to say Yes when he had said No. These stabs in the back were inevitable in the kind of career he had had, but he never could emulate the splendid, business-like calm of some of his American rivals who coped with such things in their stride and were altogether far less sensitive. His private opinion was that he had risen artificially high, was on slippery ground and cut a somewhat foolish figure.

Sometimes, in the evening, he would look back with longing to the gay and carefree period when life was made up of simple and un-complicated satisfactions. His old companions and his girl-friends in the back streets of Paris seemed, in retrospect, much more alive and real than all the sycophants and the over-publicized lady-loves with whom he had come into contact since his dizzy rise to fame. He was bored with the lot, if the truth were known. There was too much make-up on his face, and he didn't like the character he played.

The sea was getting up. The motion jolted him out of his brood-ing and he decided to go below and sleep it off. Sleeping it off was a habit he had developed on his bad days in Hollywood, and it could pull him round, mentally and physically. This tendency to look on the black side must be due to tiredness. So he did not go into dinner and every diner, male and female, was sorely disappoin-ted. Eyes fixed on the grand staircase, they expected any minute to see him walking down it, looking young and springy. But the First Irresistible was all by himself in bed, a lost soul in that crowded ship, lonely prey to depression that gripped him in its tentacles like a giant octopus. You would have thought, to hear his breathing, that a child was sobbing somewhere.

The crossing, from the first morning out, assumed a carnival atmosphere. The sea was tranquil and by ten o'clock most of the passengers were tramping round the decks in brilliant sunshine. As he dressed, humming a catchy tune he had picked up in Paris, he could hear their footsteps through the bulkhead. It was going to be a splendid day and when he, too, appeared on the first-class deck, in tweeds with just the right touch of emphasis (he and his tailor had a reputation to think of), his mood matched the weather. His manager was waiting and they set out to do their twenty circuits as though records were at stake.

The passengers reacted, interestingly enough, in different ways. The men regarded him approvingly because he didn't put on airs,

and women with escorts gazed piercingly from a distance but ten-
ded to switch off at close quarters. Only one woman, a poised,
beautiful creature, looked expressionlessly at him when they passed,
as if he were not there at all; and that sort, experience told him,
were the easiest in the end.

However, the last role he wished to play this morning was that of
Don Juan. He felt as he used to do, well and in good spirits, and
happy to be where he was, with this brief freedom from the grind
of publicity that was the penitential part of his film career. It was
like a truancy; he could be his real self. Cheerful and relaxed, he
went whistling along to the barber's shop where Ernest, would
attend him as usual and bring him up to date with all the news and
details of every noteworthy incident and petty scandal of the last
few crossings.

And while listening to this budget with half an ear, his attention
was riveted suddenly by a young manicurist whom he did not
remember seeing there before. She glanced up from her customer, a
white-haired American with rugged, juvenile features, and gave him
a ravishing smile of recognition. A dark girl with blue eyes and a
lovely face. The look was one of frank adoration, the exchanged
glance set his pulses racing.

She blushed violently and bent once more to her manicuring; but
this, he thought, is going to make the trip, and he went on staring at
her. Ernest, questioned in an undertone, revealed that she had
joined them only a month ago. She was good at her job, Marcelle,
and anything but flighty, for there had been several propositions
already which more forthcoming girls would have considered very
flattering, but she had turned them down. Married? No. Probably
had a boy-friend or a fiancé, though, for whenever they docked at
Le Havre the same young man would be there, waiting, and she
always ran to meet him; not exactly prosperous, by the look of
him, but respectable. The hunter's instinct stirred in Heart-Throb
Number 1 and his heart began to pound. He couldn't go wrong,
surely, after a glance like that, and as for his own feelings, this was
love at first sight as he had never known it. It wasn't only the pretti-
ness of her; there was something so fresh and innocent about her, and
she seemed *nearer* to him, somehow, than the others ever did – the

animated, celebrated dolls with whom he'd been entangled since he
was a star.

He was in love, to cut a long story short, just as he used to be in
the good old days. He could hardly credit it. What a miraculous
thing to happen! The ideal way of getting to rights with himself. No
pretence and no publicity; all simple and straightforward, no
photographers and no reporters. And what he needed was a manicure, that very afternoon; without looking at his fingernails, he
knew he did. Right, a manicure in his state-room at five o'clock.
They would be alone. He could forget the feminine fan-worship that
had swept him to the heights because it fancied his attractions, and
forget the gilded-puppet life he led, and be able to talk to this
delicious child, this real flower in the synthetic ship-board hot-
house; and she would understand.

By five o'clock the Irresistible was in a state of ferment. In the last
hour or more he must have paced four miles at least and smoked
enough cigarettes to cover a similar distance if you laid them end to
end. He listened to the beating of his heart and realized with astonished delight that this was It. This was what life was all about! No
more nonsense, no more doubts, the genuine thing.

A timid knock. He grabbed a magazine, sat down in the armchair
and called 'Come in! in a casual voice.

The door opened and there she was. Charming, shy and pretty.

'You wanted me here for five, Monsieur?'

'Oh – yes. Yes, Mademoiselle, I did. My hands are looking awful.'

As a quick inspection made plain, it was exactly two days since
he'd had them done, and she tried to smother a smile while agreeing
how awful they were. She laid her things out and began to work.

He trembled as she lifted his hand and pressed hers lightly. She sat
still, head bent, then, as he continued the pressure, looked directly
up at him and said how perfectly wonderful it was to be here. She
went to all his films, she cut out all his photographs. He was such a
marvellous actor, so natural always, and if anyone had told her she
was ever going to meet him, and actually do his nails, she wouldn't
have believed it; it would have sounded like a fairy-tale. Happily he
watched and listened, more and more convinced that everything was
perfect, while she continued cutting and polishing and telling him

how thrilled she was. At last he could contain himself no longer, and taking advantage of a moment when she was finding another pair of tweezers, took her in his arms.

'Don't be frightened; nothing to be afraid of. You're so lovely I just can't help it. . . . Let me kiss you.'

He held her to him, and had to hold her hard to keep her there. She was shocked and startled, her rapt expression changing to one of fear the second it dawned on her what he wanted.

'No, Monsieur, no, please. Don't, don't. You mustn't.' Thinking the struggles were pretence, he roughly tried to kiss her. She only went on begging him not to.

Something, a table or a chair, fell over. Somebody stopped in the passageway outside. He recovered himself and let her go and saw, shocked in his turn, that she was heading for the door, tidying her dress as she went. Wretchedly, he stammered out excuses.

Marcelle, shaken and upset, wept. She certainly didn't want to leave like this and hadn't, after all, come here to play the lead in any such impromptu drama. Then, as he appeared more downcast than angry, she managed a rueful smile.

'I do beg your pardon, Monsieur. Don't be cross with me. You mustn't be cross, I should feel dreadful if you were. But do please understand. You're a sort of dream-man to somebody like me, just to be admired, you know, nothing more than that. Nothing less either, of course, but what else could I expect? Anything more – well, my whole life would be ruined and as far as you're concerned I'd only be another girl. Leave it like that, Monsieur, please. It's a terrific compliment, you know, your wanting me: who am I, after all? And it's something I'll remember all my life. Think how wonderful, following you in the papers, and going to the pictures and nobody knowing about it! You see, I don't love you, Monsieur, I admire you, which is altogether different. It couldn't mean a thing to you, in your position, but I must think of my fiancé. I've nothing but myself to give him, and his trust matters more than anything in the world to me. I can't be looking at anyone else, and I can't be looking above me, either. I'm not that sort, and I'm not grand enough, anyway. Please, be nice, Monsieur, and don't be angry with me. I don't want to leave this room until we've shaken hands.'

He heard her out, defeated, understanding so exactly what she said that he felt almost sick. The admiration was all on his side, for this enchanting Marcelle. With all his heart he dearly envied her young man in Le Havre. Lost for words, he went over, took both her hands and kissed them gently. If he could have spoken he would have said: 'No, my sweet, I'm not cross.' He held the door open.

And that evening you might have seen the First Irresistible in the first-class dining salon, on his third bottle of champagne, dancing far too gaily with the poised, distinguished person who had seemed so totally oblivious when she passed him on the promenade-deck earlier in the day. That night he added her name to his list of conquests and was finally, miserably aware that this, presumably, would be his life so long as he was numbered with Hollywood's Top Ten. And all the time, all over the world, there were people like Marcelle who put love first. Innocent people, who thought straight and spelled LOVE in capital letters.

'THE HIGHEST-PAID PERFORMER IN THE WORLD'

Three thousand seats, all booked up for weeks ahead, and as many people again queuing outside; special prices, too, so the takings were enormous. I really was something, I can tell you. And the whole of London plastered with posters dinning it in that I was 'The Highest-Paid Performer in the World'. The impresario concerned thought this sensationally good publicity. To me, personally, it was terrifying and vulgar beyond words. Apart from which, it put me in a dreadful position, for my salary, although justified, as advanced bookings proved, from the business angle, was still scandalously high and all wrong psychologically.

The label of World's Highest-Paid is scarcely the best of recommendations. Think of having to make people laugh with that round your neck. But the manager, when I pointed this out, was not to be moved. It was inspired, he said, and I was going to be what he termed 'a hell of a hit'. It was all right for him. He wasn't the one who had to go on the stage, armed with nothing but a straw hat and a dinner-jacket, and face what I knew to be a most difficult audience.

The rather uninspired first half of the programme went off well enough. They were chilly, but nothing worse, and expressed no active disapproval. Chilly, all the same. Then it was up to me, and I stood before the vast auditorium of the Dominion Theatre. It was packed to the doors, men and women in evening dress as far as the eye could see. A long, friendly round of applause. Then before I so much as opened my mouth, there came the yells from the gallery. 'Hallo, Maurice!' 'Welcome back!' they cried. My mixture of French songs and English patter was still, apparently, the right one. Their first, polite laughter soon warmed up, and warmed me with it. Then they were really laughing, and really clapping their hands. That was it. We got going beautifully and never lost momentum – a complete success. Not that it had been by any means a foregone conclusion, as the morning papers noted. They all agreed that I had triumphed when I might easily have done the opposite. But for the whole of my fortnight London came crowding in. Records were shattered at the box-office and I am proud to say that my half-share of the takings surpassed by several hundred pounds the minimum they had guaranteed me.

Now I suppose I am being a bore again, perpetually going on about earnings and all those huge sums and percentages. I can quite see it must be a rather dreary subject and it is, I must admit, embarrassing to talk about. Yet these things are part of my career and therefore part of the tale I am telling you. And I haven't overplayed them, if you notice. I haven't hurled any figures at you for several chapters now. You did notice? Good. Nobody likes to be tedious. To clear matters up, however – and clear is, alas, the word – I should add that what I gained on this particular roundabout, just nicely equalled the sum the French and American tax-gatherers, on their swings, happened to have in mind.

What a universal, international balancing-act taxation is! 'How much do you earn?' is a silly question nowadays. More to the point is: 'How much do you hang on to?' You can say good-bye to a straight half, to begin with, and above a certain amount they take some more; and if you go over that, more again, until they have spirited about two-thirds of your money away, and then you can start worrying about how to live on what's left. So, if other people's dazzling prosperity ever bothers you, don't let it, I beg you.

Personally, though it's an awkward confession to make, I never laid hands on anything like the fantastic riches that rumour credited me with. Most of the cash was paid away to those charmless gentlemen whose mission in life is to think up taxes and sting us for every penny we have.

I have been much derided in my time for habits of economy, along with a lot of other things. Tedious again, I suppose, but like all my compatriots I have a saving disposition. Every Frenchman does his best to provide for his old age and his family's future. Among my many terrors, that of slipping back into poverty has never left me and has made me prone to think of rainy days. And what is wrong with that? Since when has a little self-respect done any harm? A player of the improvident grass-hopper type is doubtless more appealing, and a benefit night is all very well, but I prefer to make other arrangements, if nobody minds.

We French are thrifty by nature, with a stocking-under-the-mattress mentality. I have lived well but, considering the fortunes I have earned, simply; and I have managed to put aside a fair sum at which, as the years go by, the State is chipping away at an ever-increasing rate. I should have adored a more luxurious existence as the reward of my exertions, mental and physical. But it is very hard to decide what to do about money. If you are a saver, modern taxation will sap you, either gradually or with alarming speed; if you are open-handed, you are beggaring yourself for the future. We inhabit a world that makes nonsense of plain rules for prudent living.

TELEGRAM IN NEW YORK

Sunday, and a grand gala for theatrical charities at the Metropolitan Opera House. How could anybody with pretensions to stardom possibly refuse to help? It was a brilliant programme, with all the great names in New York and I, too, had promised to take part.

I was due on stage at about ten o'clock and by the afternoon was in the grip of the worst panic I had ever known. I could barely breathe. I put it down to nerves and my constant fear of being unable to justify my colossal reputation, but fighting for control that night was like battling through a jungle. The ovation they gave me made no difference and I almost staggered back to the hotel, convinced that something serious was the matter and determined to call a doctor if I felt no better in the morning. In the morning I received a telegram from Paris to say Maman had died.

The shock of it vibrated through me, seeming somehow a result of the black depression of the night before, but I could not take it in. I re-read the message, finally understood and went dizzy, as though I had lost half of myself and half the blood in my own body. Half my reason for living and working was taken away. My heart drained like a holed bucket and this extraordinary physical sensation lasted I do not know how many days, during which all I could do was sob. When I stopped from sheer fatigue the realization swept over me again, and again I was a child, weeping like a child. You wouldn't believe how much a man with any feeling at all can cry. These super-types with their stiff upper lips, how do they do it? The child I once was might have grown up but he had certainly not grown tough. I was lost and wretched and a very long way from home. Not even to have said good-bye to the only person who really mattered to me, who was my whole life, my guardian angel! I tortured myself, remembering our days together, ever since the Rue Julien-Lacroix. How sad she had been when I came away the last time. And I should never kiss that beloved face again, or feel those wrinkled, old-woman's hands stroking my hair for hours and hours any more. *Ma Louque, ma petite vieille!* It was a hard burden, alone, in swarming, vast New York.

We were making a film called *The Smiling Lieutenant*. Half dead and trying to look normal, I had to get back to work. Everyone knew what had happened, they were all very sympathetic and said how sorry they were; but the picture wasn't finished, there were millions of dollars involved. So the Lieutenant pulled himself together, as he must, and smiled, resolutely, as he was supposed to.

MY PROFESSOR: CHARLES BOYER

In the year of my mother's death I had also parted from my wife and was consequently living, unattached, the glittering, noisy, feverish existence of an international screen idol. Hollywood gossip was, of course, very busy with me and this my darling Marlene Dietrich did not like at all. What had been a happy relationship became intermittent and less and less comfortable and I was clearly expected to realize that that was that. Well, no one could say I was a hard man to get rid of. People only have to tell me; I was never one to hang on to anything or anybody. Pride, perhaps; or is it self-respect? I may know damn-all, but at least I know when I'm not wanted, and I have a lucky star, in any case, that always seems to take over when the various dramas die away.

And sure enough it did so now. French dinner-parties have been a feature of life in Hollywood ever since there were any Frenchmen there to give them, and it was at such a party – fellow-countrymen in search of fame and fortune – that I had encountered Charles Boyer. I already knew him by repute, for he was the most outstanding of the younger actors in Paris and I had admired him at home. For the most ridiculous reason, however, I had never sought his company. I thought his world was quite distinct from mine and I believed that any attempt at friendship, despite my golden opinions of his work, would quickly disappoint us both. Music-hall artists and actors are vastly different animals, actors being cultivated folk, which we are not; or at least we seldom were in my time. They are players, they interpret parts, while we are just ourselves, presenting ourselves on the stage; and we are nearer than they are to the circus, too. We have begun to draw together now, for singers are not of the same origins today, but this doesn't go back very far: I have known great stars of the *café-concert* who could neither read nor write. The two worlds, moreover, knew nothing about each other. They never mingled, and the theatre nourished an ill-concealed disdain for the *café-conc'* and all its works. But, gradually, singers began to try their luck on the legitimate stage, where they developed into excellent actors, with the directness of approach found only in the music-hall. We were regarded with growing and appreciative interest.

At the risk of sounding boastful I may add that I, too, have been repeatedly urged by leading dramatists to become a straight actor. Henri Bernstein and Sacha Guitry, among others, have wanted to write for me. But although I have considered these flattering suggestions very carefully, I have always preferred to stick to singing, limiting my aims and ambitions to becoming what one might call a *comédien mélodique*.

I hope this long digression has helped to explain why I felt in my bones there was a barrier set between Charles Boyer and me. Yet when I did meet him, far away from home, in Hollywood, I very soon changed my mind. He was so modest for such a brilliant actor, and he had that marvellous brain. To me, in the depths of loneliness and shaken by recent events, he seemed sent straight from heaven. In my own profession I had never come across a friend, a real friend, of his sort, and friendship was probably what I had been missing all along: they say it can be stronger than love. Freely and unasked, Boyer offered me his friendship. Desperately in need of a mainstay, I grasped the hand held out to me.

He had come to Hollywood originally to make the French version of one of Wallace Beery's epics, and, falling in love with the life there, decided to see what he could do in American pictures. He could speak no more than a word or two of English and spent several determined hours on that language every day; nobody in the length and breadth of the land, except the French in Hollywood who knew him and his work, had ever even heard of him; for stars and producers he might not have existed. At that point I could not understand how anyone so famous in his own country could resign himself to such obscurity abroad, but Charles never seemed to worry. It was as though he had forgotten what he was in France.

I liked him more the more I saw of him. We had long, long conversations, and though I couldn't have found a word to say to anyone else on some of the things we talked about, with him it was dead easy. We met, at this period, every evening, dining at his house or mine, and in the end were always invited together to the

Hollywood parties where the cinema world forgathered. I introduced him everywhere. 'That charming friend of Chevalier's', people said. Increasingly I relied upon his company and in time there was nothing he didn't know about me. He was so percipient, so very reasonable and wise, and it seemed to me that this friendship should benefit us both.

Charles was a truly educated man. He knew absolutely everything, there was nothing he hadn't read. He possessed the learning, and the schooling, I had missed. My own contribution was an instinct, a quality of common sense, an energy and, most important of all, a sincerity he cannot have met very often in the rather too literary circles he had moved in since the day he bore off the first prize at the Paris Conservatoire. We were complementary characters and solemnly vowed to be the best and firmest of friends.

I was 43, I had everything to learn and a delightful prospect opened out before me. For now at last I could get down to it seriously. To start off with, never having read anything, I read all he told me to and stocked my library from booklists he compiled. The future was bright and full of promise.

Meanwhile, in all these months, Boyer never went before a camera. He just slogged away at English, day and night. Then at last he made the attempt, in a film of Jean Harlow's. He played her chauffeur, as little more than an extra on the screen for a few seconds only. A line or two to say, the expression on his face – it was hardly a part at all, but it was enough to make actors and producers sit up as soon as they saw it. 'That friend of yours has got something, Maurice. Not bad, not bad at all. That bit he did was beautiful.' It was no use telling them he was the best French actor then alive. In that case, they wanted to know, why hadn't he stuck out for something bigger? But at least I knew now what he had been doing all the time. Charles Boyer had deliberately risked twelve months out of his career and spent them in America to learn the language and try himself out in unimportant roles. He had gone back to the bottom of the ladder, in the fairest and most conscientious way, with no pretence and no blowing of trumpets – the foremost actor in France, he came to the international screen and started humbly on the lowest rung.

We used to write to each other, pages and pages which, on my side, were so many demonstrations of educational progress. I am sure I demonstrated a bit too hard, and lifted all sorts of styles from the classics that were my daily fare. I wanted him to see, in black and white, how I was mopping it all up, and I aspired to literary subtlety which, as you realize, isn't really me. But I was madly doing my best to improve myself. Improve myself for what? you may ask. To be more clever? More erudite? Be that as it may, reading certainly brought me new and unsuspected pleasures. It was like talking to the most intelligent people for hours on end, and these talks always went with a swing since I never had to reply and reveal my ignorance. And when I wrote to Charles I fairly put my goods in the shop-window. I should love to re-read those letters now, with their laborious flourishes. They must be very funny.

Well, I made these enormous cultural and social efforts at the height of my career, but the results weren't up to much and I soon abandoned my pretensions. I suppose it was Ménilmontant working in me, urging me to be merely my natural-born self. But things were going well, the tide seemed set in my favour, and I drifted happily with it. It is my own problem, and my own fault entirely, this insurmountable problem of polishing myself up, and mixing in higher circles. Yet the star-society of Hollywood is charming and courteous and welcomes one with open arms, of that there is no question. So what was the trouble? The answer is, me. I was the trouble, with my eternal inferiority complex and my urchin mentality, my pigheadedness and ineradicably Parisian attitude to life.

And now I was getting on for 46 and had behind me seven consecutive winters working between New York and California. Seven years on top of the tree, on the happiest terms with the public of America. They had loved that Paris style of mine and had taken me to their hearts. We had got along perfectly and we could part friends. What was my best course at this juncture? Hang on, fight to keep my Hollywood position? If I did, I knew I never should be reconciled to the fuss and glare of publicity that any star must cope with. And there I was, what was more, 46, divorced, surrounded by sirens and gorgeous women, with my every instinct liable to land me at any moment in God knows what sort of situation. No, it was good and time to get home.

I was neither young nor ambitious enough to enjoy the struggle to maintain a footing in that strange and wondrous world, kind as it had been to me for the marvellous-while-it-lasted, seven-year stretch. I was off, back to France, there to think things over and decide whether to return or not. Several offers came in for films in Hollywood and revues in New York, but I could think them over, too, in a week or so. With no fixed plans for the following season, I packed up and went home.

A DIP AT PICKFAIR

Before we leave Hollywood, a chapter about a joke, a joke Douglas Fairbanks played on me one day and which was almost literally the death of me. If I seem to have taken it the wrong way, then I can only plead that I have my little peculiarities like anybody else and, like anybody else, don't always see what's so funny when the on-lookers go off in gales of mirth at my expense. One does one's best to look unconcerned and mock-serious, but what can one do? I am either amused or I am not amused. It's the same in the theatre – I have seen hundreds of people laughing till the tears come while others, sitting right beside them, never bat an eyelid. Not a gleam. Just a different sense of humour, that's all.

Well, to return to the near-fatal joke. In Hollywood we had a regular Sunday gathering at Pickfair, the royal demesne of Douglas Fairbanks and Mary Pickford. After the siesta the guests swam or played tennis and our host was in his element. A virtuoso of the diving-board, he would go through his enormous repertoire of front, reverse and sideways dives, dives from the springboard and dives from his club house roof. It was a non-stop exhibition and one really had more than enough of diving and devilry and happy, contagious laughter. He had a laugh that just went on and on, with overtones of somewhat mortifying virility.

Behold me, then, beside the pool at one of these week-end parties,

arrayed in elegant grey flannels – London-cut and quite resplendent –
when Doug like Tarzan takes a flying leap at me and grips me round
the waist with arms of steel.

'What's the idea?' I protested.

The idea, I thought at first, was to give me a scare. But no, not a
bit of it, he was really and truly trying to push me in. And push me
in he did, for he was much the stronger and I could not struggle
against him. Head over heels I plunged into the water, going under
to yells of merriment. It was only a Hollywood gag, a Hollywood
joke, but my own reactions were something like this: one expensive
English suit, say good-bye to that; one silk shirt, that'll survive.
Then, one platinum wrist-watch; damn. Buckskin shoes from
McAfee's in Dover Street; low scrub by rivers and streams is said
to please the buck, so we might be lucky there. Tie, socks, braces
and so forth, unlikely to be improved by total immersion; but we
need not dwell on details. Mentally I reviewed the list while playing
the shipwrecked buffoon to the joy of all beholders. I surfaced,
shocked and gasping for breath and thankful at least that I could
swim. I had swallowed a lot of water and must have suggested the
ghost of the ghost in *Hamlet*. Doug was laughing his head off, but
I detected a shade of anxiety in his eye.

I clambered out, more like a dripping dog than anything else, and
couldn't think of a word to say. My wet clothes were suddenly cold
and I shivered in dread of congestion, pleurisy, heaven knew what,
and the probable effect on my voice. I stood there with my teeth
chattering and all the Americans thought it was terribly funny.
Which is where the American sense of humour parts company with
the French.

Quick, what was I supposed to do? Obviously, join in the general
gaiety and put a good face on things. This I attempted, though I
could have wept. Was I going to manage a laugh? 'What fun!'
perhaps. No, impossible.

It was impossible because my roots, birth and background all told
against laughing. I had known poverty too well when I was young
ever to look on the ruin of a decent flannel suit as any kind of joke;
had longed too hopelessly for a cheap watch to raise a convincing
guffaw when the watch I had now was soaked and broken. It was

the same with the buckskin shoes, all cockled and spoilt. I could afford these luxuries perfectly well, I know, but I cannot help it if every fibre of my being cries out against sheer waste. I have no time for people who throw good bread away for the hell of it, or light cigarettes with a banknote worth hundreds of francs. That kind of pleasantry is just beyond my understanding. So when Douglas clapped me on the back and cried, with another ringing laugh, 'Come on, Maurice, you have no sense of humour!' I entirely and utterly agreed with him: I had no sense of humour. But there it is. As I said, the same things do not amuse everybody; what makes some people laugh may well reduce others to tears. The Japanese, we are told, are in their seventh heaven when committing *hara-kiri*. Speaking for us all in Ménilmontant, we find a glass of good red wine has the same effect exactly.

After all of which I feel bound to add that I have in fact had few French friends of the same stamp as dear old Douglas Fairbanks – bless his soul.

MEMORIES AND AWARDS

I lay stretched out in a deck-chair among my fellow passengers and the horizon appeared to me like a giant screen which showed remembered faces, one after another.

And what nice people they were, I reflected, and what a lot they'd taught me about men, to say nothing of women – lessons that had become a part of myself. They were different, of course, and a dyed-in-the-wool Parisian like me might easily find their emotional behaviour odd at times. The way they smiled when they were upset, for instance, smiling on and on through thick and thin. But then, I suppose one must admit, there is something feminine in the Parisian character. We are not mere male brutes in our beloved capital. We have more temperament than we know what to do with, every variety of temperament, and realize the fact only when we live with foreigners, especially in the young society on the far side of the Atlantic. You have to be so much tougher over there. Nerves and temperament are all very well up to a point, they add a dash of something to one's vital forces, but when you get to the moment of truth you're better without them.

These men and women I was thinking of had greeted me with open arms. They welcomed me freely into their super-world and when they waved good-bye it was having said and done all they could to make me feel they had enjoyed, appreciated, my incursion among them. This was perhaps surprising, for ours is, after all, no more than a profession that peddles art to the public just as a shop-keeper sells ties, or a schoolmaster sells knowledge, or a tart sells pleasure. It is all a question of merchandise, some good, some bad, for customers, some gratified, some not. All the high-flown nonsense that one hears comes down to the law of supply and demand. One brings a product to market and another buys; one to create, and another to savour the creation. 'What have you got for us?' they say. This? That? Yes, yes, I like that. And there you have the basis of absolutely everything, without exception. A man has to earn his daily bread and look the world in the face, and this he does by way of blows and setbacks, with his heart's blood as well as the sweat of his brow. But granted all this, there is also a personal angle to think of, and all the downright nice people one desires to please. And, when I thought about it, hadn't I met the most amazing people in America? Hadn't there been some incredible things to be learnt about this world and how to cut a figure in it? About being *chic*, as we would say?

With very little effort I could imagine a playbill the height of a skyscraper rearing before my eyes, chock-full of names, as though the owners had come, jostling together, to see me off. Mary Pickford first, the uncrowned queen who had found time, among all her interests and occupations, to welcome us, always, as if we were part of the family. The World's Sweetheart was one of those rare natures who confront approaching age with untroubled serenity. I remember her saying one evening: 'The cruel thing in this business, Maurice, is all these new young folk, waves of them coming up the whole time; and how they all get on, and sweep us out of the way.' But even as she spoke she looked, with those enormous eyes, more like a dismayed child than anything else. She was a charming person.

Next, Jeanette MacDonald, whom Lubitsch discovered in Chicago and who rocketed straight to the top with her first picture, *The Love Parade*. She came fresh to Hollywood, bubbling over with talent, and there, with so many gifted and beautiful women competing for the prizes, she made herself a place and stayed in it, year after year. How could she, people ask, remain at the top so long? But then, how couldn't she? There was her slender, red-haired beauty to begin with; and she could act, which very few singers can; lastly, and most important, she had a voice as true and pure as a mountain stream. Even without her voice, one felt, she could have been a great star, but that nightingale advantage made her the unmatchable star she was. She was also the most dedicated of women and artists and what struck you on close acquaintance, more than any of these dazzling gifts, was the firm way the pretty head was screwed upon those lovely shoulders. She had everything, that one. Others – well, they had rather less; not in the same school. We made four films together and they were for me a marvellous experience. I look back and remember how wonderful she was to be with and to work with. To you, Jeanette! I'd give you a rose, if I had one to hand.

And Garbo, reigning above them all. Enough has been written, in every language, on the subject of that most exquisite and thoroughbred of actresses, much of it implying that the intense reserve, the dread of crowds, are all assumed; that Garbo, like any other artist, likes to be seen, recognized, acclaimed. People maintain that she is putting on an act. But those who know will tell you that she had a genuine morbid fear of her unique popularity. She is quite appallingly shy and her famous reserve, that almost insultingly self-contained withdrawal of hers, so foreign to every accepted rule in the American publicity game, has in fact engendered hysterical mass-curiosity and more Garbo-worship than would have rewarded any efforts of an opposite kind. This is an extraordinary thing but, on consideration, logical. If you are possessed of an inimitable talent, and if you make yourself the least-seen, the hardest to meet, glimpse or get at, then of course the unslaked multitude will fight and struggle for a fleeting glimpse of you. Seclusion will have turned you into something more than mortal. So, if that's what you want, it's simple: go to ground!

I met Garbo on several occasions, but I could never have joined the adoring entourage. She was a curious creature; one moment funny, sparkling, brilliant, and the next, with no warning at all, she wasn't there. The absent, desperately sad expression would settle on her face, and there was nothing to do but leave her alone. Questions were fatal, she needed solitude. The clouds would clear, and come again and clear again. You couldn't keep up with her. All very fine if you happen to enjoy switchbacks, but a bit disconcerting otherwise. Yet she deserves sympathy, as does anyone who is too thin-skinned and sensitive. They go through hell for nothing at all, poor souls.

And so I sailed away, proffering roses as I went from my imaginary bouquet to those beautiful women of Hollywood. The images grew misty, the figures on the giant screen wavered and dissolved into the air. Perhaps the ship was pitching rather badly. My own eyes were misty too. I remembered the elderly lady who wrote to me every day for all those seven years – letters to Paris, to New York and California – just so she could shake my hand for a second or two in the clamouring crowd when I set off or arrived somewhere. So many things I remembered, charming, odd or awkward, from my transatlantic life. And now I was leaving of my own free will. Getting out unbeaten, as Gene Tunney did. Making my best bow and saying thank you and quitting the American arena on my feet, not flat on my back. In sport, the theatre and the cinema, I had seen that merciless slide downhill, had had pointed out to me so many men and women who were kings and queens of Broadway – for a time. And that, I thought, is not for me. If anything like that is going to happen, let it happen in France, among people I understand, whether the rest of the world thinks we're dotty or not.

Irving Thalberg's parting words were: 'Well, Maurice, you're off. Fine, that's how you want it. Still, we might lure you back again one of these days, in at the front door, the way you're going out. You know – when you're old and your hair's gone grey. Good luck till then, God bless.'

Really, Americans can say things that leave you feeling quite peculiar.

RESTING-PLACE

To reach the little graveyard where my mother lies you have to go along the Rue Caulaincourt, with the big Gaumont cinema on the right, and then climb upwards. It was a journey I wanted to do on foot, for the climb somehow seemed important. I went there as one mounts to Notre Dame de la Garde at Marseilles, as the faithful visit chosen shrines in certain holy cities. It is the right and proper approach to a sacred place, above our common earthly level and you feel you should be raising your arms in supplication. I, too, was visiting my saint.

I certainly wasn't going to bother whether anyone turned to stare, and as certainly nobody saw anything special about the silent, dry-eyed man they passed, or knew what this particular moment meant to him. Mine was plain despair, unnoticeable, undemonstrative, but I felt as though she were drawing me on that upward road, and must have looked half-dead myself.

'Not your usual happy face, Maurice': a boy in the street, disappointed at the sight of me without my screen smile. I could not even bother to glance in his direction. Just then I couldn't be a film-star, and a face scored with sorrow is hardly at its best.

I continued up the slope and over the viaduct from which you are suddenly confronted with the vast caulaincourt cemetery. Its tombs have an obtrusive, over-insistent air, as though they had tired of their sombre station in eternity and marched forth to plant themselves squarely in the land of the living. 'You up there!' they seem to be saying, 'we can see you, you know. And you'd better have a look at us, too, and give us a thought, whether you like it or not, for this is where you'll get to, sooner or later. And it might be sooner than you think, what's more. Sinister sort of exhibition, isn't it, crosses and flowers and white stones out in the sun like this? What do you imagine we're doing down here, where you can all pass by and have a good look? Might be to make you think a bit, mightn't it, living your lives as though the world went on for ever? We are watching you, ladies and gentlemen, from behind the gravestones here, just as if they were window-panes. And some of you seem to be in a pretty poor way, too, blood in your veins still, but some of it's running thin. As for us, we've done with it all, we can look on and criticize. You make us laugh till we rattle, you lot, with your complications and agitations and intrigues. The trouble you give yourselves! Talk about crawling between heaven and earth!'

No. For my mother I had chosen a more reticent and private place higher up, at the very top of the hill.

'God!' I heard someone say, 'hasn't he aged!' All that registered was a woman's voice, the words meant about as much to me as the knife to a patient under an anaesthetic. Aged. And where, pray, was she going to find anyone who hadn't? Odd as it may seem, no man or woman with whom I am acquainted ever gets any younger. They care for and pamper themselves and dye their hair and have treatments and massage, and operations and face-lifts and toning-up courses, but still the wrinkles gain on them, still they put on weight or they begin to shrink and nobody is deceived at all. None of it adds to their charm, either.

Growing old. Had I ever noticed she was growing old, the woman I was going to visit now? Had she ever noticed it herself, I wonder? I don't think it ever really occurred to either of us. She was well, or she was ill, and that was all. On the whole more ill than well, poor darling, with the life she had before that son of hers managed to make things a bit better for her. Besides, with her white hair and the fetching old-ladies' bonnets she wore to go out in, she just grew more and more beautiful. She would as soon have thought of stepping through the front door without one of those bonnets as she would have thought of flying; it wouldn't have been the thing. She was extremely feminine, La Louque, and she liked to look nice. She had dignity, too, and did not care to mix with anyone unsuitable.

Nearly there now, and a lump rose in my throat. Only a minute and I'll be there, hurrying, hurrying to you as I did that day from the *Enfants Assistés*. It's been so long, too; I've been on my travels, you know; all the places I've seen and the things and the people, I'll tell you all about them. Put my head on your shoulder again and tell you everything....

The *Cimetière Saint-Vincent* struck me at once as a pleasant spot. It was soothing. Impossible to have found anywhere that more perfectly suited her. I was not familiar with every cemetery in Paris, but could think of none, among those I did know, that was in fact so entirely like her. It is a little withdrawn, it is distinguished, attractive and quiet. The grand, the imposing, the self-advertising are not in its character. I could sense her approval of the small, endearing burial-place and almost smiled. I probably looked quite young for a second; a pity that the good lady who had exclaimed at my ravaged countenance couldn't see me then. But only for a second; the thought passed very quickly.

I felt my face set as I went through the cemetery gates. I had such a clear vision of the way she used to get ready for my visits, making herself pretty with a touch of rouge on her cheeks, so as not to seem too pale. It was her one and only vanity, not wanting to look ill; she required no one's sympathy and felt obliged, as the mother of an artist, to keep up appearances. A brief after-lunch nap restored her and she would be waiting to see her son. You can come in now, Maurice. I'm ready.

I stood by her grave. Well-kept, solid, plain and simple as could be. Nothing rich or fancy, no carving or sepulchral ornament. There were flowers on it. I read the incised gold lettering, mechanically.

My thoughts jostled together and pulsed like fever in my head. I wanted to give way, but managed not to. She would wish to inspect me from head to foot, and hear every scrap of news, as she did whenever I came home. I had an extraordinary impression of actually looking straight into her eyes, of touching her face, with its two spots of rouge, and taking into my own her wrinkled hands as delicate as a queen's; of saying to her '*Bonjour, ma Louque*'. And then – nothing. I could not even speak to the memory of her, nor even to myself; and that upset me again. But it would pass, she would understand and I had so much to tell her.

The bad moment was over and I was calm once more. So calm indeed, that I could see, though without quite putting it in so many words, that it was probably best that this unbelievable thing had happened while I was away. A peaceful death, they said. There was just no more oil in the lamp. Yes, it was probably best. She might not have been able to see me. And what if she *could* not have seen me? I could not have borne to have her wrenched away from me as if I were not her son, someone she did not know. And I couldn't have stood the funeral either, however tightly I might have clenched my fists in my pockets. I should have broken down, I think, and started to shout at them. This way, the blow had been tempered, at least, and I was here and not in a mental home.

We have not lost one another, either; not by any means. Do you remember how long we took saying good-bye when I last left you? And how tired you were. But you weren't a piece of machinery; you couldn't go on for ever. Anyone gets tired. But I could feel the way your heart fluttered slightly as you breathed. And now we're just the same as ever. As surely as I'm sure of anything, you are here. I am here talking to you, so you must be here. It wouldn't make sense, holding a conversation with the air. Can you imagine, a great idiot chatting away to himself! But you are so vividly present and alive. Alive, that's it. 'Alive' was the word I used, did you notice, not the other? The other is a fearful, awful word, a torture for anyone who has people to love and remember.

And so, *petite Louque*, I'm back in France. I'm not running away from hard work, or anything like that, but I'd got as far as I possibly could over there. It wasn't even my own language, and now I've shown them what I can do in English, let someone else have a turn. Funny, the way your children have plenty of courage but no desire to push themselves. We try to make a good job of whatever it is we're doing, and leave it at that. A curious lot, the Chevalier family. They wouldn't lift a finger to help their own progress but they keep jogging on. And after all, work is work. You think I'm on the right lines, don't you? For now more than ever I wouldn't for the world do anything you didn't approve of. You remain what you always were, my reason for living. More than ever you were, in fact, now that I'm alone again. You knew about Yvonne and me? The separation? I know you thought it would work out. You were fond of Yvonne and she always liked to please you, spoil you. It's a stupid business altogether and I can't explain it properly. It just *didn't* work out, that's all. One of those situations you can't resolve, where you have to get out and look somewhere else for breathing-space, some understanding and a little hope in life.

You, whose flesh I am, know I always try to do what's best for anyone I love, as I try to in my work. But I'm no different from other people; I can't be right all the time. Things turn murky and complicated, life gets into a ghastly mess and people who love one, or imagine they do, start making difficulties because one's attentions may have been a little clumsy. Nobody's love-life, I am sure, is ever simple. You can see the failures wherever you look. So, the least one can do is to make one's own failure as seemly as possible, since fail one almost certainly must. You knew the world was not an easy place, and many's the time you told me so – when I was quite young, as far back as Ménilmontant. It's simply not possible to be on happy terms with the whole human race. As somebody put it once, you can't please all of the people all of the time.

Oh, I'm sorry, Maman. I was trying to be witty and you don't like it. Forget that bit. I only said it to impress you, so you'd know I'd been reading all these books. I can't remember who it was, anyway. That'll teach me to show off.

It's a very true saying, though, and I agree with it. Think back to the Rue Julien-Lacroix when father went off and you were ill in the *Hôtel-Dieu*. They were all so sorry for you. 'Poor Madame Chevalier, what a terrible thing! Husband left her and now her health gives way. And the children too – that little boy – how will they manage without her?' The neighbours nearly wept when they mentioned us. But you came back home, and we got sorted out, and the money got easier. We hadn't much, but enough to live in a small way, decently, without having to ask for anything or bother anybody. And then, of course, they all took umbrage. Now it was, 'Thinks a lot of herself, that one!' You, of all people! Awful things, they said. 'Stuck-up, showing off about her boys. And the young one wanting to go on the *stage*! Oh, yes,' they said, 'he does. Sticks that absurd great hat on his silly great head, when he ought to be learning a trade like everybody else. Makes you want to spit. The lads in the Passage Ronce soon put *him* in his place, little swank-pot, and a good job too. That *hat*!'

No, it was very difficult. But people always gossip, wherever you are. Love me, love me not, like cherry-stones. You'd have to be very nippy to dodge the unkind comments, even when you've done your level, absolute best. It's the way of the world.

Ça va, ça vient, ça fait du bien,
Ça va, c'est sale, ça fait du mal!
It's all very well if it turns out right,
If it all goes wrong, then it's not so bright.

Then, suddenly, off they go on another tack, baying after somebody else and you're back in favour. It's a seesaw and one can't get off.

How right you were, too, teaching us to be on our guard the whole time. (And one can be taken in repeatedly, even so; I know it is better to be deceived than to deceive, but still, enough's enough.) You taught us, too, the rule of honest-to-goodness work, and there again you knew what you were doing. There's nothing to touch it in the long run. Neither priest nor doctor knows a more efficient remedy and it always does the trick. Keep on hoeing your own row, you said, and don't worry about what the next man's up to. Right, again. How could life go on if we all had to bother all the time with the activities and opinions of the rest of the population? Keep on keeping on, that's the thing, and if anyone can do any better, good luck to him.

I can remember so well our days in the Faubourg Saint-Martin, and what an excellent psychologist you were. It is only now that I realize how excellent, for you were never wrong about any of those friends whom I brought home to dinner. There you'd be in the kitchen, busy seeing to the meal and quietly listening to what we said. When we laughed you knew what the laughter meant; you studied the look, the expression of a newcomer. But you never said very much yourself, just enough to make them feel at ease.

'Maurice's mother is sweet', they used to say. 'You should see how she looks after him!' And when I got in from the theatre at night the door of your room would be ajar, for you couldn't sleep until I was safely back. I'd hear you stir, and come and sit on your bed to say good night, and you would give me a character-sketch of the newest friend, whoever he was. There was no question of your trying to impose your opinion; only, when you thought it necessary, of making me stop to think. Where did he come from? you might ask. Was he any good at his work? What sort of life did he lead? And once you had the facts you would add them to your personal impressions and draw your own conclusions. And you'd sum him up for me, *ma Louque*, as clear as day. He'd have to be a clever man to get past you if he were in any way below par, and a very convincing actor. It was as though you could see right through people. I used to think you were a little too severe, and exaggerated things. I used to pick and choose among your verdicts. Mothers! I thought, worrying all the time, like hens after a lot of chickens. But always I had to agree with you in the end; always. I can admit it now, but then, of course, I was trying to be grown-up and judge for myself. Because I brought home the housekeeping I was, or so I fondly thought, head of the household. You'll have to forgive me. I was young and silly, and young men are slow to underestimate their own importance.

Ah, now you're smiling and I know you understand. But you had the measure of some of those boys in an hour when it was to take me ten, twenty, thirty years to see what they were really like. A long time to discover what you could see at once, and so distinctly. That, *ma petite vieille*, was genius. You were a genius. Oh, yes, you'd better curtsy and say thank you, for you were. Common sense, that was your great gift. Often, while I've been in Hollywood, I have wondered what we should have said about it all, you and I, if circumstances had been different and you had been there too. I could laugh at the very thought! It's my belief that the whole show would have got on top of you and left you speechless. I can see you looking at me as if to say, 'What a fate!' And you would have been thinking: 'Well, what do you expect, my son? You would come, and here you are in this super-land of your profession, with super this and super that. There's super good and super bad, too, the same as anywhere else. Nobody on this earth, howling success or not, is ever perfect. We all have our little peculiarities, whether we come from Holly-wood or Saint-Ouen.'

Can you really see yourself in Hollywood? I should have had to teach your English to begin with, can you imagine that? 'Mrs Chevalier,' they would have said, 'how are you, Mrs Chevalier?' 'Very well, thank you,' you would have said. 'May I introduce you to Mr Sam Goldwyn, dear Mrs Chevalier?' And you again: 'How do you do, Mr Goldwyn?' What a thought! I am letting my imagina-tion run away with me, but I could have done with you out there, you know, with all the traps I managed to fall into. You might have helped me to steer a slightly more sensible course, and as it was I behaved like a lunatic. And now I'm getting on a bit, and showing it too, yet still I always ask myself, what would her advice have been? What would La Louque have said I ought to do? So I'll tell you what my next plan is.

I thought of taking a few steps backward and starting off again; a more down-to-earth career this time, with a lot less fuss attached to it. Do you agree that it's a good idea? Right, then, this is what, discreetly, I shall do.

I want to go back to my old, one-man programme, for when you've done everything there is to do in this profession you realize the freest thing is the hard, satisfying task of peddling your own songs. It isn't especially glamorous, but it's decent, honest work. You're all by yourself in a dressing-room where somebody else was all by himself the week before; by yourself in a hotel bedroom in the provinces, or abroad, anywhere in the world. You feel very homeless at times, but you're beautifully independent, too, existing by your own efforts. It's a workmanlike life, part of the music-hall round that is distinct from anything a player does in theatre, revue, musical comedy or films. All those things are team-work, and with team-work you get jealousy, cabals and intrigue, obligations and slavery. Congratulations all round if the show's a success, and if it's a failure everybody's up and off after the next job without a backward glance. Now that I find dreadful, and I find it infinitely rewarding to work alone. The happy feeling that comes on a good night – I'm going back to *work*, my Louque, and I know that you approve. I can just see you, listening to me with your thumb under your chin and your forefinger on your right cheek, that special gesture of yours that I inherited from you. Whenever I think anything out, I copy you unconsciously.

But now you must be tired. I've been running on and wearied you with my concerns. Inconsiderate of me. Shut your eyes, drift off, sleep well; I'll be back soon. But I did need to talk to you.

I knelt to caress with my hand the gold-inlaid letters that spelled 'Josephine Chevalier' on the stone, glancing up involuntarily as I did so at the windows round the small graveyard; but filial love is not out of fashion yet, and the watchers, if there were any, would not think it strange. Then, slowly, through a hedge of monuments all seemingly aware and sympathetic, I walked towards the gate and out into reality, out into the streets and the city of Paris. Protectively, her shadow followed me.

SITUATION REPORT: SUMMER 1935

If this come-back in Paris didn't work the consequences would, I knew, be serious. I could fairly hear the chorus of: 'He's finished. We've seen it all before. Same old mannerisms, same old profile – let's have something new, someone else, not him.' My name had grown all too familiar during those years of cinema. Films are seen in every town and hamlet from one end of the country to another, and one of them has hardly gone the rounds before the big drum starts beating for the next. It all goes on and on with the mixture as before until the film-goers, fed to the teeth, reject their erstwhile idol. The face that brought a fortune to the box-office has only to be glimpsed on a poster and they stay away in droves.

I have seen this happen to dozens of people I could name, and in my case there were imitators all over the world as well, hundreds of them, who had made a steady living from their more or less accurate renderings. After that interminable sequence of straw hats and jutting underlips, that constantly obtrusive and by now classic profile, it was quite a problem to recapture a public barely recovered from my glaring publicity-campaigns. And all those films – some had been good and others not so good, but every last one had been rammed down people's throats as a masterpiece. And now I had to stand up alone under the Casino spotlights, like some sort of ghost revisiting old haunts, with that blasted straw hat which would probably date me anyhow. Well, we should just have to wait and see. What was certain was that my singing career, taken up where I had left it, was my only hope of escape from the cinema. *Beloved Vagabond* had been a flop after three months of hard slog between London and the Riviera, and two other pictures for French studios did only moderately well. It was plain to see the current had set against me so far as

9. Return to civilian life; a performance at the Gâité Rochechouart in 1919

A poster for the Ambassadeurs in 1919

10. With friends from the days of Mayol, Boucot, Mistinguett, etc.

With Douglas
Fairbanks and Mary
Pickford in 1926

films were concerned. So I made a firm decision. Rather than trying
to fight it, I was going to concentrate entirely on singing and refuse,
from now on, to do anything else.

THE SORT OF FACE THAT FITS

I was thinking about Charles Trenet. Before going to America I
had heard him at the Bobino where, as a very young man, he was
singing in a double act, and when I came back he had conquered
Paris. He conquered me too. This was surprising, for you could
hardly hear him at the Bobino and I was not even sure he *looked* the
part. And having the right sort of face can mean a lot, I assure you.
It counts for a great deal in personal popularity. Politician, actor, or
whatever you like, appearance is tremendously important, perhaps
50 per cent of the battle.

Should all such persons, then – all politicians, actors and so forth –
be as handsome as Adonis? No, that is not what I mean. For a man
it isn't a question of being handsome so much as of having some
quality that makes people warm to him, something human. And you
don't look human just by wanting to. It has to come from inside. It
is in a man's smile and his expression; it is individual, personal to
himself. The open and outgoing man may have it, or the man who is
slightly awkward; not the man, however, who is too open, or too
shy. The quality we are after isn't as easy as all that and you can't
fake it. If you could, the world would be full of clever fellows being
human and warm for all they were worth.

It wouldn't do to be too solemn, for that would be dull. Nor yet
too cheerful, in case one appeared a trifler. Anyone who looks too
lofty may be thought to be assuming airs, and if too friendly be
written off as a low flatterer. Among our lords and masters, our kings
and ministers and important politicians, those who possess this
quality and those who do not are distinct as night from day. People
know in a moment, and never get them wrong. There is no need to
quote examples, you can think of them as well as I can. The non-
possessors, however clever they are, can never get away with it,
either; one slip, and that's the end of them. They may have a very

good understanding with the public, like a *mariage de raison*, but the first time they stray it comes unstuck.

The truth is that popularity is a good deal more than everybody saying how marvellous you are. My own theory about popular singers, for instance, is that the man in the street will pick those who are personable and gifted enough to make him proud to own them as his representatives, those who give him a lift up in the world. And he wants a lift up, not a push down. He doesn't want to subside into the depths; he's all for improving himself and getting some polish.

For one can belong to the streets, own up to the fact and glory in it, without being in the least bit given to low life. Vicious characters are looked at askance in working-class districts; feared, complied with, but nobody finds them lovable. There what people need is an ideal, something to keep them going, and any one of their number who betters himself betters them all. It is well to remember that appealing to the baser instincts is no way to their affections.

My apologies if I am getting heated, but I cannot help it when I am expounding my convictions, and it's not like getting heated over nothing. This is not a triviality. I, too, came from that sort of background and I know they hate being put off with anything second-rate, just as I do myself. What we demand is quality, hand-finish, the real article, not a lot of patronizing idiots simpering down their noses at us. We want the Mistinguetts and Carpentiers of this world, with red blood in their veins. Nor do we much appreciate anyone who tries to crash into favour out of turn: let him do the decent thing and wait till we have made up our minds. It is we, after all, who stand and freeze in the theatre queues; we are the connoisseurs, and we are not going to accept inferior goods for anybody.

We like our love and affection to be returned, what's more. High and mighty characters are easy to detect, and never welcome. Believe me when I say that those we choose we choose for life and make our very own. We rally round them loyally, and they must never, never desert us. Once they are constituted part of ourselves, they cannot throw us out. We love and adore them and they have to pay attention to us all the time. We are demanding, not to say tyrannical, and they are in the situation of someone who inspires a great passion, with all its attendant perils and blessings.

I am personally the first to cheer if any outstanding new talent emerges; I ask nothing better than to be persuaded and behave accordingly. But after all my years in the business I think I may be allowed a word or two on the subject; and if not, then how much longer do I have to wait? I would issue a warning to young performers who exude contrivance and artificiality and who would so love us to love them: they themselves should learn to love, before they do anything else. And let them forget the idea that films or radio can manufacture a genius in a week. The instant genius is a non-existent creature. Faces and voices, more or less pleasant in their varying degrees, are the things that exist, and the brains that make them tick, some more and some less vital and creative. The rest of it is work, work, work.

All this I can say frankly, for I am near the end of my road and standing in nobody's light. I merely ask that the rising generation of artists play fair the game, that's all. No cheap tricks and no tedious padding. Play fair by the public that provides your daily bread, and do your utmost – give it of your best. If drink makes you ill, then think of your public and stop drinking. Smoking upsets you? Gives you a sore throat and affects your memory? Drop it. Put up with things, go without things, the rewards are worth it. What does a little self-discipline matter if you want to be a popular idol? Well, popular idols there must be; but do remember you need a will of iron, too.

1938–1944

The months that followed my come-back were tranquil and happy, seasons at the Café de Paris alternating with the foreign tours I made with Nita Raya, that most charming and delightful of companions. She took to the world of the music-hall with terrific gusto and, but for the storm-signals in Europe, life would have just been about perfect. But there were political movements everywhere, demonstrations, strikes and disturbances at factories.

When the Phoney War came, in the winter of 1939–40, things were not too bad at first in Paris. We had air-raid warnings but no bombing to speak of. Our eyes grew accustomed to the black-out, but you couldn't have called life gloomy. Gracie Fields came over for a French charity concert and one morning an R.A.F. plane picked me up at Le Bourget and took me to London. There I appeared at an English matinée and was back the same night to sing at the Casino, as if I'd never been away. It was more or less Business as Usual that winter with charity events, concerts for the troops, and petrol rationing. Nita and I used her little Fiat, and then only when we had to.

As for Nita, she was unfailingly marvellous to live with and the nicest person imaginable. There was nothing stagey about her and she was happy with the simplest things. I blessed my luck and congratulated myself on ever having found her and was entirely content. The Casino was still playing to full houses, with a succession of famous faces to be seen in the boxes – soldiers and politicians. You had to pinch yourself occasionally to realize there was a war on. Until that morning of early May 1940....

That 1 May and its consequences are matters for qualified historians. It is to history that they belong, and my own personal memory is of the steadily dwindling Casino audience and how it marked, for us, the progress of the German invasion. We closed at the end of May and at first light one morning the little Fiat took Nita and me on to the highway among the long, sad straggles of people from Belgium, from the north, from Paris. There was misery incalculable, ruin and despair wherever you looked, and we were all in the same boat.

Where were they going? Few, I suppose, had the faintest idea, but we were luckier in having a destination. We were bound for the Dordogne, to two dancer friends of ours, to share their house and housekeeping. The Dordogne was an excellent countryside under the circumstances – you could see what was happening for miles around. My riviera property was out of the question; the Italians were up to God knows what down there and the house had been requisitioned by the French Air Force. So we threaded our way through in the tiny car and got to our refuge at last, a lovely little spot near Mauzac. But the sights we saw were pitiful.

And eventually Radio Paris summoned me. 'We want you to do some programmes for us: your usual sort of stuff.' Well I could see what that could lead to if I said no outright, and tried to box clever.

I invented delays and excuses. I couldn't be in Paris for more than a week or two.... My family was in the south.... I blushed slightly and the Radio Paris man gave me a piercing look. I should have to be back there in October and again December. (This was in summer, 1941.) I felt I got out of it pretty well on the whole, managing not to provoke them, while making it clear to my own people, by my short stay in Paris, that I was doing only what I was forced to.

But after this came an official request to visit prison-camps and French volunteer labour-brigades in Germany. Volunteers and captives both, it appeared, wished to hear the national singer sing. The Germans could promise me a phenomenal success if I then went on to the Scala in Berlin. They pressed me, they kept at me, but I refused to perform in Berlin, or for their French workers. I also refused to sing in the prison-camps, but agreed in the end to do a single concert at Alten-Grabow, where I had been a prisoner myself in the First World War. I also refused a fee, but stood out instead for the release of ten men, who were to be sent home to their families in Belleville and Ménilmontant. This, I thought, was a patriotic thing to do. I stipulated that there should be no publicity – I was going merely as an ex-soldier, to bring a ray or two of hope to the inmates of a prison-camp. And I was getting ten of them out of it, too, which seemed a fair bargain.

I went incognito to Germany and nothing appeared in the papers. The afternoon at Alten-Grabow was a moving experience and the men were overjoyed to see me. But next day, when I was supposed to go home, attempts were made to delay my departure. Admiring German actors, Emil Jannings at their head, would like to organize a reception in my honour. No, I said; no, thank you. I have a household waiting for me at home. Oh; then when I was singing in France could I not manage to ridicule the English a bit? A side-swipe at Churchill now and then, perhaps? Sorry, no, I couldn't. They became insistent. Expressions turned suddenly hard. Somehow I wriggled out of it and found myself on the train for home.

It had been a narrow escape from the edge of a precipice and I must be careful in future not be drawn on to any such perilous ground again. It was fatally easy to be up to your eyes in no time, before you even knew what was happening. However, I heard in

Paris that my ten men were safe, and I couldn't get off to Cannes fast enough. (I was back at the villa now.)

Before many days had passed the newspapers of both the Occupied and Unoccupied zones broke the compact and came out with long articles on my visit to Alten-Grabow. Not one of them emphasized that it was the only place I went to, nor mentioned my having bargained my single performance for the freedom of ten men. They shouted instead about 'Maurice Chevalier in Germany' and 'Chevalier Visits Prison-Camps in Germany', and generally implied that Maurice Chevalier had been off on a tour of Germany.

A horrified English friend contrived to send me a cutting from a London daily with a headline stating that I was pro-Nazi and had sung everywhere in Germany except in prison-camps. But, with all the nonsense I have seen about myself in print at one time or another, I didn't let it worry me too much, thinking people would sort out the truth for themselves.

The atmosphere of Cannes, meanwhile, was as oppressive as that in Nice. With every day came the whispered news of an arrest. Whose turn was coming next, one wondered, and how soon? Tonight? Tomorrow? Some of the young girls were said to take Gestapo pay for acting as informers and I would rather die than sing in a France where things like that could happen. With the sound turned low, we listened at night to the French voices from London on the radio, and they helped us to endure, gave us faith that better days would come. We listened as the sick must listen to the prayers for a miracle at Lourdes, and I always enjoyed the bit where a revue-composer who had escaped to England inveighed against the heads of the German Reich and notorious French collaborationists. That is to say, I enjoyed it until one evening in February 1944, when he dealt with those of his own profession who had stayed in France. 'Unpatriotic and disloyal', he said, and he produced my name among the rest. 'They have collaborated with the enemy,' the sepulchral tones proclaimed, 'and will meet the punishment they deserve. There are those among them who will be heard no more.' It sounded suspiciously like a death-sentence on each and every one.

This came as a terrific shock to me. At the sound of my name a searing pain ran through me and I could do nothing but repeat,

'Dreadful, dreadful, dreadful,' over and over again. I had never in all my life known anything so dreadful. Millions of my countrymen must have heard that night's transmission and I was powerless to reply. I was in a state of stupor and desperation. If only I could have got to a microphone somewhere and given the correct facts, told them I hadn't sung a note in public for a year. This man, with his accusations made me sick with fear for those I loved. But I had to suffer in silence. It was a bitterly unfair blow, well below the belt, impossible to counter.

They had all heard the broadcast in Cannes and were discussing it in corners, incredulous, for they had seen me about since the armistice and perfectly understood the real reason for my apparent inactivity. Some of the Resistance people came to me and said 'What *is* all this, Maurice? Man doesn't know what he's talking about. We'll get a message through to London and tell them you're all right. They're just not in the picture there.' My friendly music-composer accordingly received a message from the actor René Lefèvre, a true-blue resistant of the Antibes sector: 'Mistake on Maurice. Ridiculous campaign. Stop. Has proved himself loyal and will do so again. Regards.'

Unfortunately, too, London had several times played a satirical record based on one of mine. Mine was called *What Good Frenchmen are Made of*, theirs gave the recipe for a bad Frenchman. The composer now ceased to include me in his blacklist and orders were obviously issued about the record as well, for it was not used again. But it was too late, the damage was done. The abominable charge was known all over the place. In Cannes and Nice they didn't believe it, but everywhere else they did. They were bound to, I suppose, a good scandal being always more of a thrill than good report.

A sympathetic English journalist now sought out my manager, Max Ruppa, and asked him to help. He wanted a front-page article for the *Daily Express* with a personal statement from me. Ruppa, who knew by various ways and means that René Laporte, the writer, was in charge of the new radio at Toulouse, concluded I could not be far away and one morning, accompanied by some English officers in uniform, turned up at the house where I was hiding. His companions, he explained, were Air Force men and journalists interested in finding out the truth. Their confidence in me was obvious and I poured out the whole story. I talked and talked, and they went off with a long article which, by way of authentication, I signed. This interview was mentioned, though guardedly, on world-wide radio two days later, which meant that my disclaimers were known. And that, I thought, might at least make it embarrassing for anyone to execute me now, when all the world was willing to believe me.

Then René Laporte descended on my refuge with, of all people, the revue-composer who, passing through Toulouse and informed that I was still alive, had announced himself ready to help me out of the ghastly position he had got me into. My first reaction was to tell René that the creature had done enough harm already, and that I should refuse to meet or greet him. It would be a degradation, I felt, to take his hand.

But René was firm. 'The Paris Resistance have had a word with him about you. They have nothing serious against you and he's very keen on getting you cleared. You really should see him and have a talk. If he comes out on your side and retracts it all on the radio it can have a tremendous effect.'

So there he was in front of me, his lieutenant's uniform festooned with insignia. Thickset and upstanding, not very tall. The blue gaze was like a gimlet, the handshake long and hearty. Emotion, shame, distress, welled up in me and instead of starting to talk I started to sob, fighting for self-control with a gesture of excuse. It passed, and I gave him an exact account of just how everything had happened. With a magisterial but not unfriendly look on his face, he heard me out. Like a judge he posed questions and finally required a detailed, signed report of all that I had said. He was going back to Paris in a couple of days and would lay it, personally, before the committee which dealt with charges of collaboration against theatre folk. He would Put in a Word, personally. And that was that. On leaving, he fervently wrung my hand once more and, chest stuck out and steely blue eyes softening a little (Napoleon, perhaps, with some trusty old stalwart in need of a dressing-down), delivered his parting words: 'I like you, Chevalier; I like you very much.' You do? I thought. God help us if you didn't.

Thus fate, as in some melodrama, had put my defence in my accuser's hands. I prayed devoutly that he might conduct it honestly; perhaps admit in a broadcast that he had been wrong about me and allude to the message from René Lefèvre. Such clear support from him, among the present wild delirium of Liberation, could make things very different for me. It would even increase my popularity, after all the doubt and horror. Great men, I reflected, don't mind owning their mistakes. To err is human and nothing to be ashamed of; you only had to look at Churchill. If he could just behave like Churchill, he might yet turn out to be the best friend I had. If he could.

I went to Paris and Louis Aragon showed what he thought of things by offering me the freedom of his newspaper as soon as he heard of my arrival. He, along with René Laporte and others, was a leader of the 'literary' Resistance on the Riviera and knew that some of the Parisian newsmen and actors were eager to 'do for' me, as they put it, once and for all. Aragon stood ready, of his own accord, to defend me openly. I had acquired no negligible champion.

He planned a front-page article for the very next day and a press-conference, to be held at my house, with the sole object of scotching all the rumours that were going round concerning me. And the following Sunday morning, the day of the annual procession to the Mur des Fédérés at Père Lachaise, he and his friends asked me to take part and walk with them. Seeing me, the people of Paris would know I had nothing to hide. Aragon was insistent and I smothered my doubts as to the wisdom of courting the limelight at this juncture and attended the parade. I am thankful to say that the article he published was very widely read, and all was forgiven. I shall never forget the relief!

From that moment onwards I was caught up, like so many theatre-people, in our nation-wide celebrations. Celebration became a business in the end. Not all those gala-performances on behalf of this or that, more or less genuine, cause, were what they seemed; or if they were, the benefits to the genuine cause were very thin. On the whole the artists would be receiving normal fees and the announcement of the show as for prisoners, or victims' families, or the Resistance, was only a pretext for charging the earth for seats and everything else. It got to be a racket in the profession. Ask anyone where he was working now and the answer could easily be, 'Charity concerts'.

As for me, I'd had enough trouble and left that sort of thing severely alone. Either I sang for nothing, or I did not sing at all. In any case, when you have an act that isn't run-of-the-mill, it is only common sense not to waste your efforts. The best policy is that of the big-scale appearance. It was not always an easy one to stick to, though, for requests came in by the dozen, invariably with that overtone of blackmail. Nine times out of ten, from pure philanthropy, you sang free but if, the tenth time, you refused, you courted as much unpleasantness as if you had said No all along. It was just one of those things and the sensible course seemed to be to keep somewhere in mid-stream, being neither too reluctant nor yet too madly willing. And meantime I sang all over the place for Americans, French and English and to the troops, who all appeared to love it.

Then, for the first time, back to the Casino de Paris, at a big gala show. Police were scattered around the packed auditorium in case of an anti-Chevalier demonstration, but everything went off perfectly, with receipts to match – not wholly to the satisfaction of some members of my profession. I was conscious, behind the scenes, of unfriendly as well as friendly faces and took involuntary note of them, with the sole intention of taking no more notice, ever. I have never been, and never could be, a good hater. Hating people I consider an expense of spirit and a waste of time. Far better put whatever it is out of mind and get on with something constructive. As for revenge, surely life sees to that, for all of us. If someone tried to kill me, I am sure the thought of the years he'd have to spend inside would prevent my giving evidence against him; and if they were going to let him off with a week, that would be enough to stop me, too.

FIRST NIGHT AT THE A.B.C.

Tonight was the night, and the whole town, it seemed, was eager to see the result. I was less on edge than might have been expected, although tonight Paris would finally accept me back or not. So far

I had appeared in the capital only in charity shows, and it is undeniably harder to hiss a man who is singing for nothing than when he
performs professionally for the sort of money that is asking for
raised eyebrows – and people always know what you're getting.

A crammed house, and the press had been invited. They had
accepted in a body, and I found it surprising really, that so few of
them were against me, and that those few were apparently subdued
this evening. They were lying low and one could spot no obvious
trouble-makers. Was this a calm before the storm? Or were they
perhaps unsure of their ground? In any case, all the best-known
actors, writers, artists and sculptors were there, as well as socialites
seldom seen in a relatively democratic haunt like the A.B.C. The
special occasion had drawn to the music-hall a marvellous cross-
section of the whole of Paris.

The first half went off without disturbance. People drifted in late,
greeted their friends, had a little gossip. The air was electric. I had
asked for no special protection and canvassed no special support. I
was going to do my best and leave the decision to fate; but I had a
feeling that all would be well.

And scarcely had I got the brim of my straw hat round the edge of
the scenery than I was met by a thunderclap of applause, as though
the roof were falling in. It knocked me endways. On and on it went,
in great waves like a storm. I could see welcoming faces, even a
glint of tears, and hands stretched out in welcome. The way people
shouted my name, I might have been miraculously back from the
dead, which, in a way, I was. On and on. The noise would die down
and then start up again, minute after minute. The incredible ovation
spent itself at last and I began to sing '*Bonsoir, Messieur-Dames*', the
first notes of which they recognized at once. I worked into it refer-
ences to the audience, to friends and fellow-artists. The laughter
came and, that initial contact made, we were all Parisians together.
It was honest-to-God laughter, too, the sort that soothes the nerves
and cancels out your worries and feels as good as a gargle. The A.B.C.
that night was France, was Paris, and most of the audience were men
of good will, decent and genuine. The scanty opposition was powerless against the forces of light. I sang for an hour on a full tide of
enthusiasm.

Overwhelmed, happy for me, my friends came back-stage with their congratulations. The loyal ones, that is. The wait-and-sees, of course, did no such thing. They would be sitting on the fence till later on, when the papers had clinched the unarguable success and everybody knew about it. Then, even former enemies were to water their comments down a bit. There might be tepid reservations about me personally, but accompanied by cries of, 'What an artist!' and 'Streets ahead of anyone else, you just have to forgive him!'

Jane Marnac and her English husband gave a small supper-party for us afterwards and I let go and relaxed. I had my complete professional victory, which nobody could deny. Never had I been on happier terms with the public.

And yet, for all that, there remained a flaw somewhere. Had persecution broken my heart irreparably? Planted permanent bitterness and rancour there? And indeed I wondered whether I should fully trust anyone's handshake ever again.

Part Two

A NOTEBOOK OF PEOPLE,
EVENTS AND IDEAS
SINCE 1945

MAURICE GREY-HAIRED

And that is my story up to 1945. What I have done since, travels, films, concerts, all the stuff of theatrical biography, you know as well as I do if you ever glance at a newspaper. But I am now at an age when exterior events mean a good deal less than those of one's inner life.

I hardly had time, as a young man, to bother about what was going on around me. Not that I was blind or deaf to immediate circumstance, as I hope you will have gathered; it was simply that the urchin from Ménilmontant had very little leisure in which to enjoy his new prosperity and none, certainly, to spend in assessing all that had happened to him. But now he has. Now he can jot down, day by day in a notebook, anything that strikes him. So the rest of this book, if it's all the same to you, will be observations, impressions of people, anecdotes arising from a life which is still full and fascinating. I have picked them out of my diary just as they come. You like that? Good. Then please read on.

WRITING FOR YOURSELF

Since God, or La Louque, or both of them, bestowed on me this taste for scribbling and for writing songs, my whole existence has altered, for you can escape from a lot of depression by scribbling and song-writing. To produce a decent chapter or a good number gives me a genuine lift. I'm very fond of women and I'm very fond of love – still – but I wouldn't trade the loveliest, most co-operative lovely in Hollywood without a stitch on for the delight of getting a new idea or a vivid impression on to paper.

HOW AND WHEN TO STOP

I look at so many artists whom I used to admire unreservedly, and I give much thought to retirement. Their later careers have been pitiable, always, it seems, because of money problems. People who were fans of their younger, dazzling days don't realize they have to stay in harness simply because they saved so little.

DEATH OF A PLAYER: FELIX MAYOL, 1942

'Listen, Maurice,' he said, 'quite soon, when I die, they'll sell all my mementoes and things for the estate. No, listen to me. That Madeleine Lemaire of mine, someone will buy it because she painted it, not because it ever belonged to me. And you know what it means to me, that picture; a sort of Paris diploma, a record of what I like to look back on, when I was young. When I made my name in Paris – all that kind of thing. I only hope it goes to somebody I'm fond of and who's been fond of me, who knows and understands all that. Someone who'll take it home and hang it up and keep it, for my sake.'

I had expected to find Mayol broken by his illness, but he showed superb courage and never so much as murmured. 'I've lived for patter and singing, and the time has come to pay,' he said. He faced death without complaint, stoical and serene, as though at the end he was reverting to the old great-heartedness that surely helped to make him what he was. That Provençal voice is stilled for ever now but he will not be forgotten quickly. He was acknowledged, in this profession, as the best, the most charming and popular among the four greatest names of his time and that must gratify him, wherever he is – the highest possible praise for a decent fellow who spent his life singing his heart out to give people enjoyment.

Yes, he was homosexual and all the rest of it, but the main thing to remember is that he exalted the work, the pleasures and loves of common folk: all just as important in humble as in 'gracious' living. He was a good man, Mayol.

EDITH PIAF

Went to hear Edith Piaf at the Étoile. She's one on her own, a small phenomenon with guts of steel; a pint-size glory of the music-hall, alive to her fingertips. I was impressed, as ever, by the way she

11. A game of boules with Charlie Chaplin in 1930

With Charles Boyer at about
the same period

12. Another
picture with
Charles Boyer

With the publisher
René Julliard and
M. Daniel-Rops

works. Incredible, how that little thing goes on getting better and better. Yves Montand, in attendance, is a tall, agreeable young man.

She and Jaubert, moving spirit of the *Compagnons de la Chanson*, yesterday invited me to dinner at one of the best restaurants on the Champs-Élysées. All superbly done, as things should be when we fête each other. Piaf really wanted me to enjoy myself and when I admitted that the doctor allowed me a glass of Bordeaux with my meal she made them produce the best they had. 'Nothing is too good for our *Grand Momo*', she proclaimed, and meant it seriously. She drank water herself, because eighteen months ago, when Montand was in the running for the lead in the film *Portes de la Nuit*, she made a vow to stick to water for two years if he got it. He got it all right, she kept her vow and still has six months more to go. This I thought was very bright of her, for not only had she managed to feel she was helping her beloved Yves, but had also kept away from the drink which was said to be undermining her not very strong physique. Last night showed me what Edith Piaf is like, and the nearer you get the nicer she is.

THE GREAT DIVIDE

One has enjoyed, and even organized, sundry sorts of meaningful love-affairs along the years and one reaches a point when to continue is to court heartbreak; the point at which one begins to live on hope and self-deception, and suffer the consequent disillusion and despair. But why, oh why, having grasped this fact, should one lack the strength to say, 'I'm not playing any more?'

Life for me seems to have been concentrated until the age of 52 from the waist down, and now it had better concentrate itself from the waist up – right up to the top of my now gradually whitening pate.

M

'YES', SHE SAID, AND DIDN'T MEAN A THING. 'NO', SHE SAID, AND GOT FULL MARKS

Two brief encounters, which must serve to confirm my badly-kept good resolutions. One was with a 22-year-old actress, not startlingly pretty, but by no means ugly either; not terribly feminine, though you couldn't call her forbidding; neither my usual type nor the type that puts me off. All right, I suppose, if not too satisfactory. It was a lot of bother for nothing, really; nothing at all.

Then the other, a charming girl who came to take a photograph. Told me quite simply and artlessly that she was 'good' and aimed to stay that way as long as possible. 'Life's complicated enough,' she said, 'without going round asking for trouble.' Sensible, sensible girl!

ON TOUR, *1947*

I am happier in my work than ever before. This Belgian tour has proved me absolutely right about my new act. It goes like a dream and the money is rolling in. Last night for the sixth show at the Beaux-Arts we were sold out and had people sitting in the gang-ways and jammed on the stage itself. An atmosphere of foregone triumph.

How I adore this profession! The public can have all the love and strength that remain in me to give. As for *l'amour*, I have had my fair share and am convinced that friendship and liking are a good deal more important. I am dedicated for the future to my work, heart and soul; to my own folk, for my mother's sake; to friendship and the interchanges of affection. And to hell with the rest of it.

I have always thought that if I could go back and start life over again I should never waste time on all the easy, obvious women. I should wait until I found in one woman everything I wanted – beauty, brains, the gift of peace, and understanding. And I should wish to do, say, achieve, something that really mattered, to create something fine. Now, however, my great aim must be to grow old gracefully. Age ought to improve the patina of a picture and one should do nothing to spoil it whilst ever life lets one keep hold of the paint-brush.

A lost sheep of 57, taking to serious thought! Quite extraordinary. And what a world it opens up! I shall never be completely alone again. Heart and brain and pen have formed an alliance to solace my later years. Destination unknown, but there are ample new horizons, and all manner of delights are promised for the voyage. I am aware of satisfactions I never knew existed and henceforth refuse to get entangled and unhappy without good and sufficient cause.

It's all a matter of how you choose, of course. So-and-so isn't worth the misery, leave her alone. Such-and-such? Well, might repay the effort. This being so, pray forgive me if I hang my sign out, 'Do Not Disturb'. It's going to be a new life for me, I can tell you, and I only hope that something of my mother's spirit will make me recognize my luck and help me to rest on intellect and affection for the remainder of my days.

BOOKS

Have been reading André Gide's *Journal* for 1939–42. Someone else who tried to give up smoking, I see. He says, of an enforced abstention: 'If I can carry on from here and conquer the stupid habit, which little by little has become a craving with me, it will not have been too high a price to pay for my deliverance.' A few days later comes the fall and the admission: 'I couldn't keep to it.' He just wasn't tough enough. Undoubtedly you require more than fine phrases for that particular enterprise. A touch of steel is called for.

Toi qui es-tu? by Paul Claudel is a book which fills me with regret that I never received the religious revelation it speaks of, the same conviction and unquestioning faith. How wonderful to be able to lean on such a faith, to have joy and comfort like that, to relax one's whole being in so contented an obedience. It may still come, of course, and devotedly I long for it, but it would have to be the real thing. The true, strong revelation, flooding through.

The book at all events brought up a word which I seem to see written large these days: Chastity, from now on the most important of all words for me. Delicately I explore it. No, I grasp it firmly. A new element, a fresh source of strength. And if strength is granted me, chaste I intend to be, or nearly so, and an excellent thing too, at my time of life, from every point of view. After all of which I shall look pretty silly whenever I succumb. Well, I renounce possession for the future, and bow out.

Re-read *Le Petit Prince*, by Antoine de Saint-Exupéry. There is a fine melancholy about it and that little prince is a marvellous creation, born of the author's emotional hunger, of his need to bestow affection. You entirely love and admire him, he is so charming, good and attractive. Even when I am fed up or tired he has the same effect on me, and I can cry over his death as, though for my own nearest and dearest.

KEEP ON KEEPING ON

René Clair was most reluctant to give me the lead in *Le Silence est d'Or*, his first post-war film in France, but I persuaded him, after much argument, that I should be perfectly splendid.

'You're still too attractive to be playing a man of that age, Maurice.'

'That's as maybe, but I'm 58, you know. Anyway, I know if you don't and I'm after parts that take account of the fact. And if you don't believe me, look at the life I lead. I might as well be a hermit.'

It was a decision that led to many other things. I stuck to my guns because I knew I was right. Whatever anyone says, 58 is 58. I had been the most juvenile of juveniles in my youth; then I typified the younger generation; and then I was about the oldest young man going. Please God, I shall now become the youngest old man, for a change.

Last day but one of the filming. I arrived on the set and bade everyone good morning. René was there and I bade him good morning too. He came across to me, seized my hand, gripped it firmly and looked all round the studio, anywhere but at me. I waited, in some consternation, for enlightenment. Finally, abruptly, he hauled me off into a corner and made his halting speech.

'Maurice . . . I really do think, Maurice . . . you've made it, I think. I saw a run-through last night . . . first time . . . I was shattered. Really. Marvellous. Not a bit like anything you've done before.' And so on and so forth, all in the same vein.

I hung on to him, in my turn, like a woman on the verge of hysterics and battled with the sudden, overwhelming wish to cry. Artists! Actors! Temperamental girls, that's what we are.

THERE'S GLORY FOR YOU

Here's an exemplary anecdote. I have been a tall man since the day I stopped growing, getting on for six feet or so; and I may claim to have been in the public eye for, well, quite a long time now. And I have for the last five years had with me the pianist, accompanist and gifted composer, Henri Betti, who is, as it happens, a small man, about as high as my shoulder. One day, then, we are strolling together on the Champs-Elysées and we hear a girlish squeal behind us,

'Ooh, look! That's Maurice Chevalier!'

And a second voice, lukewarm, replies,

'Oh, yes? Which one?'

Last night at the theatre, by way of contrast: 'Telephone, Monsieur Maurice, the Duke of Windsor wants you.' Well, I wasn't falling for that one – jokers adore the telephone – and told them to say I was out to supper with Napoleon. This morning H.R.H. in person rings me up at home. 'Maurice Chevalier, is that you?' Well, it was certainly him all right, as simple and sincere as you please. A very grand party tonight at his house in the Bois de Boulogne, and could I come along after the show and sing a song or two? I said yes at once, as you may imagine, and looked forward to the honour of meeting him. I don't know – you might as well be in a fun-fair one day, and the next you're sought out by the ex-King of England. *What* a profession!

STILL LEARNING: INTRODUCTION TO PAINTING,
1946

Went with Gisèle d'Assailly, my publisher's wife, to the Orangerie,
to see an exhibition of works of art stolen by the Germans and now
retrieved (summer, 1946). This friendly, cultivated woman introduced me to some of the greatest painters of many countries and I
loved Rembrandt, Fragonard, Goya, Chardin and Monet on sight,
in that order. At 58 I was looking at pictures for the first time, but
recently awake to such things and greedy to learn. With all my new
pleasures I seem to be making progress, and intend to visit exhibitions and museums to form my taste and judgement. I shall have to
pick and choose and prune and look carefully. I shall have to find
my own favourites, in painting as in literature. My time is short and
it becomes increasingly silly to waste any of it.

Later, in Chicago. A visit to the Art Gallery, especially the French
pictures. The collection is magnificent and we were shown round by
a young public relations man on the gallery staff. The hour and a
half I spent there seemed somehow to raise my aspirations. How can
anyone dream of success who does not try constantly to improve his
art? You can see it all the time if you study painters and their
development, for pictures from different periods of their lives will
show them aiming ever higher, striving to do better and more
beautiful things.

Why does a great painter occasionally produce bad pictures,
though, or a great writer a poor book? What makes a master
sculptor carve a bad statue? The subject once arose in conversation
with René Laporte and the painter Van Dongen, and the answer was
plain and direct. Inspiration comes unawares, from unaccountable
sources that have nothing to do with planning or intelligence. Let
it cool ever so slightly, and you are left, pen or brush in hand, with
no inspiration at all. Gifted people need not, therefore, make a song
and dance about being or supposing themselves superior. They
simply happened to be born with that fortunate, subconscious
equipment of theirs, and the mystery exists independently of intelligence or ambition.

And a glimpse of Utrillo. I took him recently to the church square at Ménilmontant, which he is going to paint for me – a Christmas present to myself. We left the car 200 yards away in the Rue Étienne Dolet opposite the church, and were almost alone in the street. He had with him a photograph I had taken a day or so before, and he wished to study and digest the shade of the stone and the colouring of the houses round about.

Bit by bit I wandered farther off and he didn't even notice. I had ceased to exist for him, absorbed as he was in contemplating the church and making it his own. He tottered slowly towards it and his gaze, still wonderfully penetrating though clouded and old, went from the building to the photograph and back again. Then, in the midst of a positive storm of expressions that chased one another across his ravaged features (ravaged is the perfect word for them) he blinked, and the incubation was over. He relaxed, he wanted a drink. The bistro in the Rue Ménilmontant was all unconscious that its *vin rouge* was slaking one of the great thirsts, and the thirst of one of the great men, of our time.

A SAD DISPLAY

Le Sabbat, the memoirs of Maurice Sachs, is an account of the career of a truly vicious but always clear-headed man, in all its unbridled excess. Is he then to be condemned, waved contemptuously away? I think not. Sympathy would be more in order, I am sure, for thraldom like his to the lower instincts can lead so often to such bitter despair.

These journeys to the shores of fevered delight imply journeys back again, and it always ends the same way. We are unfortunate wretches, left to struggle on against hearts that are prone to sudden leaps and senses suddenly aflame, against feelings intoxicating or wildly out of place, and sweet reason offers us no help at all. Who on earth could stand up and swear that he knows a single person who is incontestably, thoroughly, *pure* – heart, soul and senses? I'm damn sure I don't. Evil demons lurk in every last one of us, and lead us astray as they wish. If those demons stay quiet we can come to terms with them. If not, we finish like Maurice Sachs, vomiting shame and despair on to paper as others might beat their breasts or hang themselves. Either you possess the strength to say No, or you do not. And if you do, be thankful.

BROADWAY, *1947*

My new-style programme. After the dress-rehearsal I got through the day all right because it had gone well, but panic gripped me as I waited for the curtain to rise on the first night. The thought came that this was in fact a challenge to all those who think that actors should never try to improve their acts, and that it was going to antagonize them. But this morning my return is greeted by the entire New York press and we shall see whether the public agrees. I feel as if I had just won first prize after the most searching test of my career. I ask myself, sometimes, why I do it; why do I always have to be surmounting obstacles like this? Can it be the cravings of an inferiority complex?

The one-man programme is almost a minor theatrical revolution, the admiration of Broadway. 'The one and only, the master, the greatest', they say. Everything's going my way and I never scored such a hit in my life. Now it's happened I can't believe it. I'm a bundle of nerves and I can't sleep. But it really is terrific, with people clamouring for seats and being turned away at every performance. So, as they all advise, 'Relax, old boy, relax!'

Now that I'm over here again offers are pouring in for American radio shows. Very tempting they are, too, since rating, production and fees are all unbeatable. Yet something in me hesitates. My old instinct tells me you cannot do so many things at the same time. My present solo programme is a complete success; a new film career is opening up in roles suitable to my age; I am wholly fortunate in this new pleasure of writing and my books do well. Surely that's enough, I tell myself, if you want to do it all properly. Count your blessings with your three new prospects and be content. Faith in your own capabilities is one thing, letting ambition run away with you is quite another.

I have therefore surprised everyone by turning down all the offers. I shall be extremely selective in future and work as and when I see fit; here and there, and nowhere very long. No point in ending up the richest man in the cemetery. The temptations life presents when you're enjoying a good streak might as well be poisoned sweets – so enticing and so very, very dangerous.

MAN AND HIS WORK or PROFESSIONAL SUCCESS IS FINE, BUT WHAT ABOUT YOU?

I should love someone to explain to me why people with more than their fair share of genius, or even of plain ordinary talent, always split into two people, the artist and the other one; and why, of the two, it is only the artist who gets any sort of a deal? The being who trundles on in the wake of a talented other half usually finds himself jettisoned along the way. Effort, thought, ambition, are concentrated exclusively upon the ever-receding objectives of his other, artist-self.

He, the ordinary half, is only the poor remnant trailing in the rear whose well-being the other, generally speaking, has never had time or sense to think about. This surely explain why so many great artists and men of genius are so infantile, so neutral and so lacking in character behind their marvellous gifts. The genius in such a person has devoured everything, and left as residue a dulled and more or less simple creature, often enough the victim or slave of other people: people who have cleverly avoided the quagmires of art and so have nothing to do but get on with the business of living.

One has seen and read of it repeatedly – great artists, revered as such, whose lives are tragic failures. They come to pathetic ends, married or managed by dreadful women, a prey to complexes and misery. They are at once too lofty and too petty, for in every great man there co-exists the other, the rejected, the straggler. He, unfortunately, is the one who has to live on this earth, and eat and drink and love and suffer and die – in a poor sort of way most of the time – while the great-man half goes soaring up and onwards, out of touch with mundane facts. It should be possible to husband and reserve some of the mental power that allows this half to rise so high, and put it to the service of the hapless shadow who invariably ends up unsolaced, bewildered, out in the cold. To put it simply: artistic achievement is all very well, but wouldn't it also be something of an artistic achievement to combine it with a better, more comfortable grip on everyday circumstances?

CATEGORIES

More and more clearly I see that artists of all kinds are divided into two camps, according to whether their understanding is from the heart or from the head. For those in the blessed first category, it seems to me, everything is wonderfully simplified – life, talents, work, everything. So much so, indeed, that those of the second by contrast resemble a collection of cripples, forced to compensate by all manner of shifts and techniques. Oh, the hairsbreadth set between the really great actor and the fool pulling faces!

THE BUG

You have to be really and truly bitten to succeed in this profession. How do you explain the mystery of a calling that gets under your skin and makes a slave of you? I, for example, could live a lovely life, petted and pampered and made a fuss of, in Paris or at my country house. And instead I go on and on, touring all over the place – one town after another, hotels, dressing-rooms – driven by the professional urgency, the perpetual hope that I can do that little bit better still. It reminds me of Grock's famous gag about being hit on the head with a hammer – it was so nice when it stopped. My situation exactly. The more panics I endure on the stage the greater the relief when the show is over. Then it's marvellous – I can relax and forget about it until the following night.

WHAT I OUGHT TO DO

Simplify. Stop bothering with the non-essentials. Having devoted my life to my work so far, I should reap the harvest and learn how to live the rest of it properly. You can be lazy at last, so enjoy yourself, man. It's time now for trees and grass and growing things. You've nothing to be ashamed of on your road so far, you've done your best for your work and for the public. So now be content, settle down and concentrate on playing the last act gracefully.

A SLICE OF LIFE

This incident, which happened at Vichy in 1947, shows how a slice of life turns out when you are getting on. I had noticed a great dearth of pretty women in the place. Few were either taking the cure or staying to keep husbands or lovers company. Girls of varying ages dispensed the water at the different springs and my own ration was doled out by a knee-high child with a fetching little face. Very humbly born, I should say, and when the manager of the Casino sent me two tickets for the ballet it occurred to me that she might enjoy an outing.

'Go and ask your mother if she'll let you come to the theatre tonight. She will? Good. You be at the main door at nine o'clock. Dress up and look nice!'

We entered together, she neat and pretty in a little grey, hooded cloak; when she reached up to take my hand her head was level with my waist. Down we sat like any staid old couple and I wrote a few lines on the programme for her. In the intervals we strolled on the terrace, with everybody staring.

They are an enormous family, she tells me, with six of them younger than she is.

'So you have to be a mother to them all?' I said, and she nodded, unsmiling.

At the end she clapped, pleased, but with no affected show of pleasure. Small as she was, she was a serious woman already. Then, 'Have you far to go home?' I inquired.

'Quite a way, yes. But the road's quite safe, Monsieur Maurice. I can go alone.'

'I never heard of such a thing. Take a lady out and not escort her home! Besides,' I added, 'I could do with a breath of air before bedtime.'

So off we went. She was used to walking with her father and kept up with my long strides and soon we covered a kilometre. Really, I thought, this was the decent thing to do, and what a nice evening I had had, giving her a lovely treat. A second kilometre brought us to the outskirts of Vichy, where we cross a bridge above a railway line.

'Is it much farther now?'

'Well, yes. But you should be turning back,' she volunteered.

'And leave you by yourself on a deserted road? Certainly not.'

Another fifteen minutes. Conversation lapsed, for we were a slightly weary team by now; at least, my old legs were weary.

'Much more?'

'Quite a bit, yes.'

A long, unlighted climb. I was no longer holding her hand and I was thinking, thinking. Every step of this journey, so ran my thoughts, was going to be just as long in the other direction. Virtue brings its own reward, all right. We reached the top of the hill.

'Much farther?' I inquired.

But here she really stopped me, almost stamping her foot, and ordered me to turn about and get off home to bed. It was only about another five minutes' walk and no danger, nobody was about. Exhausted after squiring her so patiently, I bade her good night and retreated, though I could not suppress a guilty feeling as I heard her pattering footsteps break into a run on the home stretch. A slice of life. But really, Maurice, at your age!

TOUR DE FRANCE

Today, for the first time ever, I saw the riders in the Tour de France pass the end of my drive along the Route Nationale to Cannes. After Cannes they were going on to Nice, and then to San Remo for the night. They were due at two o'clock in the afternoon and as we all went out to cheer them, it was nearly tea-time when we sat down to lunch. They were clustered together in groups, labouring as they rode and looking grim. One expected a combat and saw instead this array of jaded and seemingly indifferent men, but I think it was because one of their number, Vietto, came from Cannes and there was tacit and friendly agreement to let him take the lead as they went through.

They will be in Cannes again tomorrow, 15 July, for a break, and I shall then have a journalist's view, for I am to follow the two stages to Briançon and Aix-les-Bains for *Paris Presse*. We begin in the early hours and at Aix I leave them and come home. These two laps, with their endless hills, are said to be the most gruelling of all.

Why have I been thinking all day of those ancient galleys whose progress depended on the desperate exertion of slaves down on the rowing decks, with the lash to urge them on? Nobody lashes the cyclists, who do this, one must suppose, as their one and only way to fame; but they make such Herculean efforts to amaze their friends and admirers, and suffer so much in the process, that the comparison is inescapable. For them the incentive is placing and public applause. They are slaves of the world of sport, for whom the slave-masters are glory and competition.

Well, I went to Cannes and saw them all come back from San Remo. It reminds me of a Barnum and Bailey circus parade, with the attendant cars, the loudspeaker vans and the blaring newspaper advertisements, and the watchers waiting for hours; and a circus parade, of course, is exactly what it is. And here they come. First the pilot cars, sirens wailing; then the last-minute burst of speed whirls by, an eddy of men crouched on their machines, jaws set, through waves of cheering from the thrilled ecstatic crowd.

Now, Briançon, after my first full day in the midst of the great event. Most exciting it has been, too. I have not yet digested all its various physical and mental shocks and impacts, but there is an hour's interval in which to jot down a few hasty notes of a newcomer to the Tour. Let me begin by a frank avowal that I was never particularly keen on this sport myself. My two rides in theatrical races

have been disastrous. When I put on a spurt the speed affected my
chest, the bicycle started wobbling wildly and shot me over the
handlebars. The same thing happened on both occasions. On the
first I broke my left collar-bone and on the second my right, and
if there's one thing I hate it's repeating myself. It was not, therefore,
as an accomplished enthusiast that I turned up at half past five this
morning – half past five – but as an all-too-feeble exponent of the
art. At six the Tour left from a point opposite the Cafe des Alleés in
Cannes, and these are my impressions.

A good crowd despite the early hour, a great fuss made of any well-
known faces present. Cameras on all sides and dozens of reporters
there, Belgian, Italian and French. They took pictures of me from
all angles with the Tour de France people. I wrung the hands of
champions of every nationality and then the caravan set forth. I was
in the *Paris-Presse* car with two renowned journalists, Jean Antoine
and Gaston Bénac, and our chauffeur, an amiable character called
Tanton with whom they had been on this assignment thirteen times
before and whose experience was invaluable. It is quite an art to
drive with the field, to draw ahead and let them draw ahead, to speed
up, slow down and make a quick dash as required. Clearly, too,
everyone who mattered like Tanton and all seemed pleased to see
him. We led the file of cars immediately in front of the riders and
found the main streets of Cannes already packed and colourful with
enthusiastic onlookers. From everywhere came cries of, 'Bravo,
so-and-so!' 'Good luck this lap!' 'Keep at it!' I came in for my fair
share of recognition too, and when someone approached the car
and peered in my direction, I had my bright smile of acknowledge-
ment ready and waiting – only to be ignored completely in favour
of Bénac. *Vive Gaston Bénac!* he yelled. It was Bénac who took the
bow and we drove away laughing. Climbing towards Grasse we
could hardly sit still for the excitement and stood up in the open car
to get a better view.

One of the riders made a break on a downhill stretch and at once
every car in sight put on a spurt, all accelerating together to leave
him a clear run and avoid possible accidents. But soon the others
caught him up and they were in a bunch again with, presumably,
nothing to look at but the the calves of the man in front. We went

through Provençal villages with plane-trees shading the pleasant central squares and the inhabitants out along the route, a chorus of encouragement. Bénac scribbled away on loose-leaf pages with a thick black pencil. He says – and I took a mental note – that he cannot write without a thick black pencil.

The favourites were ahead, Bobet, Lazaridès and the Italian champion Bartali, whose youthful appearance makes a nonsense of the opinion, expressed in some quarters, that he is on the way out, past it. The Tour came into sight to a chorus of screams from a covey of girls who had been scanning the horizon; little more than children, 14 to 16 I should think, and the noise that issued from their pretty kitten faces was indescribable. Bénac was writing, writing all the time and handing the sheets as he filled them to a man on a motor-cycle who would telephone them on to Paris from the next village we came to. As he wrote he spoke of other things, mainly about cakes. There were, one gathered, not nearly enough *pâtisseries* in the places we traversed and sticky cakes were obviously his great besetting weakness. I was told how old he was; in a whisper, because he didn't like anyone to know. Over 65 and incredibly young, lively and on top of his job. He never stopped joking, catching some graphic detail, getting it down on paper.

We drove to the hill-tops and pulled up for a minute to watch the riders on the road below. A fine sight. From this distance they look like animated toy cyclists and the colours they wore, red, blue, yellow, white, were fresh and gallant in the sun. Cars and observers called to one another, swopping their noisy tidings in a running cacophony of shouting and witticism and hooting of horns in riotous competition.

Then the weather changed. The sun had shone until we reached Grasse but now it was clouding over and we felt the morning chill, which is unusual for July. (And what with the Tour at our front gate I had quite forgotten Bastille Day.)

Meanwhile, I was adoring it. The scenery was superb and I thought that following the whole Tour would be a perfect way to enjoy the countryside. Why not do it again next year, see it all from a front seat, and keep a diary? I took my dark glasses off the better to appreciate the view as well as the terrific drama of the race itself. The wind made my eyes sore, but that was a small price to pay for such beauty and colouring.

At Saint-Vallier the inmates of a summer school clung like small monkeys to the railings of their playground and shouted and cheered in unison. We were climbing considerably now, with three steep passes coming up, the cols of Allos, Vars and Izoard, before we got to Briançon, which is the highest *sous-préfecture* in France. The riders stayed together, leaving their joyous escort free to contemplate the fields of purple lavender, of white and yellow marguerites, of cornflowers and poppies, all looking as though sprung suddenly into bloom to match the gaiety of the occasion.

The cyclists tackled hill after hill in unvarying rhythm. They had a way of dancing, right to left and left to right, standing on the pedals, that suggested very talented performing bears. And what enormous life they put into it. The Italians, they tell me, are very correct competitors, though a bit guarded with the French, while the Belgians are more forthcoming.

We wind through pass after pass, with the three main cols of which I spoke rearing high above the rest. Here in the mountains it is cold and one of the motorcyclists gets off and runs for a while to keep warm. At some deserted spot the local postman leans against a tree to watch, and might easily believe, with a little imagination, that the whole amazing spectacle was put on just for him. Then the huge Castillon dam and the turbulent, beautiful river Verdon. What a route it is! A girl calls out, '*Bonjour!* See you next year!' She must have been waiting there for hours. It all has a quality of red-hot excitement, to be understood only by people who appreciate what sheer exertion means. We are in touch with the vital pulse of life, with something raw and real, a wild carnival of the world of sport. And among the hairpin bends of the col d'Allos, the essential battle is joined. Now, from this distance, one thought not of bears, but of the strivings of small, anxious bees.

Robic drew clear and this galvanized the whole caravan. He was off, going like a madman. Horns and whistles blew, sirens sounded. It might have been a jail-break. There was a weaving in and out of motor-bikes as the messengers made horrifying swerves to beat their rivals to a telephone and a line to the newsdesks. Vietto, just ahead of Bobet, is chasing Robic. I should think you need several days to grow used to this atmosphere and, knowing I'm only here for such a short time, I'm letting it run away with me. Any longer and I should have to take it much more calmly. It's all right for a couple of stages, but you'd need to husband your strength to get through twenty.

Next, the most ghastly thing. The press-car of *Intransigeant* skids on the slippery road just in front of us and crashes over the precipice with the paper's editor-in-chief and four other passengers. We see it, rolling, bouncing, rushing downwards out of control, like a huge cannon-ball. Our driver went white and after the first shocked exclamations we sat in silence, too horrified to speak. But the Tour, like warfare, goes on in spite of casualties, and it continued to the shouted news of the accident. 'The *Intran* car, gone over the edge.'

Down the col de Vars the road was wet and treacherous, but the cyclists were free-wheeling at a dizzy pace. The cars pulled in to let them pass, everyone fearful of skidding, which wouldn't have been funny up here. One heard occasional swearing as the field went by. A Belgian rated an Italian in Flemish, the Italian replied with something rude in his own language and an irritated Frenchman settled them both with a short, sharp *Merde!* as he tried to get through.

Antoine and Bénac were hard at it, the former on his feet like some general in the day of battle; one of those generals who mingles with the troops. He called out the names and numbers of competitors while Bénac scribbled ceaselessly on, protesting about his *pâtisserie* all the time. Some of the riders were bleeding profusely from falls and resembled murky demons, covered in mud.

Should we ever see level ground again? Whether from all the shocks and stimulation, or from the abrupt return to normal from the high altitude, I felt suddenly tired out. We heard, thank God, that no one in the crashed car was seriously hurt, though they had had a narrow escape and were lucky to be alive. And now Robic, the French star who won the Tour in 1947, is out in front and the rain is complicating the descent. The road isn't wide and is awash with mud, a hazard for everybody. The race goes grimly on. It really is a sort of war and the swagger has gone out of the riders. They are weary men, intent only on staying in one piece.

Some way past Vars, I am not sure exactly where, Bartali drew

N

ahead of Robic and began to gain ground, unbelievably fresh after those two exhausting cols. His tactics are those of a true champion, brilliant, masterly. Then through the magnificent gorges of the Guil. Bobet, we hear, has broken his saddle and the news lends wings to Bartali, who takes a six-minute lead. Then to the top of the Izoard where an assembly, apparently dropped from nowhere, is waiting in the mist, and an announcer says that Bartali is still five full minutes in front of Bobet.

This causes immense disappointment, for Bobet, who has all the requisite attractions, is by now established as the darling of the crowds. Then, down we come from the world of snow and eagles, down to where things grow and people live, to Briançon, again, after one more pointlessly taxing hill. The gruelling run leaves Bartali amazingly calm and collected, though the others are twitching with fatigue in front of newsreel men and photographers and I imagine poor Bobet is past remembering anything much about the whole hellish day. It would be funny to see his face work did one not instinctively recognize the kind of grimace that means pain has gone over the borderline of the bearable.

He could neither dismount unaided nor even sense the camera under his nose. He could not attempt the ghost of a smile to indicate that he had any reserves in hand. It was pitiful. He was at the end of his tether, beaten, exhausted, beyond caring how it's going to look in the paper tomorrow. Two supporters helped him away, a decrepit old man with tears pouring down and furrowing the mud on his cheeks. The pleasant, boyish features were almost hideous with fatigue: it was Dr Jekyll, turning into Mr Hyde.

The vision haunted me as I lay awake in Briançon that night, for I had taken to Bobet, with his guts and his likeability. He was a tryer, too, as indeed they all were. If it came to that, so were the reporters and drivers and motor-cycle messengers and the host of followers in this annual endurance-test; a whole sustaining army, freely spending strength and energy, with no thought of sparing either.

The others – the crowds at the check-points, the masses who travel for miles and stand for hours to catch their fleeting view of the all-but-impossible contest, and those who, stage by stage, devour the press reports – haven't the faintest idea of what it's really like, however keen they are. To know that, you have to be part of it, as I had been for the last two days; admitted to that private society of the Tour de France where it isn't your name that counts, it's you, and nobody has time or inclination to be bothered with smart pretensions. You need to be tough, with that lot, for they know one another's basic worth and there isn't room for anyone who doesn't measure up.

There is something of everything in the great national manifestation. It has elements of the theatrical or circus tour. It is as pure and thrilling an athletics display as you could hope to find. Grave or mortal danger looms in every second of it. For heart, muscle and human stamina it is, in fine, the ultimate sorting process.

I had a quick word with Bobet as they lined up to leave Briançon. He looked more rested than seemed possible after the state he was in the night before, but not completely happy, all the same. He said the strain was too much and that nothing but will-power kept him going; but he gave me a friendly smile. I thought I had better congratulate Bartali on yesterday's magnificent ride, but he neither knew nor recognized me and gave the impression that my complimentary remarks were a singularly ill-timed nuisance. When someone is about to stake name and reputation, he somehow conveyed, then all but intimate friends should keep away.

Off again, and we hear that one of the roads – not ours – is barred by fallen rocks. What a July! First rain, then snow in the Alps, and now rock-falls. We pass a sanatorium with all the patients out on their balconies, cheering. A tense Bobet makes a spurt and breaks away at Chantemerle; Bartali nowhere in sight. It is a cold morning with a white powdering of snow on the heights of the col du Galibier and the view is magical. I am shivering in too few clothes and the bitter wind is a sore trial to the cyclists. Several of this group have followed Bobet and are now 300 yards in front of the rest. Poor devils, what a way to earn a living!

Bénac informs me that never before in the history of the Tour have they had snow on the Galibier at this time of year; and to balance accounts I reflected that in Miami you can bathe in January. Meanwhile Bartali has warmed up, drawn level with Bobet and passed. They are now on a wider, dryer road after several kilometres of mud, their pedals seeming to yap like cur-dogs at each other's heels. For me it all boils down to the duel between these two, one for France and one for Italy, and I am keeping my fingers crossed for Bobet.

Guy Lapébie, too, is in the chase and going well. He is the most cheerful of them all and jokes the whole time. When we pass near Bobet and call to him his answering look is weary and stubborn, but Lapébie pulls a face and gives us a wink. A hard, steep road again, through wonderful country. The struggle is intoxicating and I wouldn't change places with anybody. I could shout with sheer exhilaration. We scale the Croix-de-Fer pass, thirty-two kilometres up, with a stupendous view.

Robic is tailing off a bit, despite his reported boasting a day or two earlier. Talking is one thing, keeping the lead another. Bobet is now ahead of Bartali, out alone with a big lead. A girl turns her head away as he makes water riding by. But on leaving Grenoble Bartali fairly dashes at the col de Porte. He really is a marvel! The crowd has been thick on both sides of the road for the last twenty kilometres, if you can imagine what that is like, and things are hotting up. Bartali comes down the Porte ten minutes ahead of everyone else and takes the yellow jersey to show he's in first place. Oh, come ON, Bobet! A little spin along the Entrement gorges next and a dozen Dominican monks have what amount to holy front-row stalls to watch the Tour go by: leaped over the wall, perhaps, to look? Then into Aix-les-Bains with the route a solid wall of people since well before Chambéry.

A huge concourse in the town and various well-known personalities are introduced and interviewed to fill in time until the winner's arrival. And at last he comes: Bartali, riding alone. A momentary coolness, and they gave him the reception he deserved; they were all sporting enthusiasts and appreciated the superb performance of a real, old-style champion. But it was Bobet they were waiting for and when he appeared six minutes later their applause for the others was as nothing compared with what they had in store for him. It couldn't have been warmer had he won. Bobet has earned his stripes as the great, accepted champion of the new school. He spoke into the microphone, into three microphones in fact, and made three little speeches, all different. A really nice person, charming, thorough-bred, straightforward. Two years ago no one had ever heard of him and today the sight of him makes the sun come out. He takes a few steps forward, mounts, balances on his bicycle, spins the pedals and rides away.

This was the point at which I left the Tour and returned to Cannes, there to lie at my ease at La Louque-*m'enlouquer*, I call it – in the Riviera sun; the only sun there was, it seemed, in this peculiar summer when the seasons, like everything else, had got in an awful mess. A new devotee, I follow the final stages in the press. My Bobet, understandably, is finding it hard going and there is talk of a crack-up. Bartali they rightly describe as a master, and this no more than a week since such an expert as Gaston Bénac declared in print that, as a cyclist, Bartali was fine on a toboggan. 'Loosing his Grip.' There's a good subject there, and a good title.

In sporting circles they are all full of admiration for Guy Lapébie, the determined life and soul of the party – of this particular party, anyhow; for the spirit he shows and the way he hangs on and keeps going. I devoutly hope that Bobet can muster physical strength to tide him over his depression and leave his courage and determina-tion unaffected. Room at the top is never cheap.

At any rate, he knows by now how tough it can be – racing, winning, losing, weeping tears of blood, and all at the fullest stretch of muscle and nerve. It has been the most searching test he could possibly undergo and Bartali may well prove the best friend he has, for from Bartali he will have learnt much of what constitutes the long-distance champion, if he has eyes to see and wit to take it in. He will either come out of this race a future star of the Tour de France or, if he isn't the right material, with heart and strength broken past praying for. But he will have had a good try, whatever happens, like a young whirlwind, with his true French dash and drive, and that's what matters. Louison Bobet – what an endearing name! Good luck to him.

THOSE ENVIABLE MODEL-GIRLS

How interesting to observe the posturing of the young women who model couture clothes and see how the shyest of them will assume an air of aggression at times. How arrogantly they advance, how abruptly they turn and retrace their steps and dart their unseeing glances right and left into an audience that sits there looking critical and wondering, really, what it ought to buy. The delectable creatures are most of them working-class and they not only do their stuff to perfection but also, I shouldn't wonder, get a great deal of pleasure out of it thus spurning the customers on whom their living depends. At Dior I noticed one in particular with a determinedly disagreeable expression although her face and figure were in fact extremely attractive. The dress helped, too.

It is an act they put on, this icy disdain. If you ask them the price of a gown they are polite enough, if cool, and among themselves or talking to the saleswomen they suddenly drop back to being the well-favoured, lively wenches they actually are, the belles of Paris. Class is a *very* funny thing.

THE PROBLEM OF THE OLD FLAME

Cravings. Cravings for tobacco, alcohol, women – once you find the right dodge for ignoring or getting round them, and the desire is past, then you see them for what they are – cravings, nothing more.

BRIGHTENING UP ALADDIN'S CAVE

I have become very friendly in New York with Louis Arpels, the jeweller, who is a distinguished sort of man. Sometimes I visit the shop on Fifth Avenue several times a day, for he has the most elegant clientele on Broadway and I find it fascinating to watch pretty women choosing jewellery. I was chatting to his brother in a corner yesterday when Louis came over from where he was showing necklaces to a couple of American women, and took a ten-dollar bill from his pocket. His brother covered it without a word and I, marvelling at their manoeuvres, demanded an explanation.

'Oh,' I was told, 'it's a little side-bet we always have. Sale, I win; no sale, I lose. Makes it more interesting and gives us something to think about. Gets boring, you know, sales-talk.' Ah, well!

WATCHING THE TOP STEP

No one who does an act entirely on his own should fail to see and study others. He can always learn something. Having to hold a theatre full of people alone for two hours at a stretch can reveal a lot of cracks, and it makes you long passionately to win and keep their attention. In this you may well succeed, but put a foot slightly wrong, and all's to do again. There is too much at stake ever to relax; the famous are not allowed to falter. The hint of a weak note, a second's hesitation in the course of a show, and immediately you can feel, as it were, a pull-back from the audience. How quickly they desert you!

Also, they know to a minute, in some inexplicable fashion, when an artist has no more to say to them. His public, his success, turn from him as a man breaks off a now-sterile conversation. They arrive at their pitiless verdict how and when they please and it's no use trying to hang on afterwards by any means, dignified or otherwise. They only say no thank you. Once the enchanter's vial is broken the charm doesn't work any more.

STICK TO WHAT YOU UNDERSTAND

Met Paul Géraldy, just back from several months in Morocco. A delightful man, polite, considerate and very shrewd, who made what was, for me, an immensely encouraging and sensible remark. Had that marvellous land inspired him, I asked; had he written any poems there? He replied like a shot: 'No, I certainly haven't. You should only deal with what you really know, subjects you understand.

You produce artificial nonsense otherwise, that doesn't mean a thing. Falsehood, in fact.'

It gave me positive pleasure to hear him say so.

NOT THIS WAY

Visited some of the Miami night-clubs to see the cabarets. There is no denying that these American stars have talent and attack, but their notion of what you need to get to the top beats me altogether. The forcefulness, the things they choose to sing about, the unrelenting, watchful domination behind the smiles they bend upon their raving audiences – it is all so laboured as to depress me every time I see it. They are gifted, but they seem to have made so little progress towards what must be, after all, the goal of any worth-while career. There is a certain kind of laughter and applause you just have to avoid if distinction's what you want.

WRITING THE STUFF MYSELF

More and more, these days, I enjoy expressing my own ideas in songs I write myself, and when the public likes something that is All My Own Work I find it far more satisfying than when they were applauding someone else's.

The critics are beginning to write stray articles about the solo programmes with which I am winding up my career, wanting to know why I should have risked any such innovation. What is the motive behind it? Well, I am a *café-concert* singer who wants to raise the *café-concert* to new and greater heights and at last, I think, they realize the fact. Certainly the shows are popular and we are taking record receipts.

I have become, I think, not a 'type' any more, not a 'character', but a man, and a Canadian woman journalist seems to me to have explained this very well. Analysing my development as an artist, away from the low patter and broad jokes of my early days, she hits on the song '*Quai de Bercy*', as representative of the later Chevalier, and this encourages me to enter further still into the realms of human sympathy and feeling. She calls me a spreader of friendship, of happiness and hope. What more could anyone wish?

I have divested myself of my straw hat, and unless the song calls for it I use no hat of any kind; so there is nothing special about my head, any more than about the rest of me, these days. And I write my own songs, showing my own thoughts. I dig my own principles out of my own depths for people's benefit, so what they are getting is not an evening of songs but an evening with a new brand of philosophy.

The one-man show confers enormous independence on an artist. You need do only what you wish, in the way you feel is best to do it. You are your own producer, stage-manager and executant. Add to all this the supreme joy of quarrying the material from your own heart and mind, and so interpreting it the more sincerely, and you have something perfectly satisfying. And to think of all those poor stage and film actors, drilled and dragooned by everyone in sight, in thrall to their scripts and their fellow-players, listening with bated breath to prompters and producers!

A FEW MORE PEOPLE

We might begin with Pierre Monteux, who must be among the best unofficial ambassadors this country ever had. Music-lovers flocked to hear him in all the big cities of America. Last night he came to see us, little, fat and 72, with an international reputation and not the slightest trace of affectation or self-importance. A thoroughly nice, ordinary person who chats away as simply as if he were the man who made your shirts, or the mayor of some village in the Dordogne, or any decent soul from anywhere else in France. That he is a decent soul is proved by the fact that his character, tastes and way of life are all unchanged by the long triumphal spell abroad. In this he is blessedly unlike so many theatre people, who drive you up the wall with the facile way they adapt themselves and run round imitating everything.

I attended yesterday's concert at the San Francisco Opera House, and it was a revelation. I must admit to being unashamedly Philistine, for nothing has ever managed to make me appreciate music of this kind; but here it was almost a caress, a wave of sound that carried you along. There was an awareness of uncoercive beauty, something which gently penetrated the mind and spread a feeling of content, so that Monteux, conducting his hundred or so musicians, seemed to conduct my thoughts, too, to unaccustomed heights. Nor was there the least over-emphasis or attitudinizing in anything he did. He is a genius who works at music, humbly.

Next, Sarah Bernhardt. I am reading her biography by Louis Verneuil. A woman who knew the cost of fame, and it is consoling to learn that the divine Sarah, too, had all those ups and downs. Her name on a playbill did not, it seems, automatically ensure success and she lost a fortune on dramas she fancied and the public didn't. Well, what a lesson it is, to be sure, and what a comfort also. There isn't an actor born who doesn't have to bow to events at some time or another; the greatest have been known to come a cropper. And if that happens to you the main thing is not to stay down, but to get on your feet again, make a fresh start and succeed. Succeed *quand même*, in spite of everything. *Quand même* was Sarah's proud motto. The main thing is to conquer circumstance.

And now another courageous woman, Lucienne Boyer. She had a lunch-party yesterday in the apartment they rent on Park Avenue, and prepared everything, unaided save by one sleepy, feckless servant. Seeing her busy between table and kitchen, going backwards and forwards to the stove and waiting on us all – there were two couples and me, beside her husband and herself – working like the three good maids she really needed, I had to compare the attitudes of French and American women. Lucienne may seem a fragile creature at first glance, but her reserves of nervous energy are amazing. She has spent years in cabaret, which is a tiring and tricky profession; she is always travelling; on top of which, as if she hadn't enough to do, she takes on the wear and tear of running a house and practically being her own charwoman – and this with a husband and small daughter to look after as well. It leaves her a bit breathless at times, but she laughs and says: 'It has to be done, or everything would collapse.' A French sparrow with the heart of a lion.

Then, Colette. Colette all truth and mystery. I was in the Rue de

Beaujolais and suddenly, as I passed her house, I thought of her. She was sure to be at home for sickness confined her to her bed, a little longer every time it struck, and there she lay and wrote. I decided to chance it.

They let me in and meeting her made my day. Seventy-six and mortally ill and not in the least downcast, she observes her malady with unforced cheerfulness: well into old age, joking at life and her own approaching death, accepting the inevitable with a saint's exemplary grace.

She says that writing costs her more pain than the business of dying. She swears she never had any vocation for writing, never liked it and took to literature to earn her daily bread. She has endured torment from pen, ink and paper; the purgatory of having to fill the empty sheet. Writing has worn her out and spoiled her whole life. She is a born contemplative, she says, a word that makes one immediately aware of how extraordinary she is. To be in that tragic state and still be able, by virtue of sheer feminine perception, to analyse the slow development of inner beauty as her body wastes away! A literary phenomenon.

I hope she may survive a long time yet, but I see her as one of those people destined to sail serenely off, like a dream, into the infinite. She is magnificently poised and humble. Colette will doubtless miss the life down here but step forward to the shadows, interested and agog, and protesting in advance against the difficulties of writing all about it for the angels and the legions of the blessed to read.

Another genius I have encountered is Pierino Gamba whom I saw at Ostend – a child with his load of superhuman gifts. I was singing at the Casino where he was rehearsing with an orchestra the same afternoon, and until my dressing-room was ready I settled in a corner to watch. He stood on a high rostrum, in the sort of clothes he might wear to go on the beach, and they somehow made his genius more believable than ever. Five or six times he takes his musicians through a *pianissimo* passage that is not soft enough to please him. '*Piano . . . piano*', he hisses softly, 'ssss . . . quieter. Very quiet. Like this. . . .' The boyish voice breathes a clear, sad note. 'You see?'

They do it again. And again. And again. 'It is not yet soft enough. More soft (which comes out as *plou piano* in his Italian accent), nearly nothing. Like this.' He hums in his throat. One of the players ventures to point out that the resonance in the empty hall is making a *pianissimo* somewhat difficult to achieve.

'Yes, yes. But it was empty the other day and you were *plou piano* then.' And the next attempt vindicates him completely. He obviously has a perfect ear. Then he requires 'a little more emphasis on the C, gentlemen, if you please. C *plou appuyé*.' He leaves the stand and comes down to show somebody where the firmer note is wanted.

'You see, Monsieur? If you do not actually draw your bow as far as it will go the note is *plou joli* and more sustained. Try taking it just as far as there. You see?'

He is unerring and it is pointless for anyone to argue with him or answer back. Whoever did so would merely make a fool of himself. The *crescendo*, the *pianissimo*, he asks for is always irrefutably right.

'Rest, gentlemen.'

They relax like soldiers from parade, or students from an enjoyable lecture. He exchanges a friendly handshake with the first violin, who smiles back at him in unaffected gratitude. During the break he chats with another boy who has been sitting in front and goes over the rehearsal with his teacher, Arduini, who makes a few suggestions. Then to work again, plunging straight into it with not a minute lost.

One of the violin-cellos is late on a phrase and he tells him so. No diffidence about this, and no mistake either, for the player was definitely behind the beat. Yet one has no impression that the young brain is overcharged, or unnaturally developed in any way. On the contrary, everything seems to be clearly thought out beforehand and beautifully ordered in his head. Nothing he does appears nervous or forced, there is no sign of mental strain.

'No, Monsieur, no, no. E natural. *Natourel, comprenez?*'

And the master was just 11 years old.

PATHETIC

In America I visited a new homosexual night-club with a very smooth floorshow and dresses that would have made a Hollywood star green with envy. Obviously, they were out to impress. Queer all right, but distinguished queers, who left the low stuff to the sort of little dears you find in the dives of Montmartre. The keynote here was reserve, an aristocracy of vice, and somehow the effect was blurred and lacklustre. They are neither men nor women and what they do on the stage is as indefinite as themselves. It is a pitiable state to think of and surely a tragic one to be in. Each and every one of these poor people is landed in an impossible situation, with a mental and physical make-up quite unnatural to him, forced to wrestle with a hopeless problem. One can laugh at the outrageous pansies, but these are different, and one is desperately sorry for them.

CHARITY: THE REAL THING

I made a radio appeal for uncared-for children and afterwards this letter came: 'We have heard you on the wireless and here is our contribution to your good cause. Two old women in the *Quinze-Vingts*.' The *Quinze-Vingts* is the Blind Hospital. There were two banknotes enclosed and those two poor old ladies haven't even signed their names.

CHARITY: IN THE UPPER ECHELONS

Inaugural dinner of the Monte Carlo Summer Season. Presiding were Edward G. Robinson and his wife, who emerged as a painter some few months ago and has since become an enthusiastic holder of exhibitions in New York and Paris as well as Monaco.

Where else could you see such a gathering? Seven hundred and fifty guests, most of them internationally famous. Lovely women in wonderful gowns, and men with famous faces; people whose names were made and unassailable, names from all over the world. All present and correct, anyone you could think of, the famous charmers and the plutocrats and those most accustomed to the good things of life; all, apparently, disinterested in the extreme.

'Isn't that King What's-his-name over there?'

'Oh? Really?'

'Isn't that Rita Hayworth?'

'Really? Is it?'

Not a flicker. Not a flicker for Sacha Guitry who was there with an ex-Minister and a friend. Nobody gave the slightest indication of having noticed anyone else at all, and this generated a curious feeling of dissatisfaction, as if none of them in the least appreciated the luxury they lived in or how lucky they were. It was a weary, dreary business. They had to be there, because if they weren't they didn't count, but they seemed bored to death with the whole affair. There was a terrible crush, too, and the service suffered accordingly.

Edward G. was in a constant fuss in case anyone's glass were empty. I was sitting by his wife, who never stopped talking about her pictures and the admiration showered upon them from all sides. I lent a sympathetic ear as best I could, being myself in a professional fuss at the thought of having to sing in this very same place at the Prince of Monaco's reception for the local Red Cross an evening or two later.

The acoustics were absolutely dead. When that evening came it would be like singing into cotton wool, or in a railway station. Mrs Edward G. went on and on. Dwelling on these gloomy thoughts I replied to her in monosyllables, and then not always with the right expression.

The toastmaster announced her, a microphone was brought and with entire self-possession she rose to thank those present. Polite applause. Then it was her husband's turn and he launched blithely into a speech in French which, at any rate to begin with, was a nice surprise. He speaks the language fairly well, but thinks it like an American and so is apt to fall into oddities and turns of phrase which strike a wrong note with these hypercritical hearers, so quick to condemn shortcomings of taste or tact.

When he had finished the band left the platform, by way of urging the diners into the gambling-rooms; and at that point we went home.

WHAT LAUGHTER COSTS

The public buy their laughs cash down, but the artist pays in more important currency. It is a well-known fact that celebrated jesters are the most melancholy of men, yet anyone who amuses people on a big scale is invariably pictured as entertaining his fortunate family and friends to a non-stop funny turn. But what makes the jester melancholy? It is the balance of human nature, which enforces rest as the compensation for carelessly-dispersed vitality of the kind he needs. The batteries run down and have to be re-charged. No one in this world can spend himself without having to stock up again afterwards. Those who trade in laughter and animation have, as it were, nourished the public and become exhausted in the process – as a mother might be exhausted who has fed her child and has to make more milk to feed him again next day.

EMBLEMATIC MEETING WITH A YOUNG MAN IN BRUSSELS, 1948

Much stir and ado in the beautiful Place de l'Hôtel de Ville when I go, accompanied by the Burgomaster and the French ambassadress, to offer my straw hat and dinner-jacket to the Manneken Pis, presiding genius of Brussels.

The little figure has an enormous wardrobe, donated by many famous folk; elaborate costumes, coats hung with rows of gleaming medals, and the like, all kept piously in his own museum. This, however, is his first present of a performer's actual working dress. The crowd thickens as we approach him and begins to go a bit wild. We struggle through as best we may, to find the Manneken draped for the occasion in an ample tricolour flag, and I address him as follows.

'Manneken Pis, *célèbre petit*, drawn by your charm and impelled by the Belgian blood I inherit from my mother, I have come here today to give you the dinner-jacket and straw hat in which for fifty years I have sung on stages all over the world the songs we ordinary people sing at home. You are now the most important of my imitators, and for once the imitator is more famous than his model. Not that I am jealous of you. On the contrary, I should dearly love to return the compliment and do as you do in the main square of every capital city I visit. But that, I fear would lead to complications. No – I just hope that the affection linking us today may be an emblem for both our countries. Manneken Pis, my heart goes out to yours.'

MAN TO MAN

'*Penser juste*'. I was thinking of these words as I left the presence of the Prince Regent, escorted by an A.D.C. The sentries outside the palace in Brussels saluted as I passed. *Penser juste* – decide aright, consider carefully. Words that underlie all we have said in an hour-long audience that had gone by like a flash.

The Prince had wished to receive me before, but he had had flu and the meeting was postponed until this Sunday morning at eleven-thirty. There had been a short delay, the A.D.C. came back to summon me and with a thrill of excitement I saw the double door open to reveal a huge apartment, something between a grand gallery, a salon and a sort of royal board-room. Coming towards me, hand outstretched, was a tall, slim man who looked quite pleased to see me.

'Monseigneur, I appreciate this honour very deeply.'

The door shut behind us and he moved to two chairs near the fireplace.

'I must tell Monseigneur that I shall do all I can to conform to the rules of etiquette and speak to him in the Third Person; but I ask that he will not take it amiss if I get it wrong, for I have not had much practice.'

With a barely perceptible twinkle he replied,

'No, we'll forget the protocol and talk man to man, Monsieur

Chevalier. And if you really want to know, I'm far more scared than you are!'

I thought I couldn't have heard aright, but he repeated that some-one in his position had so few human contacts, compared with someone in mine, that he had good grounds for apprehension. We were off to a flying start.

What did we talk about? Philosophy chiefly, and people. Those who help you and those who take you for a ride; the unreliable, tiring chatterboxes and the shy ones who do much and say little, whose natures are loyal and profound. We spoke of the need for toleration when a man's known character justified it, and of the way some people have of simply being there, wordless and strengthening. He wanted the tale of what had happened to me during the Occupation.

'It must have been very hard,' he said, 'when they were running after you and angling for you all the time. You must have had to consider carefully.'

Oh, that considering carefully! The words went home. Consider the for and against; consider what this one says, consider what that one means. Grasp the truth in the tangle of truth and lying, unravel all the intrigue and come to the tiny core of fact. Weigh things pro-perly, let everybody else get on with it, decide what you think is right and then go forward fearlessly. This watchword presented to me by H.R.H. will form part of my mental furniture from now on. The rest of the conversation was, so far as I was concerned, no more than embroidery on this theme.

And careful consideration, surely, means standing back, not necessarily for the proverbial leap forward, but to make, or so one hopes, some wiser choice; perhaps to find some way, better suited to one's age, of doing more in life. This question of retirement, for instance. People refuse to credit it when I tell them I shall soon give up the stage after my fifty-year-long career, their great argument, among many others, being that I could not bring myself to relinquish my popularity, let alone the money. But programmes such as mine, I keep telling them, demand physical reserves which are gradually decreasing when you reach 60. I point out too that, having got as far as I possibly can, I can only go downhill in any case. I might as well talk to a brick wall. They make bets and lay wagers and swear I could never live without the drug of nightly applause.

And I am so sure that my decision is logical and right. Oh, to be free of this awful feeling that comes over me about four o'clock in the afternoon whenever I have to sing; insects crawling round my stomach, the strung-up feeling that is agony to conquer, all because of the evening show. When I don't have any evening show there will be none of that to face. I should leave it all without a shadow of regret. I should live on the Riviera for the best seven months of the year; make an occasional film and even sing if I had to; radio now and then, some television; writing and composing and doing a little journalism – these are what I dream of. You can see how a different sort of life is calling and tugging at me. Well, we're nearly there. I'm on the last lap now. So – shoulder to the wheel.

THE REAL THING

Life is a struggle against the forces that worry and waste one, that tend to throw one off course and fill one up with lies. In the end, instinctively, one turns away from them, back towards what is true and human. There is absolutely no future in 'society' with its distracting, empty-headed chatter. A sane and fruitful life must have a basis of serenity and truth and the deliberate rhythm of repeated effort. Avoid, then, coteries of unhinged and fraudulent hysterics of whatever persuasion. People – and they are few and far between – – who confine their enthusiasm to what they actually understand, should seek one another out and cleave together. Best to keep away from the half-demented merry-go-round. Refuse to have anything at all to do with it. It's too much of an insult to the intelligence.

NOT YET PAST TEMPTATION: *La Bocca, 1 January 1949*

New Year's Day and into my sixty-first year. So, where am I? Marvellously happy in my work and living a bachelor life again. *But*, I am in a receptive frame of mind, which I haven't been for ages. ('Oh, get along with you!' do I hear somebody say? 'Sorry,' I reply, 'it's in the air.')

How pleasant it would be to, I keep thinking, to have a sort of child-wife, someone who enjoyed living quietly, someone artistic who loved music, painting, literature, philosophy, that kind of thing. I know the snags and dangers in these unsuitable relationships, but I can see this one coming and cannot resolve to say no.

Oh, risk it! Everything's a risk anyway. Risks begin the moment you set foot out of doors in the morning and get worse as the day goes on. You've got to take them to live at all, and some prove riskier than others. And when do they ever stop, for heaven's sake? It's a complete gamble – work, health, love. And I am on the point of falling in love with a girl of 22.

Old man, young girl, I have sung many a derisive ditty about just this situation. Funny when you think, but there's very little I can do about it, I'm afraid. The idea grows on me and the thing is suddenly happening. Moreover, it occurs to me at this very moment, why should I shut the door on any chance, however small, of brightening up the rest of my life? And what if I drop lucky, and this girl turns out to be the perfect companion, the perfect inspiration, who will adapt herself to my existence? At 22? I get carried away at the thought of it, and I shall take the plunge.

It will cause a stir, of course. Twenty-two, they'll all say, and *how* old is he? Yes, well, there is a slight difference when you reckon it up, but I can't see that the notion is in any way foolish. I am entertaining it only because the girl appears to me teachable, loving and sweet-natured, and if she really is all that, then perhaps I can make her happy. I shall certainly try.

Why, why not? Other men of my age have done the same thing without necessarily coming to grief. I am setting about it with so many different feelings (and desire the least among them), and who's to say that I may not have gained a daughter in the end? Not exactly as *pure* an arrangement as convention might perhaps demand, but from where is one supposed to summon up resolve to reject her spring-time propositions, I should like to know? It is a kind of adoption, really, the adopter being someone whose days are sadly solitary in the midst of all this applause they talk about. There are those who attach themselves to dogs and cats and parrots, or who, rather than be alone, live their lives out with partners who drive them mad and end up bitter enemies, hating the sight of one another. But this adoption might be a wonderful solution, if all goes well. And how encouraging to others of my age, a demonstration that one should no more give up when it comes to love and human relations than one should give in over work.

But . . . but. . . . In the Champs-Élysées again I see a mother with her daughter. And, 'Oh, look', cries mother with a gesture of recognition, 'there's Maurice Chevalier!' to which the younger generation replies: 'Big deal.' (*Ben merde alors!* is the phrase she actually employed.) End of another anecdote.

Also, I find it upsetting, when I am with this girl of mine, to run into some woman I knew in her youth and beauty, and see the years have passed and how much less young and beautiful she is.

Oh, hell, it's better to *live* and die sooner than to have been half-dead and prudent all your life. But I must remember not to be jealous, ever. That way I should make a damn fool of myself. Either her thoughts are not straying, which will be marvellous, or they are; in which case, well – off you go, my pet. And now see where imagination's getting me.

The odd anonymous letter comes from time to time: people hugging themselves in anticipation at the thought of the wretchedness in store for me when this affair is over. And I have grown jealous. Jealous of the attraction she has for everyone she meets, and for one or two especially. She is very aware and responsive and I see the slight flush on her cheeks in the presence of anyone who, as I know instinctively, finds her desirable. My heart beats in my chest. So soon! I must not let this sort of thing run away with me, or God knows what I'm in for. Sixty years grin back at me and I see this love of mine in all its painful and depressing aspects. I have always been prone to jealousy, but I could fight it on equal terms, before.

Isn't it only natural that an artist should at some time or another fall victim to his own power of stirring the emotions? But this dream of mine, unfortunately, seems to be turning into a nightmare.

No, all is well again. Back to normal. Getting back to normal –

that's life the whole time. You either succumb or you do the other thing, and that's the height of achievement.

I have just made the break, and it took my last ounce of will-power. Now I must try to get a grip on myself, accept facts and realize that one cannot play the passionate lover at 61. It was heaven to start with, and it has landed me at the gates of hell, which is far enough, I think. Time now to concentrate on work and on making a good finish – head held high, and a proper understanding of one's weaknesses and limitations. Time now to become a real, nice old gentleman; gather up the bits and pieces, it's the law of life. Meanwhile, my head's affected, my heart's affected, I'm affected all over.

'How're you doing, Maurice?' they inquire.

'Oh, I'm *very* well, thank you.' I tell them. 'Doing fine.'

And now the storm has passed. I find that one can settle ill-wishers better by a certain sort of smile than by open reproach; that some people are less disagreeable than they are supposed to be – they couldn't look so sympathetic otherwise; and I am convinced that it is better to have felt too deeply something that wasn't worth it than too little about something that was.

NICE TO BE APPRECIATED

Two of the best comics who ever came out of Marseilles were Gorlett and Rellys. The former, with his irresistible, quick-fire local humour, has gallantly taken up the threads of his career after a personal loss that nearly killed him, while the latter, who has always set his sights high on stage and screen, has earned the regard of every true professional. About a week ago, then, I received a whole collection of photographs, on a huge paste-board mount, illustrating my personal history. I am there as a boy. I am there blowing the candles out at my sixtieth birthday-party. Enclosed is a letter of extreme artlessness asking me to autograph this trophy before the sender, who signs himself Rellys, takes it to be framed. Intrigued by the name, I write to ask whether he is by any chance related to Rellys the music-hall artist? He is Rellys, he says, and I am astounded to find any actor these days capable of such single-minded devotion.

Here is someone, doing very nicely, who needs to ask no favours from me and doesn't even know me very well, and yet feels about me as strongly as this! I invite him round to collect his parcel, so we can shake hands, and he duly arrives, diffident, afraid he is being a nuisance, and telling me that in his younger days he used to trail me along the Allées de Meilhan at Marseilles. His modesty and real feeling moved me intensely. I could hardly believe my ears and had to stop myself hugging the man. Then off he went, cherishing his paste-board like a treasure under his arm – simplicity out of another world, another age than ours.

BRAVE MAN

He was 20, tall and thin, with rather girlish good looks, and he used to seek us out in the days when the young hopefuls of the *café-concert* gathered in the Rue du Faubourg Saint-Martin. He was not a singer himself but an acrobatic cyclist, the funny-man of one of the most popular troupes on the music-hall and as an admirer of mine he resolutely imitated my make-up and the outlandish costume with which I then festooned my scarecrow form. His great gimmick was to accompany the music between one trick and another with a thrumming, sonorous *zoom-zoom* noise. His name was Maurice Nicholas and the act was *Les Abbins*, but no one of our particular circuit ever called him anything but Zoom-Zoom.

Everything I did he copied; I couldn't wear a new sweater or a cap but Zoom-Zoom sported a similar one next day. What with his grace and his gymnastics, women simply loved him and he had a high old time. Then the war came, and after that I moved away and saw him only at intervals. Eventually he found himself a lovely and excellent wife named Georgette and left the acrobatic world. They opened a luxurious little bar in the Rue Pasquier where he saw to things generally and she was a charming hostess. Life was good to them.

Then things went wrong. He became paralysed while still a young man. Treatments and consultations proved useless and he was condemned to his bed for the rest of his days. He grew worse and had to be washed and fed and helped in every physical function. His wife was wonderful and some of his old friends made it their business to visit him regularly. He lived in a room adjoining the bar, his body dead but his brain as active as ever, resigned to his condition. He still had a head on his shoulders, he could still be of some use and assistance. Then came the mortal blow. Georgette had a seizure and died very quickly, leaving him unprotected, at the mercy of all and anyone, the hulk of a body with only his eyes alive.

Thanks to his friends, a man was found to run the bar and so provide an income for him. Men and women alike, they took turns to sit with him and fate, repenting of its harshness, sent him a nurse who warmed her own loneliness by looking after him. As well as could be, a life was fabricated and this man, who once had everything, behaved like a hero. It was as though all the lost physical strength had flown to his heart and spirit. He could still go into fits of laughter, joke about his own dependence, refuse the very thought of pity. When I went to see him it was not friendship alone that drew me, but the prospect of doing myself some good as well. He seemed to me, what he undoubtedly was, an example of enforced abnegation and plain, ordinary courage. For several weeks now my Sundays have been arranged round the visit to Zoom-Zoom.

The sight of his face as I go through the door is itself enough to make the expedition worth while. Carefully I shake his fingers, shrivelled and cold because the blood no longer reaches them, and frankly tell him I am here for what I can get from him. Yet his eyes, so full of answering affection and friendship, mist over as he says,

'Whenever you come, Maurice, I feel as if you've blown me up like a flat tyre.'

But that happens to be how I feel about him.

I have seen many, many people face to face with adversity, but none with guts to equal his. It does him good to hear me tell him so. Then we fall to reminiscing, going over our young days, remembering the girls we loved, and the great old performers who flourished round about 1908. In the end the small, dark room is ringing with our laughter.

At last I have to go. But down the stairs and into the street I see his expression still, the way his heart looks out at you, the directness and the comprehension which belongs only to people who live cut off from the world around them. *Zoom-ẓoom*, he used to sing. *Zoom-ẓoom.*

ON TOUR.

One thing you realize, travelling round, is that towns can affect you just as people do. Some are vibrant, glowing, generous, advancing to meet you, hands outstretched, while others seem to keep their hands behind their backs; on the defensive, suspicious, hard-to-get. Others again are sapless, worn out, uninteresting. Fists tight-clenched, these, giving nothing away. You can sense an atmosphere as you go along the main streets on the way to your hotel; the place is friendly, distant or detached. But is it the people who affect the towns, or do the towns affect the pepole?

CRITICISMS

A rather chilly wind seems to be blowing, these days, in my direction and several newspapermen and satirically-minded critics have started picking on me. They object, apparently, to my doing anything out of my usual line, and even to my getting enthusiastic about it, as though it annoyed them that anyone should take life as seriously as that. All this upward striving makes one, in their opinion, a bore. Well, I see their point of view all right. They probably enjoy distractions to which I have said good-bye and rewards which, nowadays, are not for me. But one doesn't have to play the same game for ever, from the cradle to the grave, and one may surely be allowed a little variety. Nobody *has* to listen to what I have to say, or read a word I write, or in any way give me his blessing. I potter along as well as I can, with my own aims and objects before me, and if this annoys anyone, he doesn't have to bother with me. These attacks are no bad thing, in any case; they keep the ball rolling. Heaven knows, nothing they write about me could be worse than what I think of myself, and if they run short of material I could show them a few of my failings they appear to have missed. I know me a great deal better than they do, and I know my own weaknesses are so very weak as to be quite appalling, but these people seem to think I should let them demolish me without any defence at all. It's a bit much, I must say. I refuse to be swept from the scene until I am swept away for ever. For the moment I remain alive and kicking and quite capable of speaking up for myself; and, as they ought to know, I was never one to aim at a minimum score. Bloody idiots.

BRAVE WOMAN

A telephone-call from a young and beautiful woman whom I saw dancing in a Paris night-club a couple of years ago.

'I want some advice, Monsieur Maurice. It's really important.'

'Well, come and see me at the Variétés. I'm usually there by half past eight.'

She was at the stage-door that same evening.

'I can't spare a lot of time,' I said, 'what's the matter?'

'Monsieur Maurice, I can't talk here. Might I come upstairs?'

This, I thought, was a bit of a bore, but told her to follow me. Then she asked me not to wait but to let her take the steps slowly. I cursed her lack of agility and was surprised as well as irritated, for the two flights were obviously giving her trouble. But when she caught me up there was a charming smile for me, and an explanation.

Since the time I heard her sing and had given her praise and encouragement, she had met with a stupid but serious accident and had a leg amputated. The effect of this, she said, still smiling, had been to make her love her profession more than ever, and she had cultivated this slow walk to hide her plight from fellow-artists and managers as well as from the public. But now she was beginning to fear that people might find out and jobs be harder to come by. What ought she to do? Admit it openly, or go on hiding it as long as she could? Which was the more honest course?

It was a moving story. In her place, I said, I should treat it all as something to be proud about. Why not preface her act with a simple announcement, made as gaily and bravely as she had been making it to me? Not bidding for sympathy but demonstrating, rather, that the disability was not as strong as her love of her job, and that the job was helping her to conquer and ignore it? With a catch in my voice, I told her she was a wonderful example. She looked at me, suddenly grave, put up her face to be kissed and then went halting away, leaving me to sing scales furiously before I could utter a note myself.

NICE COMPLIMENT

Some journalist now detects in me elements of Sacha Guitry – shades of the Third Person, of theatrical pomp and circumstance! – and any irresponsible boy whistling his way round Paris. ('At my age', is the implication.) A Sacha-*titi*, in fact. Curious mixture.

INTERLUDE AT SÃO PAULO

Well, I have seen the streets where the *pétasses* and the *patarasses* lived in the Old Port of Marseilles, and the street of the *cagoles* at Toulon and the *pipeuses* at Bordeaux, and basically they were all the same, just streets. Streets of wretched women with very few attractions, getting a wretched living. But how to describe the Bom Retiro in São Paulo, whose three streets of brothels run together like triple claws and market the lowest wares that the trade of sex could spew up anywhere?

We went to see this place, mingling in a stream of men, some there to pay and some to draw the profits and all of them like animals, eddying round dung-heaps repulsive enough to discourage the most virile male alive. Men only are allowed in here and police outside search them in turn for guns or knives. That done, they may enter the Rua Aymores, which consists of whore-houses and nothing else.

The doors, which more resemble shutters, are in continuous rows. The men look through them and the women show what's on sale in hope of custom. The very thought of making love in those pox-ridden cabins is sickening, but there are dozens of them. A complete nightmare. Many of the women are white, mingled with half-breeds and glistening fat Negresses.

News of our being there soon got round and from behind the shutters our names were called, not always with a foreign accent. Before one of the dens a Frenchwoman stood marvelling as if we were visitors from heaven.

'Oh, Monsieur Maurice, I was listening to you last night on the radio! Do you like São Paulo, is it nice to have the theatre full?'

She sounded decently-educated, lower-middle-class. Forty-ish and tolerably attractive still, with fine, firm breasts.

'How long have you been here, Madame?'

'Twenty-four years, Monsieur Maurice. They brought me here when I was 16.'

'It's always been your job, then?'

'Oh, no, not in France. I came from a nice family in France.'

'And later, in Brazil?'

'I've always worked here, yes.' (*Fonctionné* was the word she used.)

'Twenty-four years of it?'

'Yes, Monsieur Maurice.'

'How many customers a day, average?'

'Average? Oh, twenty or thirty, sometimes more, sometimes less.'

'Do you actually live here?' I inquired.

'Oh, *no*. I'm here from mid-day to midnight, then I go home. I have my own home, in the town.'

'Any family in this country?'

'No, Monsieur Maurice. I live by myself.'

A thin, dirty man emerged from the next-door shutter, assuaged, exhilarated. A crowd was gathering, my name flew from doorway to doorway. Some of the shutters opened a little, and one saw the repellant goods within. A group of grotesque homosexuals on the opposite pavement were posing like reluctant but excited girls. The woman continued: 'Monsieur Maurice, come in. Would you like some coffee?'

'No, Madame,' I said. 'Thank you, but I have to get back to my work. I'll say good-bye. Good luck, keep smiling!'

'Good luck to you, too, Monsieur Maurice. God bless you.'

We took a final look along the street, from end to end of which the news of our presence had temporarily halted the market. Then we turned and walked without speaking to the car. Behind us everything started to 'function' as before.

ON BEING TAKEN DOWN A PEG

First lesson. For the past three months my new posters have been attracting a lot of attention. They are by the gifted young painter Badia Vilato, they are all over Paris, and you can't miss them. Night after night, for those same three months, I have occupied the stage of the Variétés forging, song by song, the sort of programme singers dream about, a kind of ultimate performance. And the other day I call a taxi, and as I give the address the driver turns round to me and says, 'Ah, well, Monsieur Maurice, given it all up, have you?'

Lesson Two. Some nights ago I discovered Fernand Gravey standing patiently in the queue of autograph-hunters outside my dressing-room after the show. I hauled him inside at once, surprised and embarrassed, and this actor, happier than most in his life and his career, nearly wrung my hand off and could hardly get a word out.

It was incredible, upsetting almost, suddenly to see how sensitive he is. I had always thought him colder and more self-possessed than most people and in a moment realized how wrong I was. Next day there came a letter from him, so charmingly appreciative, so shame-faced about it all, that it was my turn to feel emotional. I have written back and tried to tell him how much I admire his acting and how I appreciate his attitude to me.

And the third lesson? Charles Boyer has been in France for ten weeks' filming with Martine Carol, but since he was working all day, and my evenings were occupied by a series of fifty-five concerts, we managed to meet only twice, lunching once at my house and once at a hotel. However, before he went back to America, I wanted to introduce him to the Flea-Market, and we went there yesterday. We sat together over our meal, a couple of old cronies whom nothing now is likely to disrupt, and then, though the weather turned suddenly icy-cold, we wandered off to the cluttered stalls of the Marché Biron. As we stood in front of one of them a woman came up to me and asked,

'Are you the stall-holder?'

The proprietor, certainly, was not in evidence, but I assumed she was joking and was about to laugh. But no, she had not recognized me and was perfectly serious. So I pointed to Charles and said: 'It isn't my stall, Madame, it's his.'

'Oh, good,' she said, looking straight at our celebrated Franco-American Great Lover without batting an eyelid, 'and have you any flyswatters in stock?'

'Well, no, Madame,' he replied, 'I'm right out of them, as it happens.'

Upon which she departed to rake the neighbouring establishments, and Charles and I collapsed, with neatly punctured egos.

Later, I had this characteristic letter from him, posted in London:

DEAR MAURICE,

I shall be sailing in an hour or two. Thank you for your message and remembrances. You and I, I know, can survive absence and separation, but that doesn't make me any the less sorry to have seen so little of you. It's a great comfort, all the same, to know that this close, perceptive friendship exists for us both. Never far away, proven and disinterested and certainly, at our age, irreplaceable.

The best thing you could do just now is rest and let up a bit. Now is the moment to take advantage of your quite unprecedented success and really enjoy what you've earned and what you've done. Besides, I have never seen you in better form, or more relaxed.

We'll go back to the Flea Market for some flyswatters next year and get ourselves taken down a peg or two again.

Je t'embrasse,
CHARLES

REWARD

The magazine *Adam* has just named me France's Best-Dressed
Actor and awarded me the golden Apple that goes with this somewhat devastating honour. Well, I made a film about a tramp once,
called *La Pomme d'Or*, so the golden Adam's Apple is just about all
I needed.

THE WAY IT USED TO BE

An artist's popularity goes through unnumbered fluctuations and of
these I may safely say that I have endured some and known all. I
was fairly popular in France before the days of radio, cinema and
gramophone record; days when the people who recognized you in
the street, who smiled or stopped to give a word of appreciation, had
actually seen you on the stage. Autograph-hunting was unheard of
but I can remember how, in Marseilles especially, I only had to
wear a new sort of hat on a morning's stroll for all the young men
to adopt it without delay. And will you believe that they used to
have 'amateur Chevalier' shows? Nothing on the programme but
imitations of me, fifty or sixty of them? Such a thing has never
happened to anybody since. Yet, for all the deep and genuine feeling,
there was no hysteria. That came later, when records, cinema and
radio could make a reputation in a week or two. Then a kind of
mass-madness seemed to take over and the visit of a star could
inflame a capital city. When I was a Hollywood star I had tens of
thousands of people to meet me at the station in London or Paris or
New York, with sizeable contingents of police on duty. One would
be shoved out on to balconies to wave. It was inflamed, all right.

But what about the recipients of homage like that? Were they
happy about it? Well, they were and they weren't. They were as
far as the publicity itself went, but they weren't from the personal
point of view. All the delirium and hero-worship so enslaved its
victims, and landed them in predicaments so embarrassing that the
most avid of them begged for quarter in the end. Eternally at the
mercy of clamouring fans, the wretched idols had to lie and dodge

to get the smallest interval of peace. They were paid performers, in bondage to the crowd who hounded them like criminals until they required police protection if they were not to be lynched alive by their admirers. The morbid, maniacal adoration forced them constantly into unpleasant and humiliating situations.

So the popular idol of those days had to take a grip of himself and learn to put the brakes on. You needed enough sense to say No, to think of diplomatic excuses and generally navigate a tide which, once you let it get too strong, would sweep you off your feet. And another thing: popularity of that kind didn't last. It was self-consuming, and anyone who thought it wasn't was in for a nasty shock, poor fellow.

PLAIN AND SIMPLE, 1955

One of the most likeable people I have seen on American T.V. so far is Rocky Marciano, boxing champion of the world. His modest bearing and engaging smile, the self-effacement of him, make one long to take his hand. (Not on one's chin, of course, I hasten to add.) These qualities must stem from his poor start in life, just as the misfortunes of Marilyn Monroe's early years have a lot to do with her attraction for men. Such origins, when allied to more than ordinary strength or beauty, somehow tend to foster this particular, mysterious appeal.

For me, the things that matter are distinction and simplicity and it is on these points, I like to think, that my work will be seen to differ from that of the leading Americans for, rich in talent though they are, they all seem so terrifically, professionally sure of themselves that one cannot believe them to be 100 per cent sincere. The man in the audience needs to believe, heart and soul, in the man on the stage and I am convinced that any touch of spuriousness, however small, will affect him profoundly. I am convinced, too, that I shall be remembered for some innate naturalness, something to do with ease and contact, that makes the man more important than the artist.

DEATH OF MISTINGUETT, 1956

I have just heard on the American radio that Mistinguett had a stroke this morning. They gave her age, and she is obviously dying, The international press has been on to me and I am saying that I hope to see her when I go home, three weeks from now. It is unlikely, though, that she will live so long and, with a serious attack, one would not wish her to.

So, as I wait for further news, I reflect on the years we shared of work and friendship and, so often, happiness. I can see her now, vital, amusing and so out-of-this-world attractive. I remember how it was when I was nobody and she the queen of the music-hall, lavishing her love on me and helping me so much; how the days were, and the nights out, and the love-making at home: nights which this woman, so universally sought after and desired, gave to me, who shared both work and life with her. I recall and re-live every moment of it. It makes me think how time, in time, will get the better of anyone, however youthful, and any work, however wonderful, and all the strength and gifts in the world. Now, if Mistinguett dies suddenly, I, who adored her uniquely, jealously, shall not be there to follow her on her last journey among the Parisian crowd who, collectively, loved her just as much. And perhaps it is best that way.

I can truthfully say that before, during and after the First World War she brought me more love, more fun, and did more for my work, than any other woman. Ten years we had, including three war-years when I was wounded and a prisoner. Then everything, life and love and work, seemed to get in a terrible mess; circumstances and my own pride made the separation inevitable. But in the final reckoning no one else has ever been what she was to me, or done for me what she did. More than any other woman, she was what I mean by Love.

I have sent a cable, but I don't know whether she can possibly read it. They are talking of general paralysis. Nothing to do but wait.

Later. Ten people have rung up tonight. Mistinguett is dead. French and foreign newspapers are all wanting something and I have produced the following text, which has been sent to Paris, and recorded some impressions for the French radio.

GOOD-BYE, MIST.

You haven't gone, you haven't disappeared; you've just made a change, that's all. For me, wherever life happens to lead me, you'll always be there. Your face, your look, your laugh, will come clear through the shadowy din of places where people are too busy to know what love is. You were wife and mistress to me, and my dearest friend. You loved my mother, too. It was you who made me understand much of what, through good luck and hard work, I was to accomplish later, and when our profession came between us in the end it was right that we should separate. But our ardours, our achievements and mistakes have only secured the place we hold, each in the other's heart.

You can take your rest, Mist. You who were the Parisienne personified, more than anyone ever was before, as much as anyone will ever be again. You were the body and soul, the wit and chic of the feminine city. They all adored you, gallery, stalls and boxes, and you will remain, for every one, a shining light in the City of Light.

Always,
MAURICE

Her passing leaves me bereft. I know she was no longer young, and would have had no peace in her old age. I know she has been spared a great deal and things are better as they are, for her and for those who loved her. All the same I find myself asking, Why? There are people of whom it is impossible to believe that they will ever not be there. You think of them as more or less immortal. And when you learn with a shock one morning that they are, suddenly, not among the living, you go on your way disturbed, thrown off balance, chilled.

WHAT MAKES AN ARTIST?

Clowns, again. Why should the most dynamic comedians nearly always be quiescent, melancholy folk, even downright sad, in ordinary life? It is because too much of their capacity for joy goes into their work. Being more than usually funny or dramatic – or being just plain funny or dramatic – in front of an audience, calls for an expenditure of nervous energy far beyond the normal.

An artist has at all costs to convince, and this he can do only by, as it were, discharging his own essential strength into the minds of his audience, leaving himself correspondingly weaker until, by degrees, he can recuperate. Never trust a comic who is too ebullient in private life; his work is bound to suffer for it. No one has resources enough for both. It is the public who receive the best a dedicated artist has to give; the very highest he can aim at, he offers on the stage. The rest of the time he is replenishing, gathering himself together again.

Then, they all get stage-fright, too. What actor hasn't known it, never had to steel himself, wind himself up before he can take the plunge and walk on to the stage? And insecurity – ask the greatest among them and you will be surprised to discover how insecure they feel. I once made a film in America with a 10-month-old co-star named Baby Leroy. Such a hit he was that every star in Hollywood demanded his services whenever a film went on the floor; and Baby Leroy was burnt-out, a has-been at the age of 2.

The whole thing's relative.

MY OWN FOLK

Leading traders in the Halles central markets have a charity which from time to time entertains elderly and penurious men and women from all parts of Paris at the big Café du Globe at the corner of the Boulevard de Strasbourg and the Rue du Faubourg Saint-Martin. After a splendid dinner, with a fine orchestra playing, big open bags are distributed and they all file past to have these filled with a liberal assortment of eatables from the most tempting of the grocers' and butchers' stalls. I had agreed to do the handing out on this occasion and for an hour I saw French poverty close to. I saw, that is to say, 500 poor Parisians whose shining neatness and unassuming dignity, whose courtesy and, if I may use the word, whose *class*, evoked respect and admiration. I gave out jam in large quantities as they went by and there was such warmth and charm in the way every one spoke to me, or pronounced my name, that I could have wept a dozen times. Some of them were 86 and more, and most could recall my early days. They remembered me singing at this, that or the other place, they knew the pet-name I called my mother by. We were like neighbours from the same street, out of the same world. Grey-headed as I am, I felt like a child of theirs, and driving home to Marnes-la-Coquette that world was all about me. Ménilmontant and Belleville took possession of my heart once more until, miraculously, I was a boy again.

BITTERSWEET

The pilgrim urge is gaining on me all the time. Wherever I go there is always some pleasant memory, something nice that happened in some place or another. Yesterday it was the Rue Rodier, where we were filming in a painter's studio just opposite the house where Dorville's widow is still living. I knew her when she was 18 and took the opportunity to go across for a friendly chat about old days. Then I went and sat in a café near the former Auberge du Clou where we all used to meet so often after the theatre – Mistinguett, Spinelly, Polaire, Régina Badet. That was between 1908 and the Great War, when they were in their prime. Raimu, Dorville, the composer Magnard and so many others, they were there as well. I was back among them, I could see and hear us all as though it were just the day before. I felt like a miser, but a miser of friendship, counting over the hoarded gold of memories.

Memories. There was an old lady asking to come round to my dressing-room. Her name meant nothing to me and I regarded her without interest. But, diffidently, she repeats the name and suddenly it is 1918 again and I am at the Femina Theatre where Madame Rasimi puts on revues and is so expert at finding decorative dancers for them. And there at the Femina is this gorgeous girl Didiane, young and lovely and the pick of the bunch, carefully culled though it is from the most gorgeous girls in Paris. Didiane! And smiling

across at me was a respectable-looking person with grey hair innocent of dye and no nonsense about how old she was. A woman
whose sweet, resigned expression seemed to accept what we must all
accept in the end and to contain a hint, too, of regret that we are
allowed so short a walk along the paths of love, the most delightful
we can tread. Didiane. That night I dreamed of her as she used to
be, matchless, adorable, superb.

SAME OLD STAGEFRIGHT, *1956*

Work begins on *Love in the Afternoon*. Audrey Hepburn and Gary
Cooper, with Billy Wilder directing: a decisive landmark on my
road back to Hollywood. I am also polishing my solo programme –
the last one, I trust – for the Alhambra next month. All seems to
be organized. Nothing now but to get on and make a success of
it.

Wilder holds a first run-through of my early scenes with Audrey
Hepburn at which I am trembling like a leaf and as nervous as a
tyro, so much so that I begin to wonder how I shall possibly manage.
The part is more or less tailor-made for me, yet the English lines
have a paralysing and disastrous effect. Audrey then informs me
that she, too, is worried about working with me for the first time,
practically knocked off balance by the awful prospect of somehow
not 'jelling'. Gary Cooper, shy, long and lanky, appears to be in
the same state as well, and the sooner we all get going the better, I
think. We are like musicians tuning their instruments. Actors
exchange more than words when they rehearse. Shades of feeling
emerge which will in time produce the speeches, or the music – and
on occasion a good deal else besides.

MY POPULARITY AGAIN

T.V. changes everything, the nature of popularity most of all.
Passing some children in the park of Saint-Cloud, ages ranging
from 8 to 12, I heard one say,

'I've seen that man on our T.V. at home. You *know*,' he insists, 'he sings.'

'Well what's his name, then?' inquired another.

'Oh, can't remember *that*,' rejoins the first child. They then return to their amusements and I passed on my way, suitably outraged.

THE GREAT RAIMU

It is now, 1956, ten years since Raimu died. I was 18 when we met in Toulouse in 1908, doing my song-and-dance act at the bottom of the bill at the Nouveautés music-hall. He was leading man in the weekly repertory of one-act plays with which, at that period, they finished off the evening. Those plays were, I think, the training-school in which his comic gifts were gradually developed, and helped to make him so remarkable an actor. Raimu was a sort of natural phenomenon and did his very best work with Marcel Pagnol. His talents were unique, his own, incomparable; and thanks to the cinema and, I repeat, to Pagnol's books and films, he brought to the widest of audiences the typical laughter of Marseilles, with its sunshine and its rueful overtones. He was always someone whose extraordinary figure provoked reverence in his fellow-players. Meeting him on the Champs-Élysées you didn't necessarily smile, you doffed your hat in a big way and said, *Bonjour, Monsieur Raimu.*

GLANCES BACKWARD, SEPTEMBER 1956

Having been made a Commander of the Legion of Honour for services to my profession I was guest of honour at a lunch for our residents and committee-members at the Actors' Home at Ris-Orangis, south of Paris. For those three hours I could re-live my early years on the stage, since I had known these old men and women in the Rue du Faubourg Saint-Martin when I was 14 or so. Some, a year or two my senior, had been my friends before our paths divided. One by one I scrutinized their faces and, since this was a special day with aperitifs and liqueurs on top of the usual menu, some of them grew a little exalted as the feast went on. I was back with them as an elderly man and advisedly sticking to water, but it was still a good feeling to be the local boy who had earned their regard.

And earned it alone, what's more. For when you really get down to it I have felt alone all my life. At home in Ménilmontant I was alone in my desire to be something different, something other than my father and my brothers were. It was not that I despised what they were, far from it, but from instinct all my dreams were theatre dreams. I took the risk alone and as my name got bigger on the bills I went on feeling more and more alone. And love? Well, all those delectable women who have left me memories so marvellous (or most of them have, anyway) that I never cease to dwell upon them fondly – every last one of them forced me to cut and run in the end in order to survive.

Still, I played the game as well as I could. Maybe I was just not fated to know the sort of great love that fills a lifetime and on which you stake everything you have. And now people who dislike me cherish hopes that my declining years are solitary and sad. How very wrong they are. My life is as full of affection as that of any man of my age can possibly be, for the craving for independence has led me, as it happens, to choose and cherish friends – my beloved, affectionate friends. I still play the fatherly role thrust upon me long ago, when I lived as a boy with my mother. There is always my profession, too, my life-long consolation; and the public who, in spite of all the slings and arrows, have been faithful and kind to me. There is another thing too: being alone in life bestows the absolute creative freedom that is the mainspring of my own special brand of one-man performance. And of course I am alone only when I want to be. I have nothing to regret. I have known as much, and more than as much, love as most people. As much as anyone, I have helped those of my calling. Now, though I still work a great deal, I find my most pleasant moments are passed in looking back, in grateful memory, upon the highlights of my life. And if they asked me what title I should choose among the Oscars and professional awards, the French and international honours people get these days, I shouldn't worry about being a Commander or a Grand Chancellor or anything so lofty. *Artisan de France* on a little certificate would be quite enough for me.

THE IDOLS

There is in film-land a nonsensical contrast between the way they welcome you at first, and ask you out and make a fuss of you, and the dismal lack of interest you encounter when the rites of hospitality are duly over. Nobody has time for anybody else and just as, on the set, the rule is to husband your nerves for the vital moment of the actual shot, so they seem to economize on human feeling outside the studio as well. I suppose it helps to build up their strength for the sharp about-turns and changes of opinion they are always having to adapt themselves to. Well, I may be a novelty abroad, but in France, thank God, I have become a sort of affectionate habit.

YOU CAN'T WIN

It is now six months since my doctor told me that giving up alcohol would put ten healthy years on to my life. Blast it, I've tried it more than once before now and always, some evening when things are either fine or lamentable, comes the fall. A week ago the battle was on again. As the son of an alcoholic I really should try to conquer this last, worst demon; finally earn the title of Wise Man of Montélimont and cultivate an agreeable mixture of sobriety, lucidity, serenity and so forth for the years that remain. 'And not a moment too soon', do I hear somebody add?

A doctor tells you to give the stuff up. You then dine out with friends and a famous doctor in the party observes that you touch no wine. Why not? he inquires; and promptly proceeds to undermine you with: 'Oh, well, doesn't do to take anything too far, y'know.' And there you are, locked in combat with the demon as before.

TWO EXAMPLES OF DETERMINATION

Henri Farman, pioneer of international aviation, has died (1958) at
the age of 84. In the last interview he gave, when asked how he
actually got to the stage of flying for the first time, he replied simply:
'Oh, it came, you know. One made a little progress every day.'

'A little progress every day.' There you have the right way to
go about things.

And secondly, Chaplin. I last saw *The Dictator*, I forget where,
after the Liberation, and was not particularly impressed. Yesterday
I did so again and it impressed me very much. Why is this? It
isn't the subject of the film. I think it poor taste to found a farce
upon events which so tragically laid waste the Europe we knew,
even though it was made a long way off, in Hollywood, and before
the horrors reached their peak. No, what struck me this time round
was the professional courage of Chaplin in taking his plunge into
spoken dialogue among the judiciously spaced passages of mime.

We hear him first in the dictator's long oration, with its basis of
German sounds – not altogether unlike a dog barking. He has not
yet spoken, though; that comes later. Towards that he moves
gradually, scene by scene, little by little increasing the number of
his lines until by the end of the picture he embarks gallantly, whole-
heartedly, upon what is, for him, the critical adventure of the
spoken word and gives it all he's got. He reminded me of a champion boxer who risks his entire reputation, past, present and to come,
in one grand bout with no holds barred. It fairly gripped me by
the throat to watch it and I have never admired him so much. The
old so-and-so! The kind of thing that shows you what the Chaplins
of this world are made of, despite the fact that they go off the beam
occasionally.

FIFTY YEARS ON

Lyons, in 1906. I was singing at the Kursaal, and topping the bill
was an English revue-company with an amusing sketch, *An Evening
at the Music-Hall*. Their young comedian, supposedly a tipsy

elegant in the audience, sat launching devastating remarks from a box at the performers on the stage. It was my first contact with English artists and the actor playing the tipsy young man had me going overboard for his style, so completely different from any- thing I had seen in France. And that wasn't all I went overboard for. The head of the troupe had a daughter who, in her role of singer and dancer, exchanged some hilarious backchat with my friend in the box. I had not at that date crossed the Channel, nor met an English rose before.

She was tall, she was talented, her figure a dream, her face exqui- site, and in the course of two evenings I fell head-over-heels in love with her. Easy conquest, or anything of that kind, was out of the question. She was unapproachable, very strictly guarded by a father who never missed a thing. She had, moreover, a quality of purity which earned her universal, admiring respect, especially my own boyish respect. How I loved her! Night after night I stood in the wings and watched that company and gazed at her. And my gaze obviously broke down the language barrier for secretly, innocently, she came to understand my silent declaration and seemed shyly flattered by it. She was about my own age, I suppose, a real *jeune fille*.

I began to suffer from this hopeless passion, my deep love for a creature almost too pure and beautiful, this King's daughter, as she seemed to me. And she, on her side, must have found my glance of feverish adoration somewhat upsetting. She had soft, lovely eyes and she looked at me, when no one else was looking, as if to say that I did not displease her. Indeed the contrary, it seemed, might well be true. But that was all there was to it; just these wordless messages. Nothing else was possible.

Still, we loved each other more and more and I became more anguished every day. I realize, in retrospect, this was the first time I ever was in love, with the sort of love I should not feel for any girl again.

I had a bit of a name already and the English manager, unaware that my transports had nothing to do with professional appreciation, was highly gratified to see me at my station, night after night, applauding. The girl got under my skin, became a part of me. I would have made a run-away match with her, had anyone suggested it. I was over-wrought and in despair. My heart behaved like a battering-ram if our glances crossed and had she actually tried to talk to me I think I should have passed out. My love was real, honest, respectful, passionate, and it was making me quite ill.

It did not take the English comic long to grasp the situation. He and I used to go out in the daytime and though neither of us spoke a word of the other's language we got along very well. The panto-miming was fun and he taught me to sing English and American songs; there was one, I remember, called 'Teasing', which we harmonized together on our strolls beside the Rhone. He, too, was very young, perhaps 21 or 22, a year or so older than I was. And much as I admired his acting my regard undeniably gained a certain something from the fact of his closeness to the girl I adored.

As I say, he guessed that I adored her long before I told him so. He also saw how miserable I was and undertook to carry messages, for she, as it happened, had confessed her love for me (the love of a *jeune fille*, to be sure), and was miserable too. This naturally put me in a worse turmoil than ever, for once I knew she felt the same way all my instincts were awake. I was all for making a scene, organizing an elopement. And the whole time her father, unsuspecting, kept telling his company that the French boy 'had what it takes', expatiated to them on my various abilities and had some word of praise or gesture of encouragement for me whenever we met.

The comic, meanwhile, sympathizing with my sorry state, thought he really must do something. This was for him no light decision, since he was risking his job and, what might well be worse, the ire of an irascible parent, and an English parent at that. But at last a meeting was arranged. I was shy and she was shyer. All we could do on the banks of the river was sit and look at one another, a totally inexperienced boy and an absolutely innocent girl with captivating eyes.

Her father had given my friend permission to take her for a walk in Lyons and my friend told me where they would be going. Thus, and rather hypocritically I fear, I was able to bump into them by accident. We continued the walk in a trio, while she and I communicated by means of clasped hands and eloquent silences. It was very frustrating, this having no language in common but the language of love.

Nothing else happened at all.

Then one afternoon we made a rendezvous in her dressing-room and had a few minutes alone while our ally kept guard outside. We kissed each other fervently and kissed again. He then tapped lightly at the door and we had to tear ourselves apart, trembling, breathless, fearful of discovery.

The Lyons engagement came to an end but I had checked on where the English troupe was going next and fixed my own bookings so that I could visit my new friends whenever possible. When I did, things were as blameless and awkward as ever, as I sat in some corner of the dressing-room and we all made theatre jokes.

Until, that is, the day came when they were due to open in Paris and I was met at the stage-door by a finally-enlightened father, white with rage. I was to leave his daughter alone – or else. I loved his daughter, I assured him, my intentions were honourable. But he refused to listen to reason and I was forced to give up seeing her.

Painfully, for a long time, the thought of that gracious beauty haunted me. But the months went by and gradually my work and the women who fell into bed with me, and the problems and struggles of a successful career, blurred the pain and dulled the heartache. For better, for worse, my love-life, since that year of 1906 up to this birthday on 12 September 1958, has been what it has been.

Well, the seventieth birthday made front-page news in all the papers and I had hundreds of letters; and one of these, as I was going through them, suddenly caught my attention. A long letter, wondering whether, after all these years ... did I by any chance remember the company at the Kursaal in Lyons? The English comedian? And the manager's daughter ... the young actress. ... And the warm, warm feeling there had been? More than probably I had forgotten all about it, but she would so like to know. She, too, was 70.

Fifty-two years fell away as I read the letter. It was the time of that unhappy passion, I saw her as she was and felt just as I felt then. I was 18 once more and as deeply in love as ever with my English fairy princess. I replied immediately, and in her own language, for I could speak it now; and all the long-ago devotion burned in every word. I told her I never had forgotten her, I had loved her far too much: that she had been my first true love.

The post brought a long, delightful answer back. There had been, I learnt, some terrible scenes with her father and she had left home soon afterwards, though without ever daring to come to me in Paris. She had worked for many years in the States and in South Africa. She had made a loveless marriage, since for her no one could ever replace the boy in Lyons in 1906, that young French singer who had done so well.

I sent her a not-bad photograph and asked her to meet me the next time I was in London. I can tell from her candid letter that what she says is true and that she is a fine and genuine person. I am prepared to believe that she has, indeed, loved me all her life and I know that I, for my part, keep our sad romance as fresh in my memory as though it happened yesterday. The battering-ram pounds at the thought of her, just as it did then. What is she like now, I wonder? She was so young and lovely – what does she look like now?

Whether it is in fact sensible to meet again I do not know. Shall I recapture something of the past behind her wrinkles and white hair? Or will it all turn out to be perfectly horrible? What I do know is that I am, for the moment, back in 1906, at the theatre in Lyons. Thanks to the Englishman we shall be meeting secretly, soon, in her dressing-room, and I shall take her in my arms and give her un-practised kisses, intense with everlasting love; and my heart jumps and thumps in the same old way.

Well, a day or so after all that I dined at the house of friends with my white-haired love of over fifty years ago. A charming old lady who was once a ravishing girl; decidedly a credit to that beautiful memory of ours.

They say the greatest accomplishment of mortal man is to grow old gracefully. Henceforth I shall confine my ambition to doing just that, and to giving of my best for the final performances.

WORK: AND THE REST CAN TAKE CARE OF ITSELF

Seventy-two now, and I have more important things on hand than in any single season in my life before. I find I needn't bother now with what does not concern me. I can stay simple, stay myself and jog along my own enthralling road. I don't have to blow any trumpets and far prefer to astound people nowadays with my modest and retiring common sense. Moreover I have reached that marvellous stage when nothing has to look like a performance any more. I, personally, mean more than Maurice Chevalier, the personality. It is not the actor who matters now, it is the man; and if anybody tries to persuade me otherwise he can go to hell.

I hope I shall not be past a joke when the moment comes, mad as I shall be at leaving everything behind. And I hope that those I loved will miss me, and smile affectionately sometimes when they think of me.

PANISSE & SON

We are filming *Fanny*, by Marcel Pagnol, and one of the scenes takes place in front of a garage above whose door, to suit the story, they have painted 'Panisse & Son' in English, in large letters. An old Marseilles woman sees this and loudly exclaims, 'Really, these Americans, they never *finish* anything! "Panisse and His!" Panisse and his *what*, I should like to know?'

DEATH OF A GREAT MAN

Gary Cooper is dying of cancer. At 60 he is among the great Hollywood figures, a sad, gentle man beloved by everyone. He did not want to go to hospital, preferring to die in his own bed. He always maintained that he had more luck than talent, and will be remembered for the legendary moderation of his acting and the inborn amiability that shone from one of the nicest faces an actor ever had.

FUNNY FOLK

I was out for a stroll and, coming to a poor church, ill-repaired and
with peeling plaster, went inside to see what it was like. It was almost
empty, with a funeral in progress around a pitiful coffin. Ten people
– old women, some children, a couple of girls and old men – were
obviously the family, not one of whom looked in the slightest bit
concerned. The priest, on home ground, intoned the psalms meti-
culously before the black-draped bier, bowed and crossed himself,
while another held up the crucifix. Both of them needed their
tonsures trimming. They finished off with a last genuflexion at the
little altar and disappeared through the sacristy door, their pious
task completed. A preoccupied beadle came and snuffed the candles
round the coffin. The ten people exchanged smiles and kisses, still
without a shade of sorrow, and started homewards. They made for
the door without a farewell look.

I had been kneeling unobtrusively near the entrance and one of
them, in passing, recognized me. I pretended to be praying, to
temper their surprise, but they all stopped, death and church forgotten, wondering whether they really shouldn't ask for an autograph; hesitated; then regretfully left, without shutting the door.
Even then they hung about outside for a while before tearing themselves away.

I was alone in the chapel with a dead man whom priests and family
abandoned and the feeling swept over me that I, the stranger, was the
one creature in the whole world with a thought for his mortal
remains, now the candles were out and the short service was over.

AND QUEER ENCOUNTERS

On the Champs-Élysées. Three very young effeminates, boys of
between 14 and 16, waggling their rumps and waving their arms
about and flapping their hands. The baby of the party spots me and
cries: 'Oh, my *God*! Maurice Chevalier!' He gazes ecstatically in my
direction and offers a heartfelt, '*Handsome!*'

I smiled, which seemed to embarrass him, but he blew me a kiss and walked off with his lady-friends; his friends, I mean. Then all three turned round and blew a complimentary kiss together. Quite touched by this idiotic comedy, I waved good-bye.

WHAT I BELIEVE

I believe in God, and in refusing to worry when I cannot understand all that people have had to say about Him. I realized when my mother died that the soul of a beloved person lives on beside one, and so became convinced of a mystery that has helped me to live since, to the best of my ability, as a good Christian. This is my guiding-light. I try to be as good as I can, to resist grave temptation as far as I can, to know my own limitations and humbly accept what cannot be avoided. I know that work is the best and most reliable of friends; you can live at peace with yourself by means of work. And I know you are really defeated only when the courage to try, and try again, has been crushed out of you.

This will be my creed until the day I die, because it seems to me the best way to live. I know my own weaknesses, the chinks in my own armour. I suppose they keep me from being a colourless bore and the problem of controlling them keeps me on my toes. And every day I pray the help of the Almighty to keep me from being too ashamed of myself.

All my life I have been a great one for encouraging other people and I think this has been due to nothing but my own need for approval. It is in my nature to find my happiness in the pride of working as well as I can. And I believe that there are more decent folk in the world than the other sort, more candid than depraved, more sane than disturbed. I believe in human kind.

I have never played the Great Actor nor, God forbid, the Genius. I have sung my songs to cheer up my listeners, to amuse them and make them laugh. No thought of any obscure Message, nor of Rebellion against this or that. My themes have been the joys of peace and quiet, of toil and love, a life innocent of cruelty.

And now, to finish up with. I read an interview with the pianist

Rubenstein, confessing the fear that tortures him before every recital, and calling it the price of the wonderful life he led. I know just what he is talking about, but would it not be too perfect, otherwise? There is a price to pay for everything. And yesterday, dining with Edward G. Robinson, who is a fine and perceptive actor, we agreed that the great artist must draw from his audience the maximum emotion with the minimum of 'artistry'. He can succeed no other way.

A reporter from *Newsweek* has asked what I think is the main reason I have lasted as long as I have. 'Because,' I tell him, 'people have always known that what they get from me isn't just a technical display. It's human feeling.'

THE END